Sounding Differences
Conversations with Seventeen Canadian Women Writers

In this provocative collection of interviews, Canadian women writers discuss with Janice Williamson their thoughts on writing in general and their own work in particular, on the nature of writing as a woman in Canada today, and on the links between women's writing and social change.

These interviews serve as introductions to lesser-known writers and provide informed new readings of established women writers. The seventeen writers are Jeannette Armstrong, Di Brandt, Nicole Brossard, Elly Danica, Kristjana Gunnars, Claire Harris, Smaro Kamboureli, Joy Kogawa, Lee Maracle, Daphne Marlatt, Erin Mouré, M. Nourbese Philip, Gail Scott, Lola Lemire Tostevin, Bronwen Wallace, Betsy Warland, and Phyllis Webb. Williamson's introduction sets the work in political and literary context. Each interview is accompanied by a short biocritical piece, a photograph of the writer, and an example of her work.

Their voices in conversation reflect both the passion and the critical thinking that inform their writing. Among the areas they explore are the issues of 'difference' in the women's movement which have been raised by Women of Colour and lesbians, and the current challenge to the Canadian literary canon in its exclusion of non-European writers.

The editing process in this collection has been uniquely collaborative, shared between Williamson and her subjects. The result is entertaining, revealing, and challenging; the words of these writers enrich a number of debates in both the women's movement and Canada's literary communities.

Janice Williamson is an Associate Professor in the Department of English, University of Alberta. She is co-editor, with Deborah Gorham, of *Up and Doing: Canadian Women and Peace*, and author of *Tell Tale Signs: Fictions*.

SOUNDING DIFFERENCES

Conversations with Seventeen Canadian Women Writers

JANICE WILLIAMSON

UNIVERSITY OF TORONTO PRESS
Toronto Buffalo London

© University of Toronto Press 1993
Toronto Buffalo London
Poetry and prose excerpts © the authors
Printed in Canada

ISBN 0–8020–2762–8 (cloth)
ISBN 0–8020–6808–1 (paper)

Printed on acid-free paper

Canadian Cataloguing in Publication Data

Main entry under title:

Sounding differences

ISBN 0-8020-2762-8 (bound). – ISBN 0-8020-6808-1 (pbk.)

1. Women authors, Canadian (English) – 20th century –
Interviews.* 2. Feminism and literature – Canada.
I. Williamson, Janice.

PS8089.5.W6S68 1993   C810'.5408   C92-095551-7
PR9188.S68 1993

For permission to reprint, the author and publisher are grateful to:
Gynergy Press for an excerpt from Elly Danica's *Don't: A Woman's Word*
and M. Nourbese Philip's 'Discourse on the Logic of Language,' in *She
Tries Her Tongue; Her Silence Softly Breaks*; Theytus Books Ltd for
Jeannette Armstrong's 'Grief Is Not the Activity That Heals,' in the
Theytus / Williams-Wallace co-publication *Breath Tracks*; Véhicule Press
and Erin Mouré for 'Song of a Murmur' in *Sheepish Beauty, Civilian
Love*.

This book has been published with assistance from the Canada Council
and the Ontario Arts Council under their block grant programs.

Contents

Acknowledgments

This collection of interviews was made possible through the generosity of the writers: their patience and willingness to extend and deepen our conversations provided me with renewed enthusiasm not only for this project but for imagining a community across our differences. I am grateful to Linda Pasmore, who efficiently transcribed some earlier interviews, and to Lise Creuer, who transcribed Nicole Brossard's original interview with good cheer. I am particularly indebted to Astrid Blodgett, who contributed a writerly eye, organizational savvy, and parenthetical wit to her transcription work on all of the interviews as they circulated and recirculated as inevitably as the seasons across her desk. Generous funding from the Explorations Program at the Canada Council made the first journeys possible, and the University of Alberta's Central Research Fund supported part of the transcription. Thanks to the editors of the following journals who published the following interviews: Jeannette Armstrong in *Tessera*; Smaro Kamboureli and Lola Tostevin in *Canadian Forum*; Daphne Marlatt in *Line*; and Bronwen Wallace in *Open Letter*. My editors at University of Toronto Press, Gerald Hallowell, Laura Macleod, and Ken Lewis, approached this project with welcoming enthusiasm and good humour.

I want to pay special tribute to my teacher the late Eli Mandel, whose poetic voice, critical enthusiasm, and 'gossip theory of Canadian literature' nourished my love of literary and political conversations.

Tragically, one of the interviews could not be entirely edited by the author. Bronwen Wallace was too ill with cancer to make more than initial comments on her transcript. Her literary executor completed the editorial revisions according to Bronwen's original excisions and comments. I am grateful to Carolyn Smart for this contribution at a time of mourning and loss. This book is dedicated to the spirited memory of Bronwen Wallace, whose fighting words and community activism remind us of feminism's transformative promise.

Introduction

Entrevoir: Interviews As Intervention

While training in English studies encourages us to reread, analyse, and evaluate, the homely craft of the interview is often reduced to a secondary and debased pseudo-journalistic genre. However, in a textual universe where critical work on a limited group of writers can proliferate while others starve for public attention, the interview can make space for the writer's revenge. Just as the fluid boundaries of women's conversational gossip can disrupt more authorized forms of knowledge production, the excesses, repetitions, and circuitous routes of these interviews at times explode critical propriety. When I began this interview project, there was little critical work on many of the writers in this book; these interviews were intended to flesh out their textual concerns and provoke positive interference in canonical habits by considering the politics of contemporary Canadian women writing.

The title of these interviews draws together a cluster of meanings around the words *sound* and *resound*: 'to sound,' according to the *OED*, can mean to measure a depth or fathom a sea; 'to resound' indicates voices which echo and reverberate, or turn celebratory, to 'extol loudly or wildly.' The notion of 'sounding differences' suggests a process-oriented exploration which unsettles the critic from any mastering seat of authority. To sound ideas and questions with seventeen women writers whose experiences differ through age, class, ethnicity, race, region, and sexual preference is to hear a welcome noise; silence marks the beginnings of other conversations.

The interviews were recorded over five years in living-rooms or restaurants, during walks by the sea or the prairie, on beaches overlooking high plateau lakes, in cars along mountain highways, or en route to various airports. Filled with diverse experiences, each conversation records women's voices whose language and writing share interests and sometimes don't. Many of them write in hybrid forms which critique the thick-skinned genres of traditional literary studies. Many provide textual openings for readers to contemplate their own engendered and embodied histories. Their work refuses to distinguish in any absolute terms the role of reader, critic, and writer.

The interview genre can interrupt the conventions and power relationships which inform traditional scholarship. The voices in dialogue refuse the closure of correct arguments or final analyses. These conversations are 'thinking in process,' oral essays, good tries or close calls, rehearsed again and again. We would not 'get it right' since our process of thinking / speaking / writing was intended to expose an exploratory series of fluid dialogues over time. Not true transcriptions of a spontaneous moment, the interviews have been edited to incorporate conversations that extended well beyond the initial encounter into a revisionary process of telephone talk, letters, notes on the fly, additional questions, and expanded or excised answers. Some questions landed dead in the air between us until conversation took flight – in some cases, years later in far away locations. During this interval the exchange of new fictions, poems, or essays injected surprise to the turn of talk. Our questions could be round or sharp amidst endless revisions. What emerged from each original encounter were conversations, layered with the insights and anxieties of second thoughts. Each interview talked back to itself, re-sounding the possibilities of new extensions from what had already been said.

Gail Scott suggests that women's reading and writing are processes of self-revelation: '... when women address other women in their writing, the body and the mind are both involved in a seductive process ... of using language, of learning new ways to use it; [this] is linked to a disrobing, self-exposure.' Implicit in the notion of 'interview' is its root in the French entrevoir, 'to have a glimpse,' and s'entrevoir, 'to see each other.' For any interviewer the vulnerability of self-exposure emerges as part of the work's process. While 'interview' suggests that the interviewer can 'catch a glimpse' of the writer, the reverse is also the case. In this respect the interview/conversation is a process of continual de-authorization. When conversation moves through provisional terrain, a sense of mastery is impossible to maintain; just when one feels on top of an idea or a subject, it tumbles into new questions.

Bronwen Wallace remarked that 'the original meaning of the words *converse* and *conversation* carried the sense of "living or having one's being in or among" others, as well as talking with them.'[1] While implicated in the conversation, occasionally I turn on the tape recorder and hear my radio voice, the one that sounds with formulaic words when I intended something more 'authentic.' Caught in the spin of spoken words, I work to maintain equilibrium without holding on too nostalgically to where the conversation might have been trailing. To resist the flow of breath and currents of air is to fail the moment. In the end, I hear the writers' voices at play outside of my critical reading frames.

Any romanticized view of the interviewer brushes aside the very real issues of authority and power. Feminist critics can be marginalized or alienated in universities, which remain marked too often by misogyny. At the same time, the White[2] feminist academic with a stable, well-paying job has privilege and authority denied to many other women. Throughout the interview process I became increasingly conscious of when, as a White bisexual bourgeois woman on my best behaviour (somewhat dutiful and 'good'), institutional privilege and public voice became available to me. In interviews both speaking subjects are speaker and listener, witness and participant. The scholar's solitary armour can't provide much of a protective shield in the process of conducting more than sixty hours of interviews. The interviewer provides a continuous voice and thus finds herself on record in embarrassingly vulnerable rhetorical positions.

The Difference Within

The interviews were originally intended to confound the separate spheres of 'academic feminists' and 'community' writers – of 'elite' theorists and 'unsophisticated' activists. I hoped these conversations would enact the problematic status of this division and suggest how feminist theorizing and praxis can be interconnected in a women's writing community which insists upon the heterogeneity of our commitments. Indeed arbitrary divisions between feminist critic and creative worker, theory and practice, are impossible when 'feminism' itself remains multiple. The contributions of an active feminist creative and critical community in the 1970s and 1980s made possible a richly complex series of cultural works and interventions informed by critical vocabularies specific to our multiple locations. A number of writers interviewed here write through and alongside cultural traditions which interrupt any single-minded reductive sense of Canadian Literature.

The permeability of the boundary between francophone and anglophone texts in some contemporary Canadian and Quebec feminist work has encouraged a variety of theoretically informed writings to flourish. Lesbian writers, building on the earlier visibility of writers like Jane Rule, have explored 'lesbian images' in challengingly innovative forms. And the interventions by Women of Colour have provoked further questions, pushing past the limits of ethnocentricity. It is clear, however, that the occasion of theoretical speaking must be carefully negotiated in order to avoid intimidation. My first interview with Elly Danica suggests how critical readings can sometimes be used by intellectuals as personal armour to establish authority or distance rather than exchange. And Bronwen Wallace pointed to the limitations of a strictly textual theoretical approach to feminism. My own desire was to actively engage with current thinking about feminist issues in order to push through arbitrary splits between communities of readers while working to avoid an exclusionary vocabulary.

The selection of writers to be interviewed developed over the years. Initially my interest was piqued by a group of women writers whose work engaged with contemporary feminist theory, francophone and anglophone, and who developed cross-genre writing. Unafraid to define themselves as 'feminist,' a term sometimes demonized as narrow and prescriptive, these writers were knowledgeable about the intellectual and political possibilities of this self-naming and were conscious of feminism's difficult challenges. At a time when some 'good girl' feminists were supposed to avoid Freud or Marx, others refused to exile and vilify feminist revisions of psychoanalysis or Marxism in order to isolate a sacred body of correct reading and writing. A number of the writers interviewed here were associated in the early 1980s as editors and writers of *Tessera*, a Canadian feminist literary journal dedicated to developing innovative theoretical feminist writing. These writers included Daphne Marlatt and Gail Scott, co-founders and editors with critics Barbara Godard and Kathy Meizei, as well as Nicole Brossard, Smaro Kamboureli, Erin Mouré, Lola Lemire Tostevin, and Betsy Warland.

A recognition of a critical gap in my own intellectual work provoked me to expand beyond questions of gender and theory. My own PHD dissertation on Canadian women poets, completed soon after these interviews began, was marked by a racial homogeneity I wanted to revise. Especially from the mid-1980s feminist writers and scholars provided various forums for women writers to discuss issues of gender, race, and ethnicity. A York University conference featured various workshops and readings, and was attended by Caribbean-Canadian writers Claire Harris and Marlene Nourbese Philip, who are interviewed here. A feminist writing retreat, West Word, featured readings by Jeannette Armstrong, which introduced me to her powerful voice. Lee Maracle's speaking out at the Vancouver 'Telling It' conference and at the Second International Feminist Book Fair, as well as in several articles, made her voice central to the issues circulating in other interviews. The interviews also followed my move from Toronto to Edmonton, where my sense of cultural centres and regions shifted westward.

There are other writers I would like to have interviewed had it been possible to make an even larger volume of conversations. One writer withdrew her interviews, partly because she did not want to address what she presumed would be a predominantly White audience, but also because she felt my own cultural bias framed her responses unproductively. The book would have been strengthened by more coast-to-coast representation (no Maritime writers appear here). A writer like long-time Maritimer Maxine Tynes would have shifted the focus about Black writing away from issues of immigration and underlined the diverse histories, traditions, and concerns of Black writers in Canada. Other writers such as Ukrainian-Canadian Myrna Kostash, a creative non-fiction writer, or Italian-Canadian poet and fiction writer Mary di Michele would have contributed to our understanding of ethnicity and Canadian writing. Other francophone Quebec feminist writers like Louky Bersianik, Jovette Marchessault, or France Théoret have expanded our understanding of women's writing and consciousness and contributed inventive cross-genre texts. 'Differences' between the writers in this book are relative in many ways, and other voices deserve the attention of other interview and writing occasions.

The stubborn edge of courage is a difference between some women's writing which calls for transformation and other texts more easily managed by the status quo. In the process of editing these conversations, some of the writers described their fear of public censure. Over the years I've been working on this book, my own life has been marked by several painful attacks in response to my feminist work. At the beginning of my teaching career at the University of Alberta, I had my backyard fence ripped down after teaching Erin Mouré's lesbian love poems.[3] And last year, along with several other members of the university community, I experienced homophobic insults and misogynist death threats in the name of the anti-feminist murderer of the fourteen Montreal women engineering students. The death threats directed at me may have been linked to my activities organizing a women's peace group against the Gulf War – an ironically violent rhetorical response to a call for peace. What is certain, however, is the accumulated effect of these invasive threats. I am in retreat, sometimes too fearful to speak out. Intimidation, for the moment, has been effective. In listening to my own silence, I look back on these interviews and celebrate the power of these women's words.

On Puzzle Communities

The 'politics of difference' has a significant critical history in feminist publishing.[4] The differences in this collection of interviews include a diversity of ages, ethnicities, races, sexualities, migrations, classes and regions, as well as of formal and critical approaches to writing. Debates about the politics of difference belatedly and painfully developed out of the women's movement and made central what had been marginalized.

While the concept of difference plays a role in the transformation of our cultural and social communities, it is only useful when considered in relation to power.[5] Left unexamined, difference can be an illusionary solution. The White feminist critic/writer/reader risks imposing her own values and criteria in the name of difference when her unwitting *in*difference can mask racism or internalized homophobia. Gloria Anzaldúa writes that 'in pinpointing and dissecting racial, sexual or class "differences" of women-of-colour, whitewomen not only objectify these differences, but also change those differences with their own white, racialized, scrutinizing and alienating gaze.'[6] During the 1980s the Women's Press in Toronto experienced a painful split as one group of feminist volunteers and staff accused another of exclusionary racism. Eventually a number of the founding members of Women's Press were forced out by the group who saw themselves speaking from 'the back of the bus.' The debate was hotly divisive, but in the end it was clear that feminist presses were the only publishing community which would so actively take on public discussions about racism.

The women writers interviewed here have worked to create new communities while risking the wrath of intolerant readers. The diversity of lesbian writing disintegrates any homogeneous lesbian identity. For lesbians like Nicole Brossard, Daphne Marlatt, Erin Mouré, Gail Scott, and Betsy Warland to speak and write within and beyond a censorious and sometimes violent homophobia can provide challenges which yield inventive strategies. For lesbian writers different communities of readers offer different writing possibilities as well as possible conflicts. Betsy Warland describes how her lesbian feminist audience speaks 'different dialects. When you have a small audience, there is the tendency for that audience to want you to represent them, and obviously I can't.'

The 'ideal of community,' according to Iris Marion Young, 'relies on the same desire for social wholeness and identification that underlies racism and ethnic chauvinism on the one hand and political sectarianism on the other.'[7] However, any totalizing singular definition of a 'women's community' loses the intersecting lines of connection which define us. A number of recent interview collections on Indigenous and ethnic writers provide different contexts for some of the writers interviewed here.[8]

In a conversation that is, sadly, unrecorded, Jeannette Armstrong told me how she wrote her poetry in the margins of the official notes she took as a member of the Okanagan Band Council. Sometimes the words arrived in the midst of fevered interchanges moving towards consensus in a collective 3:00 A.M. discussion. The poet in her had no choice; poems came to her in spite, or perhaps, because of her complex engagements in the moment. In this doubled image, the writer is simultaneously active in a community and self-enclosed in solitary retreat. While particular to her constituency and work, Armstrong's aesthetic practice is relevant in other cultural contexts where the writer/artist is vulnerable to dismissal by those who make hardline distinctions between 'the social' and 'the aesthetic.'

Joy Kogawa's writing has been intertwined with her political engagement in seeking redress for the internment of Japanese Canadians. With this relation between politics and writing a central concern, Kogawa comments about one of her characters who 'believes that politics is the sacrifice of the voice from the stars, but one of the people argues that there are stars reflected in the well's dark bottom, and the voice from there also calls. And so, the artist and the political person cannot be differentiated in that sense.'

Writing is a communitarian 'ceremony' for Métis writer Lee Maracle, 'a relationship to the people in my life who need to have their lives articulated and to myself when I need to go forward out into the world.' Responding to a sense of community in a more highly individualized tradition, Betsy Warland wonders whether 'we need to explore the possibility of a new kind of commitment which doesn't rely on sameness or the feminist facade of solidarity or individual solutions'? Daphne Marlatt writes that 'the trouble with idealism ... is that it can overlook the pain of real differences in oppression for the sake of some fantasized solidarity.'[9]

These commentaries insist on our differences. The notion of community in this context is a necessary irony and leads us to consider the work of Julia Kristeva, who sees 'the role of women as a sort of vigilance, a strangeness, as always to be on guard and contestatory.'[10] It is in this context that Kristeva defines a world of 'puzzle' communities where the strangeness and differences between us help define what we share. Imagine 'a politics of difference' in an 'unoppressive city [which would be] defined as openness to unassimilated otherness, ... by giving political representation to group interests and celebrating the distinctive cultures and characteristics of different groups.'[11] This city is where I imagine future interviews to take place – an imaginary place, not one governed by a liberal pluralist politic of diversity which tends to perpetuate the status quo, but an elsewhere bustling with energetic, even ecstatic, languages. In speaking to and of each other in our new city of address, we honour our differences and make alliances. Never do we risk losing ourselves in conclusive endings like this.

Notes

An early version of this text was presented at 'Interventing the Text,' a University of Calgary conference. The proceedings are forthcoming in *Open Letter*.

1 Quoted in Bina Friewald, '"This isn't one to be told / in the third person":
   Bronwen Wallace's Life-Stories,' *Open Letter* 7, no. 9 (1991), 115
2 'White' is upper-case in response to Lee Maracle's suggestion. While 'White'
   is not an undifferentiated category, in a racist society it has a special
   purchase on social and cultural privilege. See also bell hooks, 'Representing Whiteness in the Black Imagination,' in *Cultural Studies*, ed. Law-
   rence Grossberg, Cary Nelson, and Paula Treichler (New York: Routledge
   1992), 338–46.
3 For a discussion of this harassment see 'Can't We Talk about the Alberta
   Flag?: A Conversation between Erin Mouré and Janice Williamson,' *Prairie
   Fire* 13, no. 4 (1992–3), 74–82. In defence of sunny Alberta, attacks against
   feminist academics are not site specific but have occurred across Canada.
   I refuse to call my experiences 'backlash' in light of the compelling arguments made by Janice Newson in '"Backlash" against Feminism: A
   Disempowering Metaphor,' in *Resources for Feminist Research* 20, nos. 3–4
   (1991), 93–7.
4 Critical writings from a variety of feminist ideological and critical perspectives include: Hester Eisenstein and Alice Jardine, eds., *The Future of
   Difference* (New Brunswick, NJ: Rutgers UP 1985); Elizabeth Abel, ed., *Writing and Sexual Difference* (Chicago: U of Chicago P 1982); Barbara Johnson,
   A World of Difference (Baltimore: Johns Hopkins UP 1987); and Gayle Greene
   and Coppélia Kahn, eds., *Making a Difference: Feminist Literary Criticism*
   (London: Methuen 1985). Other more recent contributions to the 'differ-

ence' debate include Julia Emberley, *Thresholds of Difference: Feminist Critique, Native Women's Writings, Postcolonial Theory* (Toronto: U of Toronto P 1993); and Manina Jones, *'That Art of Difference': 'Documentary-Collage' and English-Canadian Writing* (Toronto: U of Toronto P 1993).

5 Canadian literature, like other 'Second World' literatures, can become a critical theatre for the politics of difference. In a public lecture Australian postcolonial critic Alan Lawson discusses this literature as 'a place of negotiation ... of vectors of difference' ('Theorizing "Settler" Cultures: A Problem in Post-Colonial Theory,' 11 Jan. 1993). Himani Bannerji provides an excellent critique of 'the concept of "difference" [which] opens and closes simultaneously some very basic epistemological and social questions.' While she sees theories of difference as 'a politically or discursively expressive gesture,' their lack of 'an analysis of forms of consciousness and social relations [diminishes their] potential for a revolutionary politics' ('But Who Speaks for Us?' in *Unsettling Relations: The University as a Site of Feminist Struggles*, ed. Himani Bannerji et al. [Toronto: Women's P 1991], 85–6).

6 Gloria Anzaldúa, 'Haciendo caras, una entrada,' in *Making Face, Making Soul: Haciendo Caras: Creative and Critical Perspectives by Women of Color*, ed. G. Anzaldúa (San Francisco: aunt lute 1990), xxii

7 Iris Marion Young, 'The Ideal of Community and the Politics of Difference,' in *Feminism/Postmodernism*, ed. Linda J. Nicholson (New York: Routledge 1990), 302

8 See, for example, Jurgen Hesse, ed., *Voices of Change: Immigrant Writers Speak Out* (Vancouver: Pulp P 1990); Linda Hutcheon and Marion Richmond, eds., *Other Solitudes: Canadian Multicultural Fictions* (Toronto: Oxford UP 1990); and Hartmut Lutz, *Contemporary Challenges: Conversations with Canadian Native Authors* (Saskatoon: Fifth House 1991).

9 Daphne Marlatt, 'Introduction,' in *Telling It: Women and Language across Cultures* (Vancouver: Press Gang 1990), 13

10 Julia Kristeva, *Strangers to Ourselves* (Irvington, NY: Columbia UP 1992), 63

11 Young, 'The Ideal of Community and the Politics of Difference,' 319

Often this speech about the 'Other' annihilates, erases: 'No need to hear your voice when I can talk about you better than you can speak about yourself. No need to hear your voice. Only tell me about your pain. I want to know your story. And then I will tell it back to you in a new way. Tell it back to you in such a way that it has become mine, my own. Rewriting you, I write myself anew. I am still author, authority. I am still the colonizer, the speaking subject, and you are now at the centre of my talk.' Stop. We greet you as liberators. This 'we' is that 'us' in the margins, that 'we' who inhabit marginal space that is not a site of domination but a place of resistance. Enter that space. This is an intervention. I am writing to you. I am speaking from a place in the margins where I am different, where I see things differently. I am talking about what I see ...

bell hooks, *Yearning: Race, Gender, and Cultural Politics*

The difference is that I cannot live deferred ... And it's this same difference I ask of your body, the difference of other woman with my regard. Identical to yours. The *same like* a differential equation. Derived from our functions. Point-blank in the luminous spectrum. Projected against one another like a polysemic dream.

Nicole Brossard, *The Aerial Letter*, trans. Marlene Wildeman

Jeannette Armstrong

Grief Is Not the Activity That Heals

grief is only   a place   to begin   it is eyes
turned inward   calling up
disfigured babies   injured   battered   defenceless
open   suck   mouths
hunger shrunken stomachs
crooked bodied adolescents   cower   broken
toothed   blue   black   boot marked
tongues hanging   beaten men
bellies spilling guts   gouges
left for eyes   dry   shrivelled   scrotum sacs
mangled breasted women   legs torn asunder
teeth marks for clothes
rotting cancerous figures   float
to the surface   pieces of death
a dredging   upward   of the guttural   primal
keening   containable in no words   no descriptions
a boiling   and distilling   into bitter water
compacted into crystalline droplets of salt
to be expelled
into excruciating   sundrenched   light
the terrible   the hidden   the unbearable

to grieve   is only to find the place   to begin
the forming into words   the unspeakable
the magic   out of which   comes healing
to bring into understanding   into subjugation
the old lies   that scream and scream
to quiet the internal   quivering and shaking
of flesh and bone   the power to dispel the myths
that cling and cling   to stop the continuous
chant and rattle   of the dying   to turn outward
the eyes   into day   landscape of the living
a leaving of horror   a letting go   never to be recalled

to finally reach outward   to restructure   to allow
time   truth   trust   to pull in   warmth
to fill spaces   with quiet   a light brush of lips

across the cheek   of heart against heart
a murmur   a gentle welling up   an unfettering
of laughter   to wear brightness   fresh words
new stories   a song   the silent singing of which
pushes outward   to fill   others   in the place
to come to

From *Breath Tracks* (Vancouver: Theytus; Stratford, Ont.: Williams-Wallace 1991)

Jeannette Armstrong

'What I intended was to connect ... and it's happened.'

JANICE: We're sitting in your office in the En'owkin Centre, where you administer and teach. Could you tell me a little about the Centre – first of all, what does the name mean?

JEANNETTE: Well, En'owkin Centre is an Okanagan word and comes from the high language in Okanagan. The word, if you are to interpret it, means something like a group challenge to get the best possible answer. So it's partly referring to a consensus process and partly referring to the ability to challenge one another's thinking, to come to the best possible conclusion of any problem. Loosely interpreted that is what En'owkin means. Literally translated it means to drop something through the top of the head into the mind or brain.

JANICE: Several courses presented through the En'owkin Centre will be credited through the University of Victoria.

JEANNETTE: There are now eight courses delivered from the University of Victoria through the En'owkin International School of Writing, including creative writing workshops for poetry and fiction as well as a publishing workshop. There are also Okanagan College base courses, an introductory English course that has the open learning institute format, and a basic creative writing course.

JANICE: Your own writing is quite diverse. You write poetry. You've written a novel, children's stories, and you're also collaborating on a biography with Douglas Cardinal.

JEANNETTE: I wouldn't actually say it's a biography, although it's biographical in nature. The collaboration is really a look at the architect as a Native person and how the Native perspective has influenced not only his creativity but his lifestyle, thinking, and philosophy within his architectural work and his life. I guess you could say it's biological because it's about Doug Cardinal and his creative process, but we're really focusing on the Native world-view and philosophy as it connects to the creative process.

JANICE: When you're discussing this book with him, does your particular insight as a woman writer connect with his perspective? Are there different creative processes for female and male Native writers?

JEANNETTE: It's difficult to answer that question, but I think that Doug selected me to work with him on this particular aspect of his thinking and philosophy, first, because I am a Native writer, and, second, because I have a traditional perspective compatible with his understanding and creative process. As a Native person and Native writer, I can key into, understand, and articulate, those two things in relation to his thoughts. So that makes it a collaboration, rather than an editorial relationship or whatever. We're not talking about architecture in this book. That should be clear.

JANICE: What about the question of gender and the Native creative process?

JEANNETTE: That is interesting. Doug is one of the people I greatly admire because he understands the necessity of reconciling the two sides of ourselves in becoming a whole person. He has had to reconcile and work with the feminine aspect of power. He calls it the 'soft power' which has empowered his thinking and philosophy. For myself as a Native woman and as a writer this process is very interesting. He's working in the place where feminist thinking comes from. He has said very clearly that if males would allow their thinking to be sourced by feminine thought and the processes engendered in that, the power they could have in terms of potential change in the world would be much greater than it is at this time. As a female and also as a feminist, my interest is in looking at and understanding people who are thinking not about male or female, but in terms of feminine gender and thinking. It's critical to my thinking and philosophy to understand how this feminine process can work in healing both the world and individuals in the world, including males.

JANICE: Your poem 'Indian Woman' is printed as a double poem. On the left-hand side is a poem of pain and suffering, of deprivation and the degradation of naming the Indian woman 'squaw'; on the right-hand side there's a very powerful invocation of Indian women's strength. How did you arrive at this double narrative form?

JEANNETTE: Well, that wasn't very hard because the first portrayal is a common, stereotypical understanding that the majority unfortunately has of Native Indian women. The visual images are over-dramatized in terms of their presentation, but basically that's how people look at Indian women in Canada, and I'm talking about all levels of people, from professionals all the way down to the people at street-level. For Native women, this becomes an image of themselves, an image that they take on and help to perpetuate, sometimes in frustration and anger and hostility. But at some point the other image of Native women that is really what being woman and in particular what being Native woman is needs to be given to Native people. This is our perspective. I want to be sure that other Native women have an understanding of the perspective I have of myself, so that they can look at themselves in a different way. Juxtaposing the two perspectives together is a technical thing: this is how other people see you, but over here is how you really are. This is what we Native women must portray, understand, and pass on to our daughters and granddaugthers.

JANICE: In Beatrice Culleton's *In Search of April Raintree* there's a twinning of two women, one who suffers from abuse and prostitution and another, more affirmative woman who retrieves herself. This double representation repeats your own twinning in the poem. Are you in close contact with other Native women writers and do you share a vision of the world with them?

JEANNETTE: In the last five years one of the things that's happened is a synchronicity with other Native women writers. It's eerie in that it seems to be happening in a synchronous way for all of us. We've been in contact with one another and have tried at various times to get together and talk. When we *do* do that, we find amazing parallels. Many Native women are emerging at this point, as writers, performers, artists, or people working in political arenas. Because the women are the central backbone of the family and of the next generation, a healing in terms of ourselves first needs to be understood by Native women and carried out before healing in the family and outward to the rest of the community can take place. Many native women are emerging out of necessity and taking a real leadership role, and this was really apparent at the Second International Feminist Book Fair in Montreal, where all the top Native women writers came together. It was a wonderful experience to realize that we weren't alone in our separate corners working.

JANICE: At the Feminist Book Fair, you talked about the power of healing and the voice of Native women. How does writing and finding your voice heal you and heal the reader?

JEANNETTE: The reader is secondary to the person writing. It's opposite to the reader's point of view. I can only speak for myself as a writer, not for other writers in the world. It's a whole process of uncovering layers of mythology about what society and people should be about forced onto me by other people's thinking and philosophy, of discovering through those layers the Native principles that I've been given through my teachers, of looking at these principles truthfully and honestly in terms of how they equate with the negative myths. The process of writing as a Native person has been a healing one for me because I've uncovered the fact that I'm not a savage, not dirty and ugly and not *less* because I have brown skin, or a Native philosophy. In fact, I've found that *my* philosophy, and my people's philosophy, of harmony, cooperation, and healing has a lot more relevance today in terms of humanity and the whole world, where individualism is causing social chaos and where people are killing the environment out of individual selfish need, out of not thinking about their fellow humans or even the next generation. In uncovering my own philosophy as a Native person, I've come to realize that my people and my self are beautiful and necessary in this world, where there is sickness, discordance, chaos, hatred, and violence. That discovery continues to be a healing process. Everyday I wake up and think, 'God, I'm glad I'm Indian!' People out there who are Indian who don't know that need to understand. The suicide rates and problems our people are having are a result of being told you're stupid, ignorant, a drunk, you'll never amount to anything – just because you're Indian. To me, that's the biggest lie of all that needs to be dispelled. It's my vocation or commitment to do that, and whatever happens for non-Native people in that process is a by-product.

JANICE: You use the word *Indian* to describe yourself and I use the word *Native*. Can you talk about that difference in language?

JEANNETTE: Sure. I like to use *Indian* mainly because the word itself is not a word which is derogatory but generic. There is no such thing as an Indian person – either you're Okanagan or you're Shuswap, Mohawk, Cree, or whatever. That's what we are. If I were being fully truthful, honest, I would say I'm Okanagan. I'm not Indian. I'm not Native. I'm not whatever you classify me as. I'm Okanagan. That's a political and cultural definition of who I am, a geographical definition, and also a spiritual definition for myself of who I am because that's where my philosophy and my world-view comes from. That would be the most correct way of defining it. But because there are categories of people in North America, there needs to be some word which describes us in a generic sense, and so I prefer *Indian*, mainly because it is a word that was used in some of Columbus's writings to describe who we were, *Indian* coming from *in deo*, meaning 'in with God.' That was how he described us. I understand that this description wasn't because of confusion with India, because historically at that time, it wasn't called 'India,' but 'Hindi,' or 'Hindustani,' or whatever. We would have been called 'Hindians,' I guess, if that's where the confusion was. But my understanding is that he referred to those people he came in contact with as being 'in with God' because of their innocence, purity, harmony, and cooperation with one another. And so I prefer this word, of course, because I feel that we are in with God.

JANICE: When you talk about the pre-conquest Okanagan culture, you point to the empowerment of women within it. Could you elaborate on the power of women in Okanagan culture?

JEANNETTE: I had always known as a child that I was female and different in physical terms from men. That's something that's always there and has to be recognized because we're basically mammals and have basic instincts. My grandmother, my aunts, and my mother explained this to me. It was very clear when I was becoming a teenager, and it is a reality that you accept. I got a clear message from my grandmother that no person has a right to coerce or own another person or act in a way which determines by force that the person doesn't have a choice. No person has that right over another person.

It's not dependent on gender or authority or whatever. We are born free and are free people, but we understand the kinds of things that make up families, the customs of people. We understand the accepted relationships between people, whether they're male or female and what their places are as either the mother or the father. Those things were explained to me by my grandmother, a very powerful woman, who influenced me to a great degree. My aunt influenced me as well. I always knew as a child working with them that I owned myself, that I would always own myself. I was always the choice-maker, and what I accepted to be done to me, I accepted to be done to me. You can talk about love relationships and all of those things from that point of view. In terms of family stability, I was told that as a woman I would bear the children. I had the prime responsibility to be sure that I was in control enough of my own life to be able to provide for them. We don't just see the husband as being responsible for those children. We see both sides of the whole family – aunts and uncles and grandparents and brothers and sisters – are all equally responsible. In my family, I am responsible for my nieces and nephews and so on from both sides as their parents are. Ownership of property and work was always shared with the Okanagan people. I don't remember a time when work wasn't shared by members of our family, depending on how physically able they were. I went out on berry-picking camps with my grandmother and my aunts and my brothers and sisters, my uncles, my father and so on – we would go out and camp for a week or two weeks at a time and all the work was shared. Men went out there and dug roots or picked berries, and they also went out on hunting expeditions. Women went with them, and they still do in my family. We're a traditional family. My understanding is that that's always the way it was. I worked out in the fields when I was a child, along with my sisters, and my aunts. We used to have to do hay by hand – not cut it, but shock the hay, pile it up, and bring it in. We worked out there with the men, and there was no difference in the division of labour. Same as in the household – the work was divided equally, and I grew up *expecting* that people, if they were physically and mentally able, would take part in the work. It was the same way with the thinking process. The responsibility for the thinking in the family was shared equally. Every family has a process. In fact, my mother, aunt, and grandmother were the strongest people in terms of the thinking, the choice-making, the decision-making. My grandmother was law; she was a matriarch and what she said went. The same thing passed to my aunt, who was the law. What she said in the family – and it wasn't just out of the top of her head – it was as a result of knowing what everybody's thinking was, what everybody's reasons were. She was able to bring that back to everybody, who knew she was right, of course. So she had great power in the family, and I grew up with and understood that kind of thinking. I knew who the powerful people were in my family and they were female. I understood that it had always been that way with the Okanagan people – and I don't mean that it's matriarchal. I mean that it's shared equally. There are families where male figures are dominant and do the thinking. But it's not because they're male, it's because they're the best people for that job. In the same way, in those families with dominant females as the powerful part of the family, they're the best people for that!

JANICE: There are no Okanagan pronouns for 'he' and 'she.' Does your language encode this egalitarian reciprocity?

JEANNETTE: Absolutely. Glen Douglas, a researcher and Native elder here, who is fully versed in the language and philosophy of our people, has done research with me. I'm not prepared at this time to publish anything, but I'm documenting it so eventually something will come out about it. In looking at the stories and legends of the Okanagan people, I've found the coyote stories in particular don't dwell on female and male roles. There is differentiation between male and female, but what is focused on is the character that it symbolizes or personifies and the process that's used to develop that character. When you look at the language in connection with that, there's no way that we can refer to a person in a general sense in our language. We have to identify *how* we relate to that person before we can talk about that person. I would have to say 'my aunt' or 'my grandmother' or 'the person who has done this kind of thing' or 'the person who is in charge of this or that,' if I'm going to refer to a person – or I have to say a name directly. If I don't know the name, I would say the person who has been involved in connection with this. I can't say 'he,' or 'she.' A person is always connected or related to something, and we must always refer to that connection or that relationship. So if we refer to a person as a woman, it's always in terms of that woman's connection or relationship to us or to another person or to the work that's being done. There's no way of connecting that to gender. The culture doesn't separate by gender – though it recognizes that certain things are attached to male and female out of necessity – but in terms of who we are, what we do, and how we think and feel, and gender doesn't have anything to do with how well we do things or how as human beings we connect to one another.

JANICE: For a feminist outside your culture this Okanagan language logic appears utopian. But in your novel *Slash* you take a hard look at the everyday politics of Native life through a fictional re-creation of activities in the seventies. How did you come to write *Slash*?

JEANNETTE: There wasn't *one* decision that I took to write that story. Oddly enough, it is the question of the breakdown in our society in relation to the male role that prompted me to write about and use a male character as a focus to write from. I don't know if my working with that was fair in terms of the male role. One of the practical reasons that I chose a male character was the politics at that time – the Native male was at the forefront and engendered the thought of the American Indian movement. There were a lot of things wrong with this, including the male ego and a displaced philosophy regarding what role the Native woman played. I raged against that at the time, as did many Native women, because we knew it was wrong and false and that any movement forward for Native people, any healing, needed to reconcile this. For the historical sense of the novel it was appropriate to have a male figure at the forefront, but there's also a philosophical reason. I needed to uncover for myself what my own hang-ups were in terms of the male role in Native society. I needed to know how they affected the progress of the movement in the positive and negative sense, to understand and then present an alternative. I wanted to be able to say, well, this is what could be, or what should be, or what can happen. If you look at the shaping and progress of that character from the beginning to the philosophy he develops at the end, he moves a lot closer to the philosophy which allows changes in the male role. That's were the concentration of work has to be done. Healing needs to take place between male and female, and the males need to reconcile their own female power, compassion, love, and caring. Their need to feel and be sensitive can only be learned from the Native females, or through the long process that the character Slash had to go through. At the end, Slash is able to be what he needs to be and have the strength he needs. That is a message I wanted to pass to my brothers, so they will be able to see and understand. Native men who have read *Slash* come to me and say things that I need to hear. There hasn't been one Native male who has come to me and said 'bullshit.' They say either 'that's where I've come to' or 'that's where I need to go to.'

JANICE: When you were writing *Slash*, did you imagine yourself writing towards a particular audience? Did you intend to address Native men?

JEANNETTE: Primarily I wrote because I was so damned frustrated with the egos out there that were so big and interfering and acting as obstacles to any kind of real powerful work that could go on. And I was angry! I was angry. I was saying – I want to swear. You're doing all kinds of shit that has nothing to do with reality; it has more to do with your arrogance that has been handed to you by this paternalistic European society. It's full of shit. That's not being Indian. A lot of things, a lot of potential things that could have been really powerful, ended or were disfigured or corrupted because of that arrogance, and it continues. I'm not saying only Native males are doing that – there are Native women who go along and push and promote and support it. I was talking to them as well. I don't want to be seen as someone who's negative and tears people down. I would rather be someone who's positive. I would rather say, look at this easier and better way of doing things. I've been called by feminist groups for making the central character male, and I'm saying that's the exact reason I did it. You can spend your life cutting down and putting down men, but what the hell are your doing to change them? What the hell are you doing to teach differently? Sexism – whether you're male or female – is against doing it differently.

JANICE: Does the systemic oppression of Native peoples give you a greater sense of solidarity with Native men in spite of the differences that might exist between some of you?

JEANNETTE: Yes, it absolutely does. A number of Native people who were involved in the movement talked to me and said, 'I never was able to articulate it, or even see it in terms of the questions that you pose' – and that's what they really are, questions which make things clearer. Had a lot of people known, or questioned some of these things at that time, it might have been different for us. I know that when I travel, Native people come to the readings, lectures, and workshops and want to talk to me. The most frightening thing about writing for me is that these are the people I'm writing to and about and for, and they are going to tell me whether I did wrong or right. So far I haven't had any negative criticism, and I've really made contact with a lot of the people who do read. I don't know about the people who don't read, but I've been amazed because some of those who have read *Slash* are not novel-readers. But they've picked up this book and said, it's the first book that I've read. And I thought, 'Holy!'

JANICE: You actually began writing *Slash* on a dare, in response to there not being enough fiction books by Native writers available.

JEANNETTE: You shouldn't confuse the dare with *Slash* because at that time it was a concept that didn't have *Slash* attached to it in terms of the character and the novel. I developed the concept of filling a gap in the contemporary history of Native thought over the past twenty-five years. The curriculum project here was looking for writers who could look at contemporary history and write something that students could connect and relate to other than just a dry history of dates. The Okanagan Indian Curriculum Project began in 1979, and by 1981 or 1982 I was working as a researcher and involved in bringing together materials and selecting which periods of history we'd be focusing on. I knew basically what we wanted, although it could have resulted in a film, or a series of short stories, or whatever. Anyway, the whole thing went off-key, though it wasn't really a confrontation. We sat down in a planning session, and one of the consultants who was concerned that we get the best materials written for the project said OK, you get hold of the Native writers, and I'll get hold of the non-Native writers. We can bring them together, sort through them, and figure out what can be done. At that point I told him that there's enough Native writers and you're coordinating this so here are some names, addresses, and phone numbers, so you can get hold of them. On my own I contacted a couple of people. We had a huge meeting, and it turned out that his point of view was that there was no use getting hold of these Native writers since none of them was well known. He did try with a couple of them but didn't get a response because basically he said, who are you, what did you write, what did you publish, and so on. Anyway, he had some pretty well-known non-Native writers lined up who said, yeah, we'd like to get involved, we'd like to help out. One of them was George Ryga, who is a good friend of mine. We got together in this meeting with other people I won't mention, but who are prominent non-Native names in Canadian literature. Not only were they willing to do the work, but they were basically dripping at the mouth. And there were publishers who were prompting them, saying, yeah, get in on that because these things sell. I was in a real disadvantaged position at the meeting, and I felt pretty angry because I had three Native writers who were willing to work with the researchers. They were unpublished, but I knew they could do the writing. I got angry and just got up and said, 'I can't go along with this.' I told the guy who was my director, 'If this is your idea of turning this project into something that non-Native people are going to benefit from, then I wash my hands of it. And I'm going to make sure from this point on that this project doesn't go because I'm not going to have *my* culture and the Okanagan people exploited this way. There have been too many exploitations.' The consultant said the Native writers weren't invited to this meeting while the well-known White writers *were* invited and we need to get down to business and decide now, tonight, who's going to be writing what. I got up and said, 'Well I'm walking out of this meeting. As far as I'm concerned, this project is dead because I'm going to the Tribal Council tomorrow. If you guys don't think I won't, try me.' Jeff Smith, the director, knew that I meant what I said. None of the other people understood the influence that I had with the Tribal Council at that particular time; they would have shut the project down, and Jeff knew it. So the consultant said, 'Well, OK, then I quit. If you want to get these things written, then you can god-damn well write it yourself.' So I said, 'Sure. No problem with that.' I didn't know what I was talking about at the time, but I was angry enough to say anything. George got up and walked out with me and the other Native writers saying, 'I totally agree with Jeannette. It's Native people who should be doing this and I'll help them do it, if I'm the only one.' The other writers didn't know what was going on, and didn't know what to do or say. It wasn't their fault at all. The next day I came back in and Jeff said, 'The consultant is off the project and so are all those other non-Native people. Let's sit down and regroup and decide what we're going to do.' Two films and two books came out of that meeting as well as writing which was never published for trade but was used in the curriculum.

JANICE: The process of writing a novel is very demanding. Did you know what you were getting into?

JEANNETTE: I had no idea when I made that statement that it was going to be a novel. My concept was that I could interview people and recreate the historical situation. I had in mind a historical account or a series of short stories for the classroom situation. But when we sat down to discuss the whole idea, we decided it would be best to produce for each grade level, so we distributed the work in terms of grade. Howard Green was given the grade 10; Glen James was given the grade 8; films were done for grades 7 and 9; and I worked on grade 11, which was contemporary history. My process was to look, first of all, at all of the historical material from 1960 to the present. I sat down and tried to cover everything that happened in Indian country during that time in the States and Canada. I looked at it in terms of what influenced the thinking of the people and how it affected Indian lifestyles, communities, and individuals. Growing up through that time I knew some of it, and particularly during the seventies I knew some of the feeling as well. So once I amassed the research the first year, I did massive interviews with people at all levels of the community, not with the intention of using their words but of finding out myself what their thinking and feelings were, and where the people were in terms of their hopes, their dreams, their hearts, their rage. I documented a chronology of events and put together a profile of the thinking of the period. I submitted a six-page outline of the events to the Curriculum Department and asked them how they wanted me to proceed. The committee looked at it and said the best way would be to develop this into a novel or a story in which one character experiences some of these feelings first-hand and shows the effects on his family or friends or his people. In that way, when a person reads, they could experience the process as if they were going through it. Yeah, I thought, good idea, OK. At that point I still didn't realize what it would take to put that in place. I had never written anything as comprehensive of that nature. So I sat down and said, oh, OK, fine, but whose story? It couldn't be one person's story because no one person could have experienced all those things. One of the balances I had to create was whether that character was a non-traditional person or a traditional person who goes through a metamorphosis. I decided on the traditional because that was what I was most comfortable with myself. I did do a character sketch around the non-traditional character, Slash's friend, as a focus, but I just didn't understand enough about his thinking, philosophy, hopes, dreams, and motivation. On the surface I could, but I couldn't reconcile his feelings with the person I am. I understood that a lot of yourself is tied up in a first novel, so I accepted that I would work with a traditional character. Even at that point, I hadn't decided on male or female. I could have had powerful female characters, but female leaders in the American Indian movement were very few and unique in terms of personality and development. I didn't want to be untruthful and emulate one of those very rare and beautiful individuals like Anna-May Aquash and other women who are still alive at this time. But I didn't want to be dishonest and create a general female because I know the powerful role those unique females played and I didn't want to mess with that. They or someone who knew them very well will tell their story. For practical reasons I decided the male character would be best in my storytelling, so I looked at everything I was angry and frustrated at in the Native male who was torn between role and ego. In the end, through his metamorphosis into a personality, this character reconciled himself to his feminine qualities. By 'feminine,' I mean the capacity for compassion, love, sensitivity, and understanding that's required by the soft non-aggressive approach. We call it 'feminine' or feminist thought, but really it is the reconciliation of both male and female and the wholeness and healthiness of who we are as human beings that I wanted to move this character towards.

JANICE: If you see your novel as a teaching story, particularly for male Native readers, is your poetry writing different?

JEANNETTE: It's a very different process. The creative process for writing, storytelling, fiction or non-fiction, is a recognition and a putting together of information, a recounting of things external, so that it makes a coherent sense in retelling what may have happened. That's where my dividing line is between prose and poetry. Poetry is the opposite creative process. It's an identification of the landscape inside me, my own internal sensibility, reactions, and understanding of all that affects me as a person. Poetry is a process in which I attempt to put into words internal things that rise up out of the subconscious, out of my spirituality and my intellect. I try to make sense of them in terms of what makes me human, what makes me Jeannette Armstrong, what makes me Native, what makes me woman. So it's an identification of the internal things that I am and their coherence with the external.

JANICE: You criticize an evaluative system that would dictate what is 'good' Native writing in terms of a White tradition. You oppose this ethnocentric notion of the 'literary' with Native oratory. Can you elaborate on this difference?

JEANNETTE: It's one of the things that I'm exploring. If we were to say prose is over there, oratory lies in the middle. Some of the political oratory of Native people and my own oratory attempts to bridge two separate cultures and world-views. We are bridging a gap into another culture for non-Native understanding of the internal humanness in how our people relate to the world. In Native oratory, you're trying to draw on symbols, metaphors, and images to help the understanding of your presentation of internal philosophy. This is how some of the most beautiful pieces of oratory happen. If you look at the contemporary oratory of Dan George and James Cosnell, traditional oratory shows through because they're searching for metaphors, symbols, and archetypes submerged in our culture. They're attempting to put them into English terminology and English words and to relate to the underlying givens of European culture that we just take for granted in terms of structures. In oratory, poetry happens in a prose situation. You have to draw on poetic tools when you're trying to tell a history or a political or social reality. Some of the most beautiful writing falls into this category but is often discarded as invalid because it is 'political' or 'sociological.'

JANICE: Ezra Pound called poetry 'the dance of the intellect.' The dance of Native oratory is very different from Pound's, but how do you think about the body in your tradition?

JEANNETTE: Well that's the question that we'll be looking at in the oral tradition. Written literature hasn't been in place for European peoples for a heck of a long time. You came from an oral tradition like I did. Over generations learning has passed on in speech or oral images. How was that done? How was that transfer made through folk stories, legends, and mythology? This is connected to how one person's physical being transferred it to another person's physical being without that gap in between which is paper or a stone tablet. I'm exploring how the oral tradition connects to the body, the voice, our thinking, and our internal processes. In political oratory a person makes certain points and depends on the rise and fall of voice, the emotion in the tone of their speech, the rhythm and sound of the words, and also the animation, the posturing of the body. In my culture language depends on gestures, body gesture. In storytelling, where you're getting the ideas across in oral form, body gesture is an integral part. We hear sound, and physically sound becomes something else for us, something we interpret as understanding. When you remove the body and put a piece of paper in its place, what happens? How do you compensate for that loss of the body? In our writing school we'll be exploring and looking at how you replace the body in writing.

JANICE: This is thinking through the body in a different way, and it returns us to your discussion of the origins of *Slash*. How do you feel about non-Native writers like Anne Cameron or W.P. Kinsella writing from a Native perspective and using Native mythology?

JEANNETTE: I have real problems with it because they're putting themselves in a position which they have no knowledge of, really. They can't be Native because it takes more than reading the mythology or knowing Indian people. They present their non-Native individual personal view as a microspective of the outward, larger Native perspective. It takes being Indian, living that culture, and understanding which you acquire almost through osmosis. You can't transplant yourself as a European or whatever into my thought processes or subconscious and the symbols and archetypes I draw on.

A person can live within a Native culture and absorb or glimpse some of the culture. I don't have a problem with people writing about whatever they want to write about, but our people have been stereotyped, misunderstood, and misrepresented in many ways. This has been damaging and exploitative. People need to tell their own stories – whatever culture they're from – in order to relate to one another in a more truthful sense. We need to understand one another if we're going to survive as different peoples in this world and start combatting things like racism and classism and sexism. We writers have the responsibility to clarify for the world who we are, what we are, where we fit in, and what our perspective is. I don't have any business clarifying for someone else out there. This is a free world, and I'll speak out and say that whenever I'm asked, not pointing a finger particularly at any one person. People have to make up their own minds, but every time a space is taken up in the publishing world and the reading community, it means that a Native person isn't being heard and that has great impact.

JANICE: Liberals would say that since writing is an imaginative act, a good writer will be able to imagine what it is to have the complex experience of a Native person. But that argument doesn't take up the practical issue of who is being published.

JEANNETTE: Exactly. And that's the proof of the pudding right there. I hold people responsible. I can't do anything to stop them, but they on the other hand can't stop me from saying, well, unless you're Native, you don't have a Native perspective no matter *what* kind of an imagination you have.

JANICE: How did you come to imagine yourself a writer? Did it happen when you were a young girl?

JEANNETTE: I never imagined myself as a writer, and I still have some difficulty with that. I didn't strive to be a writer; I *was* a writer. In retrospect, I know now that I had the makings when I was a child. I was writing very early. My first worst piece of poetry in the world was published when I was fifteen. I was writing in school, and I was writing for myself at home. I was just writing because I liked it. I liked putting things down, saying things, and using the language. I was a compulsive reader, and I just liked the sound of words; it was like magic for me. I never really understood that all of that works out to being a writer. For me, it was just a pure act of something that I enjoyed. Other than visual arts, nothing else could do that for me. Answering that question is difficult because even at this point in time I don't see myself as a writer who wants to be a writer. Writing is what I have to do. Writing is what I do. I have piles and piles of stuff that's not going to be published. But I have to write because I need to map out my thinking and understanding. In practical ways I use my writing in my everyday life. It makes the world make sense and brings a sensibility, a coherence, to the world around me which would otherwise be chaotic. I find that I get hung up on issues and ideas unless I can sit down and write to put them together. It's that process rather than the finished product that is important, so I guess if you call that being a writer, that's what I am.

JANICE: Are you going to participate in the writing school?

JEANNETTE: Yes, I will be coordinating the writers who will be coming to do the lectures, readings, and workshops with the students, and I will be acting as instructor in between those writers.

JANICE: Will you do the performance work about the body in storytelling you were speaking about earlier?

JEANNETTE: Yes, that's one of the main focuses of both fiction and non-fiction, poetry and prose. We'll be looking at how the oral tradition works with performance – music, sound, and dance, and speech rhythm. We have some exciting people lined up, including Inuit storyteller Minnie Freeman; Wilfred Peltier, a storyteller and an elder from back East; storyteller and writer Maria Campbell; Margo Kane, a performance artist; and West Coast writer Lee Maracle. And we're looking at a number of people from the States as well, Native writers like poet and Native literature professor Joy Harjo, Elizabeth Cook-Lynn, Roberta Hill Whiteman, James Welch, Lucy Tapahonso, and others. We're looking at traditional storytellers, those who have published, like Ellen White from Nanaimo, as well as the non-published storytellers, including local people who are very good.

JANICE: You publish with Theytus Books here in Penticton, which has been housed in the same building as En'owkin School since 1980. Is the writing school going to have links to the Native press?

JEANNETTE: We will in an indirect sense. Our publishing workshop is not concerned with the technical aspects of production but with the critical thinking that needs to be done around Native literature. What is Native literature? What is *good* in Native literature? What is the focus? How will the layout and design of the book make a format for the book? Who is the audience and how do you reach it? Theytus Press will play a part in that they've agreed to come to do some workshops. Elizabeth Cook-Lynn, an editor for *The Wicazo SA Review*, a Native review journal at Eastern Washington University, will work with the students on the form used for reviewing Native literature.

JANICE: And who are the students?

JEANNETTE: Students have applied to us from different parts of Canada. Students have various levels of expertise and have been working in different areas, such as journalistic or creative writing. We're going to be really careful in selecting the first-year students, so we may end up with a relatively small group, anywhere from ten to twenty people, likely about a dozen or less students.

JANICE: You've just recorded one of your oratories on a tape. How did you come to work with dubb poets?

JEANNETTE: Patrick Andrade is a Jamaican person living in Canada who was really fascinated with the rhythms in Native oratory and poetry. He suggested we put together Native poetry with reggae and made the tape 'Poetry Is Not a Luxury.' My music in that piece was not set to reggae. I collaborated with Selwyn Redivo, a classical guitarist. It wasn't actually dubb poetry. In the second tape, 'Theft of Paradise,' I read poetry with reggae music. The latest exercise is political oratory and doesn't have reggae music. I was invited to deliver a key-note address to a national gathering of Native youth in Ottawa. I wrote a speech which had actually been printed up and distributed in the conference kit. But in listening to the presentations prior to mine, I realized that everyone making presentations talked down and preached to the youth, saying, you gotta do this, you gotta change this, you're seriously delinquent and so on. What they really need at this time is somebody to lift them up, to encourage and tell them, you're needed, you're useful, you're valuable. You're the next generation. You have everything in you; all you need to do is work with it. So I thought, well, the hell with the speech that I had written; I'm gonna go up there and talk to these people. So I said, well, if you wanna read my written speech, look in the kit because I'm just gonna talk to you. I talked to them in oratory style. My music group was doing the sound and they taped the speech called 'We Are Valuable.'

JANICE: You've worked with the artists in different cultural communities. What is your relationship to Women of Colour who are immigrants to Canada over the last several generations or to White women who are recent immigrants?

JEANNETTE: To be honest I haven't given that a lot of thought. We all face practical problems in terms of not being able to find a publisher interested in the writing of ethnic minority groups. We struggle. First of all, we have to speak and produce in English and fit into comfortable genres for the Canadian reading public. Female writers of any colour face the same thing because the publishing world is dominated by male thinking and male words. That's a reality for all of us. Commercial publishing is restrictive. There's a lot of good information that should be state-supported because that information is necessary, but we're all dependent on free enterprise and shouldn't be. In literature we get a corrupt picture of the world because of that.

JANICE: In the process of our conversation I found tears welling up in my eyes. Your oratory is very powerful, even in this interview setting. You have an ability to move people with your conviction, and that's a very wonderful skill, gift, and talent.

JEANNETTE: I feel good about that. That's one of the things that tells me we're connecting on an honest level. In the last five years that I've been travelling to workshops, lectures, and readings I've been surprised that European peoples have a fear of feeling and being exposed. But if I am honest and truthful and open up and touch those parts of the person where there is feeling and sensitivity about issues, it sometimes comes as a surprise to them to react really emotionally and not know what to do about it. Sometimes they even apologize for it. I say no, that's what being human is about. If we can connect at that level between people, between individuals, between sexes, races, or classes, that's what's gonna make the difference and bring about the healing we human beings have to have to bring us closer, to work together, and live together, care for and love one another, and look at change passing onto the next generation. It's not gonna be politics that will connect people. To touch and understand one another is to bridge our differences, and that makes me feel really good, happy, and clean in knowing that I've connected. I don't feel embarrassed or bad for the person. Sometimes people do feel bad, but I try to reassure them and say no, it's good if we can connect this way, it's good, it's good. What I intended was to connect that way, was to get something across, and it's happened.

Penticton, August 1989

Di Brandt

nonresistance or, love Mennonite style

(for L. & the others)

turn the other cheek when your brother
hits you & your best friend tells fibs
about you & the teacher punishes you
unfairly if someone steals your shirt
give him your coat to boot this will
heap coals of fire on his head & let him
know how greatly superior you are
while he & his cronies dicker & bargain
their way to hell you can hold your
head up that is down humbly knowing
you're bound for the better place where
it gets tricky is when your grandfather
tickles you too hard or your cousins
want to play doctor & your uncle kisses
you too long on the lips & part of you
wants it & the other part knows it's
wrong & you want to run away but you
can't because he's a man like your father
& the secret place inside you feels itchy
& hot & you wonder if this is what hell
feels like & you remember the look on
your mother's face when she makes
herself obey your dad & meanwhile her
body is shouting *No! No!* & he doesn't
even notice & you wish you could stop
being angry all the time but you can't
because God is watching & he sees
everything there isn't any place to let
it out & you understand about love the
lavish sacrifice in it how it will stretch
your woman's belly & heap fire on your
head you understand how love is like
a knife & a daughter is not a son & the
only way you will be saved is by

submitting quietly in your grandfather's
house your flesh smouldering in the
darkened room as you love your enemy
deeply unwillingly & full of shame

From *Agnes in the Sky* (Winnipeg: Turnstone 1990)

Di Brandt

'The sadness in this book is that I'm reaching for this story ...'

JANICE: Di, you write towards different audiences: on the one hand, a Mennonite community; and on the other, a feminist community. How do these communities intersect in your work?

DI: When I started writing, I had a Mennonite audience in mind, which is mostly a fictional audience consisting of the Mennonite community that I grew up in, which isn't quite the same as the contemporary Mennonite community. I was writing very much against this fictional Mennonite audience, so it was very scary writing, because I felt I was transgressing rules on every page, in every line. But the people who responded to my writing and wanted to publish it, of course, were not people from this imaginary audience. So I had a very strange sense that the people who could hear these words were not the people they were addressed to. That was the beginning of my sense of having a double audience. I'm anticipating the publication of this book [*Questions i asked my mother*] in the fall, and by now I have a sense that there is a real Mennonite audience out there, a large, very hungry audience starved for Mennonite poetry, awaiting the publication of this book. On the other hand, I'm also still very scared of the Mennonite community because my book probably asks for a bigger opportunity than most of them will be willing to give.

JANICE: Can you discuss the functional differences between the prose and poetic narratives in your book?

DI: If I think of my heritage in terms of territory, there was the territory which I inherited from my father, the language of God and truth and the self. But the storyteller in my family was my mother, and her stories were not about that at all; they were about events that happened, so I guess the poetry and prose represent these two separate territories. The poetry is somehow addressing a more intimate or metaphysical question, the question of the self or identity in a very direct way. The stories are addressing the question of the self in a much more social and more fictional sense; it's a story of experience. The fitting together of different experiences of the everyday was more the woman's territory.

JANICE: It reminds me of Charlotte Lennox's eighteenth-century novel *The Female Quixote*, where Arabella's mother dies and she's sent into the library to educate herself by reading her father's books. But instead of reading his classical books, she reads her mother's sixteenth-century romances and constructs her life in terms of relationship and romance.

DI: Yes, the prose gives the possibility of talking about the diamond earrings and bracelets, let's say, rather than asking who I am or who God is.

JANICE: So the prose passages are clearly 'feminine' in terms of how our gendered culture organizes the world, in terms of female costume, pleasure, relationships.

DI: The men constructed their identity through language, and the women did it through their things.

JANICE: And through gossip.

DI: Gossip, and organizing social events. Social interaction was in many ways controlled by women in my community, and that was seen as a lesser activity. It becomes a question of hierarchy of genres in the book. Which is important and more true? My editors wanted to cut out the prose pieces, but I said no, because that female territory in them seemed very important to the story being told.

JANICE: Traditionally, poetry has always been the terrain of expert men, while fiction is the quotidian feminine. As well as a gender distinction, there's a class distinction between the two genres.

DI: Yes, and that's what I'm trying to resist.

JANICE: We can talk of culture and community, but what of discrimination and difference? How does the Mennonite community distinguish itself from other cultural groups?

DI: In contrast to a lot of other ethnic groups who are trying to become assimilated into Canadian culture, the Mennonite community worked very hard to stay separate from a Canadian identity and define itself against the rest of the world around it, so discrimination is not quite an operating category. Mennonites traditionally wanted to see themselves as different from everybody else and in that sense wanted to be treated with discrimination and in fact they have been, in Canada. The Mennonite men did not have to go and fight in the Second World War, for example. That was the kind of discrimination that the communal identity protects. There have been privileges attached to this very strong communal identity, so I guess the discrimination has been favourable for Mennonites.

JANICE: My WASP background would lead me to see the communitarian vision within the Mennonite community as a reversal of a liberal individualist notion of the community. Is the Mennonite community simply the authorization of a very select group, where the difference of multiple voices is muted in favour of ...

DI: The separate soul. To grow up in a community which didn't have the separate 'I' is a completely different experience of the world. Most people I meet are trying all the time to find community, a way to be together and identify with other people. My problem is the opposite of that; I have this automatic communal identification with people. It's really easy for me to be very close to people and to understand them. The kind of intimacy of vision that most people in the modern world find hard to achieve is a given for me. My problem is the opposite of that. I'm trying to find a way to insist on my separate experience, my separate identity. I haven't found a way to do that yet in spite of writing this book, where I insist on my separateness. Because what happens is that people read the words and identify with the speaker instead of with the implied audience. I imagined the audience to be hostile and unsympathetic and therefore the words would set one apart, but instead, the audience listens and identifies with me.

JANICE: You came to read in Toronto at the Swiss-Mennonite Bicentennial Celebration in August 1986. As the only woman poet reading, you were nervous about the reception from two hundred Mennonite listeners. What was their response?

DI: The response was very intense and warm and in some ways the opposite of what I feared. There were a lot of women who came to me and said, 'You're saying this all for me. This is also my experience, but I'm too scared to say it.' When Mennonite women say this to me, it confirms my fear of that audience because they acknowledge their fear, and it makes me feel extremely presumptuous in having broken this public silence of the Mennonite women. I'm very visible.

JANICE: Can you talk a little bit about this question of silence? Silence in feminist discourse has become almost a cliché. In your childhood Mennonite community the sexes were segregated in church and women remained without a public voice. How do you write towards and from that silence?

DI: The whole experience of my childhood and growing up as a woman in that community was a mute one in terms of public language; there was no language for us. If I want to speak about it at all, I have to borrow language from, let's say, feminist writing, or certainly from a different tradition. I wanted to talk about my experiences in the language I grew up in, that is, I wanted to say it in English, but I wanted to talk conceptually in the language system of my childhood, which was circumscribed by the metaphors of the Bible. In talking about women's experience there are metaphors about the feminine available in that language, and they're all very sexual. They weren't meant to be used to talk literally about women's experience. I didn't change that language; I just read it and articulated from a woman's point of view, from my own physical experience in the world. This was apparently very shocking to many people.

JANICE: In this reinscription of biblical language into another context, there are lots of moments in your writing where female desire is present, not simply in terms of how you as a Mennonite woman who has left the community now articulate your own desire, but how you remember the moments of pleasure that existed within the community as you were growing up. 'Shades of Sin,' a prose poem, eroticizes the curls that escape the mother's hat. The mother sends away for a hat, and the wrong hat, a veiled black hat, is sent by mistake. You recount how she shortened the veil in order to make it less seductive. But within these gestures, you uncover an element of seduction, pleasure, and eroticism.

DI: The structure of that story, 'Shades of Sin,' is kind of a Miltonic argument about the justification of women's being in the world. I think I was reading *Paradise Lost* at the time, and I was really pissed off afterwards to find out it had shades of Milton in it. There's a disjunction between the abstractness of the narrator's language, which tells the story, and the sensuous story of seduction going on underneath the girl's experience. Holding the narrative voice to that abstract language allows that other experience to be there. I can tell the story of that child as the forbidden story if I have a framework which announces that it's forbidden. That's what allows it to be told. There are two different languages going on all the time; the one which is not really what it's about allows the other one to be there on the side.

JANICE: In some of your poems the father sounds the patriarchal voice of authority, while the voice of the female writer uncovering, remembering, dismembering her own history is transgressive. The transgressive voice doesn't come into play until you articulate the voice of authority she's speaking against.

DI: You mean, I'm coming to terms with that voice of authority first? But even more than that, it's giving ground, participating in the voice of authority. The argument is with the voice of authority, and so carrying on this argument makes a structure. Underneath, on the side, or around it, there's another story going on – the real story, the women's story.

JANICE: Would the image be of the women's story as the edges of the pool or the border of the frame, the decorative parts of the tapestry?

DI: Actually, if I visualize it, I would say it's the other way around. The narrative voice arguing with the father's voice, the authoritative voice, allows the content to be inside it.

JANICE: Is there a tone shift in the dialogic relation between the voice of authority and this transgressive female voice?

DI: Oh yes, I think there's very definitely a shift. There are a lot of voices. One of the voices is the voice of the mother, which is silent at the beginning. She doesn't answer the questions. As you move through the book, there's an integration of various disjointed voices. They all become part of the same experience, and at the end I think the speaker contains all but the voice of the mother and her silence.

Stylistically, the shift is from a difficult articulation to an easier dialogue of voices at the end. You don't have to draw the lines in terms of who has the right to speak and who doesn't since they are finally contained in the speaker's voice and have a relationship with each other.

JANICE: Different narrative codes are also integrated in your writing. The everyday and the exotic are mixed up in your work. Why?

DI: My awareness of those different codes originally comes from growing up in three different languages, which referred to different codes of behaviour as well as consciousness. We used low German at home for everyday life, things in the house, and the experiences of the body and so on. High German was the public language we used in church. That was God's language. And then there was English, the worldly language we used in school that referred to the rest of the world. So I grew up with a very early sense of different codes operating and had to be adept at jumping from one to the other. Many Mennonites deal with this multiplicity of codes and rules by keeping them very separate: you jump from one to the other and don't think about how come when you're speaking in Low German you can make all kinds of semi-obscene jokes, but when you're speaking English, you can't. I tried from a very young age to translate from one to the other rather than to keep them separate.

JANICE: How do you reconcile the various mythologies which organize your world? In terms of constructing an 'identity' or writing a female subject with a particular history, you're able to develop a very layered sense of history because you draw on these different mythologies: in the biblical myth, Diana's bad; in Greek mythology, she's devilishly clever; and in the Cinderella myth, she waits for her prince. You manage to retell the Cinderella myth with a subversive edge since she's not necessarily waiting for her prince to come.

DI: Whew, good!

JANICE: Can you expand on your 'Whew'?

DI: To tell this Cinderella story in any version and to identify with her is to risk being the princess who waits. My identity is very much made up of old stories from the past, and one of my major motives is to arrive in the present. I'm not entirely sure if I've got there yet.

JANICE: One of the ways your writing arrives in the present is through a different use of language. You talk about language as a construct given as the Word. But there's another language used in the questions asked of and by your mother, a more vulnerable language, filled with possibilities only half understood. In this language the path to understanding insists that you don't submit to the authority of the Word. How do those different forms of language play in your writing?

DI: That's an interesting way of asking the question, but I feel much more ambivalent than that. I feel a very great pull to the old language; the power of language to me is in the resonances of that old language, the metaphorical associations, and the profoundly poetic vision of the world that I grew up in. One part of me feels that the modern world I've tried so hard to get to is a world which has lost much of that power. Contemporary language is very flat and superficial and has lost a lot of the old power that it had. One half of me is pulled back to that. So I feel a great sense of loss in that I'm contributing to the movement away from the old vision. Todorov said that literature kills off the metaphysics in language, and I feel that all the time because there was a great, very beautiful power in the metaphysics for me. Another part of me feels that it's very important to climb out of it because it was a very definitive, authoritarian, and constricting language.

JANICE: The shortest poem in your series of poems is one line. After your 'missionary position' poems, you write, 'just kidding mom.' Are you ironically 'just kidding'?

DI: The line was a response to a previous poem about having a dozen lovers, and it was an awareness and acknowledgment of this double audience of mine. The part of my writing the Mennonites will respond to with outrage is not actually dangerous. The real violation going on in the book is much deeper, but there's a response deflecting it onto that level of a superficial breach of the rules.

JANICE: What is the deeper violation?

DI: The deeper violation is destroying the metaphysics in language. There's a great loss involved for me in appropriating a language that when I was a kid functioned as a kind of public language in the church to concentrate, create, and sustain a religious vision of the world; God was present everywhere and surrounding us, and language sustained that vision. In my writing I'm trying to pull that language back into my own experience all the time, so it's a violation of that vision. There's a great loss involved in that for me to make my own experience real. It's necessary but it's still sad. And in terms of speaking for women in that community or to people in that audience, it is also violating their religious sense of the world. It's violating an oral culture. My father was practically illiterate, but one of the most articulate men I've ever met – he knew the entire Bible and Mennonite tradition in his head. He didn't want us to read books; he understood that fiction and writing would be ...

JANICE: A place of deceiving?

DI: A place of deceiving and a place of betrayal, and it was, and it is. I have found the reading and writing of fiction and words to be a violation of that oral sense of the world. It destroys oral memory; I've felt this very much in my own experience. I carried around this huge memory of my own experiences of growing up in that community, and when I started writing down those experiences, it destroyed my memory of them and the rest disappeared.

JANICE: This brings me to the question of autobiography and how auto-bio-graphy, writing – the life – of a self becomes auto-graphy, writing the self: the self comes into being through the process of writing. When you talk about your loss of this oral memory through the substitution of your written account, is this part of the process of writing a new self into being?

DI: Oh, absolutely, that's what's happening, yes. It has to do with coming into the present for me and the integration of the various voices and somehow finding them all inside myself. Part of the narrative progression is coming to the possibility of inventing a self. When I started writing, I had so many rules in my head about why I can't be a writer and can't write, and one of the rules was that you can't make anything up. That's why I started with these very little memories that I had and tried to write them down as faithfully and as literally as I could. But when I wrote them down, they were just as fictional as if I'd made them up. You could slip in things that didn't really happen; it didn't make any difference to the story, and it certainly doesn't make any difference to the reader. When I read 'Shades of Sin' to my mother, she said, 'I think you made that up.' And I said, 'Don't you remember the diamond earrings? Don't you remember visiting the art gallery?' And she replied, 'No, I don't remember any of it.' So I started realizing that memory and imagination aren't very different from each other. The rule of being true to history just wasn't possible and in the end didn't make any difference. That was a release for me; it released the possibility of play in writing: you can choose what the story is going to be, or at least you can choose the story, select and change events, you can have a dialogue with the past. You don't have to just remember it or fight it. That was a very big change for me.

JANICE: Your dialogue with the past has occurred between two communitarian groups: the Mennonites and the feminists. You were involved with the CV2 collective, which continues to publish the poetry magazine founded by Dorothy Livesay. You also participated in a Winnipeg feminist collective group, 'Hiatus.' We first met as participants in West Word I, a women writers' retreat. Coming to terms with the differences, shared experiences, anxieties, and conflicts between and among women is a concern in your writing. Can you talk about what it is to write the female self within your double communities?

DI: There are big differences in the relationship between the writer and the community in those two extremes. The community I grew up in was in effect a 'pre-Renaissance' community. We didn't have separate identities. Our whole upbringing was directed towards resisting a separate sense of the self, so being a public speaker in that community meant speaking the communal truth. Becoming a writer involved insisting on my own separate experience and resisting that communal voice, which was also authoritarian and definitive. So I was writing with a progressive sense of alienation from the community. On the one hand I was choosing to exile myself from that community, and on the other hand I had no choice but to feel and acknowledge myself as separate. And then this very strange thing happened – I had expected public outrage, people throwing stones at me, you know, as in the poem where I'm surrounded by 'the old father & his wives / their greedy hungry eyes their mouths full of stones.' But instead, people came up to me, Mennonite women especially, who identified with me. So now I have this sense of speaking for a community or finding a community voice in resisting a communal identity. This was a very big surprise to me, and I still feel oppressed by that, because I have to resist that new communal identity if I want to continue writing. I can't write for all these women either. It's too big a responsibility: what if I don't say the right thing? what if these words aren't the right ones for them? If my words end up speaking for somebody, then that's the audience, but I have to be free to change what it is that I speak about. On the other hand, belonging to all these groups of women writers is very, very important to me as a writer. Being a member of Hiatus was a very formative experience for me. I don't think I could have got up the courage to publish any writing if I hadn't been part of that group. I found myself in this room with other young women who were as tentative and hesitant about their vision of the world as I was; they dared to call themselves writers and think of themselves as real writers in the world, and for me that was a very crucial contact. And then being part of West Word I, where I met people like you and Betsy Warland and Daphne Marlatt, really opened up another world for me, women who could hear what I was saying and didn't think I was crazy.

JANICE: Are there other Mennonite women writers in your community?

DI: There is one very fine young Mennonite woman poet in Manitoba, Audrey Poetker, whom I found out about after I started writing, so when I started writing this book I felt completely alone. Since then she's published *I Sing for My Dead in German*.

JANICE: How have other women writers interpreted your cultural specificity? How much do you feel a part of a community of women writers?

DI: Two summers ago at West Word, I was talking about my writing in the poetry group and I said, 'I feel like I'm not really one of you because I have this old stuff I have to write about. I grew up in this sixteenth-century community and I have to write through the Bible in all this old language, and so my project is completely different than yours.' And, I remember, somebody in this group said, 'Oh, you think you're so special? What makes you think that you have such a privileged place? Don't you think we all come from weird places and have weird things to write about? You're not any different than anybody else.' And it really stuck in my mind, and it was wonderful for me. I felt, oh, yes, I do belong to this group of women even though I'm different.

JANICE: We were all differentiated within the group.

DI: We're all different, and we're all a group, yes. I went home, and a Mennonite church in Winnipeg invited me to come and speak about being a Mennonite writer. One of the things I said to them was, 'It's hard for me to be a Mennonite and a poet at the same time. They are completely contradictory things, but since I don't have any choice, I have to be both. But being a poet exiles me from my Mennonite identity.' And the people in that community said, 'Oh, no, not at all. You're one of us. You're not different.' You're saying these are opposite experiences in the sense that with the community of women writers all their separate selves came together in their differences, whereas the Mennonite community was an identity of sameness. I know that's what the theory is, and I sort of understand it, but in some ways it feels like the same thing to me. That's part of what the problem is because I hear people saying, 'Let's celebrate a community of differences,' but in the feminist writing community in Canada, for example, you could say there's a correct feminist language developing; we read the same critics and there's a correct text. I'm not sure if it's less prescriptive than my old Mennonite community.

JANICE: How do you position yourself in relation to writers like Dionne Brand or Claire Harris, who, as Women of Colour, identify themselves as feminists but insist on the fact that they write within different traditions, as Black women with Caribbean roots.

DI: That's an interesting question because I'm also resisting this WASP power in Canada which works like the politically correct line and dominates a particular group of people. I feel an identification with Claire Harris's vision of difference in *Fables from the Women's Quarters* and other ethnic writers, too, like Myrna Kostash. I really understand her pain as an ethnic writer trying to write. I have a strong identification with, let's say, the edges of the feminist community, but then that isn't so very different, is it, from where I've located myself in that other community.

JANICE: How much does the form of your writing embody your sense of writing outside? What's the relation between your writing on the margin and your writing's margins? [Laughter.] Some of your pieces are long-lined prose narratives, and others are much more economical in spatial and rhythmic terms.

DI: I started writing very, very, very short lines, shorter than you see in this book. I felt I had so very little space in which to speak, so I claimed a tiny space for myself in the middle of the page. Learning to be a writer was trying to extend and widen that space, to push those margins over to give me a little bit more room to write. That maybe accounts for the arbitrary right margin in my writing. And I couldn't tell a story because I didn't have enough space. Daphne Marlatt was influential for me, because I read some of her work when I just started writing and I had this feeling of her breathlessness, of her being really stuck in the syntax and having to work very hard at pushing the sentences open to be able to speak what she wanted to speak. My solution in terms of syntax and rhythm is different from hers, but I identify with that feeling in her writing of not being able to write in long lines.

JANICE: What other writers have influenced your work?

DI: The most important influence was Pat Friesen, a Winnipeg Mennonite poet. I discovered his poems and identified with his writing so much. It was the first time I ever read poems that were so close to the voice inside me. When I read his poems, I felt released to be a writer, too. Then I got to know him as a supportive friend who taught me a lot about being a writer in every way and encouraged me to publish. Other than that, most of the influences are very traditional ones, like Milton and Blake and the Bible. I've also been influenced by prose writers, Alice Munro because of her relation to tradition, with the stories from the Bible, or other old stories. And her small-town geography.

JANICE: Cliché is another kind of old story. In one of your poems you write about old men, and cliché enables you to speak of a fairly particular sorrow. You acknowledge the traditional relationship of women to romance, as victim or *la belle dame sans merci*. How does cliché enable you to write against the cliché of romance?

DI: I run very dangerously close to the edge of cliché all the time in my writing, and maybe I do fall into it. Cliché is a banal contemporary version of what we did with language in the Mennonite community in dissolving our various idiosyncratic individual experiences back into the traditional language in order to be heard and to share the experience. Consciously playing with cliché was a way of acknowledging my inherited sense of language. At the same time I try to climb out of it by standing on top or on the edge of romance clichés as well as religious ones.

JANICE: The final poems in your book play along the thin line of women's submission to the law.

DI: There is a waiting which is a dislocation of the speaking voice at the end of the book. It's an integration of various voices and a dislocation of an identity which defines self against community. There's no clear resolution to that problem at all in the book. I thought this book would be a resolution of identity in terms of my heritage, but it became much more problematic and complex. The waiting is a waiting for other possibilities or other ways of discussing or exploring the problem to emerge, a waiting through loss and dislocation for the pain to subside enough to explore in another way.

JANICE: On the other side of this pain is the blissful sensation of 'seeing the world feelingly' – an integrative mode of perception. Or, embodied desire, the final 'hot, hungry love [which] waits, like you, for a new tender flowering.' Are there two separate and opposing stories, one, a story of loss, dislocation, and alienation, and the other, of recovery and the possibility of relationships?

DI: I thought this book was about finding a place, but I don't think I found the place at all and maybe that part belongs to the story of loss. The promise in the book is the promise of relationship in spite of the loss.

JANICE: Is this promise of relationship interiorized in the subject / object, the 'I' and the 'you,' in the final poems? Smaro Kamboureli's poems, written 'in the second person,' are in part a response to Benveniste's notion that speaking is made possible by an interiorized split between the 'I' and the 'you.'

DI: For Smaro, language is the place in which she lives. Well, I don't want that to be true since it's a very lonely way of locating yourself with all the voices inside you and all the real conversation going on inside your own head. Doesn't that contradict what you were saying before about the possibility of real community?

JANICE: OK, who is the 'you' in your book?

DI: It shifts and changes. It's not just one person, although you might be right that the 'you' at the end is not a different person from the 'I.'

JANICE: There's always the reader as community.

DI: Thank you. I think I have to write another book, because I'm not sure I've entirely arrived at the place of this book. I'm still floundering around trying to understand where it leaves me as a writer and a person in the world in relation to the voices and audience. I don't think I've even entirely heard or integrated my own words, which has partly to do with the fear of the audience I'm projecting onto the event of the book's publication. Part of the question has to do with where I choose to locate myself in relation to my words, but part has to do with others' responses to them.

JANICE: You've recently published a piece on mothering.

DI: Guilt.

JANICE: Guilt? You have children, two daughters. What are the benefits of mothering and writing? Does 'guilt' sum it up?

DI: When I started writing, I felt that my experience of being a mother was a very positive one in terms of my writing, because it released me into the freedom of children, of watching and being with my own children. The spontaneity and creativity of my children was a gift that I could participate in, and it was also therapeutic in that I could relive my own childhood. This book started as a recalling of the child's experience buried underneath the official language. I argued passionately for a long time that being a mother is not in conflict with being a writer but in fact nurtures it. But then the conflict happened on a practical level of finding time and space, finding enough hours in the day to balance being a mother and a writer without flying apart. This is a real problem, so I guess I would argue less idealistically now about how mothering and writing are related.

JANICE: What happens when the questions you ask a mother are addressed through your own motherhood?

DI: I would really like to write about being a mother, the story I don't think I got to in this manuscript. The experience of the mother as an absence becomes more painful in the book as you go along. This is not an intentional absence since I was trying to get to that story. While I was writing poetry, I was also trying to construct a PHD thesis about the absent mother in a patriarchal tradition, and so it's an absence that I was very conscious of in terms of both literary tradition and my own experience as a mother. There are not enough words around us to adequately articulate that experience, so I feel the absence in my manuscript as a very intense failure.

JANICE: How can it be a failure when you told a daughter's story?

DI: It's not a failure in the sense that I broke a lot of silence around the daughter's story and created a new space for myself and other women. But it's a failure in terms of the conscious commitment that I had, and still have, to not only *tell* the story of the mother, but to *be* the mother, so it didn't do enough. The sadness in this book is that I'm reaching for this story but don't get to it.

JANICE: You'll get to it.

DI: Yes, thank you.

Pelican Lake, Manitoba, July 1987

'that questioning self'

JANICE: Since I interviewed you two summers ago, you've completed your second book of poems and you're also working on a prison biography. Your first collection was extremely successful and nominated for the Governor General's Award and the Commonwealth Poetry Prize.

DI: Well, I was unprepared for the very amazing reception of this book. First of all there was this great big lovely recognition by the Canadian writing community and so that was lovely, and then the Mennonite audience that I was so afraid of actually ended up being a lot more positive and interested and affirmative, including my family. My family was traumatized by the publishing of this book, and they worked very hard at trying to understand it. The official Mennonite community also has responded with great interest and curiosity. Most of the angry people have not talked to me personally. I feel I do have the permission to write now. I don't have to defend the activity to myself, and I don't have to theorize so much about making a place for it, because there is a place for it. So it's a lot more relaxing and a lot easier to do; but also, I feel I don't have any choice because I took such a big risk and invested so much of my identity, I have to keep on doing it now.

JANICE: A Mennonite journalist, Wilma Derksen, recently interviewed you, and you were very moved by what she had to say about your writing.

DI: Oh, it wasn't so much what she had to say because she didn't really know what to say about it at all. She kept apologizing for not knowing anything about poetry and not knowing how to respond to it. But she was interested in my having written this book, and willing to listen. She quoted me at length in the *Mennonite Reporter*, which is the official news magazine in the Mennonite community. It was a very moving thing for her to give me such a very big, uncensored voice. She didn't pronounce any judgment. The interview ended with a very big question mark about everything in the Mennonite faith. I called her up and thanked her for this interview and said I can't believe you wrote it that way, and she said, 'We know that's not the end of the story, and we're all listening to hear what you will say next.' It's incredible to have this sense of an audience of women who are *waiting* for me to speak.

JANICE: In your first book some of your metaphors and images were quite girlish. Your new work is more mature and coming to terms with some of life's subtle complexities, with finality and loss.

DI: It feels like a rewrite of the same story but in more grown-up terms. It's less coded, isn't it?

JANICE: In the new poems I've heard you read, you've been digging very deep into your own history, into your relationship with your family and your own feminism.

DI: This is possible because of the permission. My other book was so transgressive and dangerous, playing around with the official story, but with so much risk. This book is different. Once you get past the transgression and take apart an identity underneath that's sustained it, it becomes a more focused critique of the culture in specific ways. In *Questions i asked my mother* the transgression took place on the level of narrative and discourse. *Agnes in the Sky* is much more about specific abuses in my culture and how they constructed me. The other book was very deconstructive; this one's more transformative. It is about what do you do after you've exploded your family story. How do you live after that? You have to just reconstruct your own terms.

JANICE: So your new poem about the healing heart which remembers being beaten as a child by your father indicates this possibility of transformation?

DI: There are a lot of other places as well. The Agnes poems, for example, are about a woman who had a very desperate life, and me trying to imagine a sense of worth in it.

JANICE: Your poem 'nonresistance or, love Mennonite style' is very ironic. Part of the process for a number of writers who are confronting incest in their histories is understanding that recuperating the memories is part of an integrative healing. How does your poem about incest compare with other tellings?

DI: The poem claims that the Mennonite incest narrative is connected to the way we were brought up to be non-resistant. That was a very central belief for us, the way we should approach the world, and it leaves us very vulnerable and with no defences at all against abuse of any kind. As a community there's a communal solidarity against the outside world, and that's how this culture worked. If there was abuse inside the community, then there was absolutely no defence against it, given this upbringing. Women and children were vulnerable in that culture to whatever kind of abuse the people in power chose to inflict on them, especially the fathers, who had all this power. Incest is the extreme version of something that was part of every woman's and every child's experience. I was beaten by my father when I was very little, and psychologically it had a similar effect.

JANICE: Do you think it's that different from non-Mennonite Canadian culture? Soon after Elly Danica published her book, the publisher Libby Oughton received a hundred unsolicited complete manuscripts on incest. Other women's stories and the popularity of books like these suggest sexual abuse of children is a very widespread phenomenon.

DI: It's widespread everywhere, and the story is starting to be told now on a very large scale. What would be the WASP version of this — I mean, it's not non-resistance, right?

JANICE: No. It's puritanism ...

DI: ... that makes you repress the sexual part which comes out in this twisted way. So that would be a slightly different version of it. I want to isolate the specific way in which, *officially*, we were supposed to be vulnerable to the world. Non-resistance means you don't resist things that happen to you. Elly Danica's story is very similar because she writes out of a Dutch identity, which demands this incredible obedience to the father. The grandmother and mother are not able to contradict him in any way. That part is the same, and my family is Dutch way back too.

JANICE: How has your sense of language changed in your writing, now that you feel more of a participant in a cultural community, more writer than interloper?

DI: I was trying to write myself into the twentieth century, so I thought that my sensibility would become very secular and less religious. My sense of loss was that through my writing I would lose my Mennonite identity and all the things that went with it like the very deep metaphorical sense about everything and the connectedness with everything around as sacred. I don't think I lost it, it just became available in a different way for me. Because words weren't owned by the people in authority any more, I could play around with them on my own terms and make them my own. Language was available to me in fragments instead of as stolen pieces from this fixed frame. At the end of the Agnes poem, for example, I imagine a heaven for Agnes. I just make up a lover for her and all the lovely things I imagined would be heaven for Agnes; it didn't feel transgressive to do that, but constructive. In my earlier book, it would have felt really transgressive to try to invent a heaven on my own terms, and there would have been more fear in that.

JANICE: So, you've been displaced from the margins, and you're now feeling much more centred?

DI: Maybe not displaced, but relocated in a place that I'm inventing. This is why I can't stop and have to keep on doing it now.

JANICE: You've been writing a book with a prisoner. How much is 'No Tears Allowed' a mirror image of your own writing? You're writing the other side of the violence your own poetry unearths. Is your writing of the Patrick Michael Marsh story an investigation and attentiveness to that other voice you've been confronting?

DI: Yeah, that's what it is, an inquiry into what would make a man violent, and – especially the part that is most moving for me – what does it *feel* like to be a violent man? What does it feel like to want to try to kill somebody and why did he feel that way and what does it feel like after?

JANICE: What are the risks of writing this man's biography?

DI: One of the risks is for me to be implicated in his life in some way. People think that I'm either romantically involved with him or that I have some sort of romance about crime. Why are you attracted to an inmate? On a practical level, there's no danger about becoming romantically involved with this man, but there's a temptation on his part to ask me for help in his life and a temptation on my part to try to help him. I resist this because I don't want to become involved in his life that way; I just want to tell his story. So that's the risk. We also both have this fear of audiences, this fear that people won't understand the story, won't hear it, or won't respect the story and him. Or they'll love to read the story, but they won't give him a place.

JANICE: How does this mythology about the romance for prisoners develop?

DI: The romance of crime. One of the attractions to prisoners is that they're the opposite of men in power. These guys take the position of the feminine in relation to the dominant male society. I think that's one of the attractions.

JANICE: So you think it's homoerotic, a submerged displaced lesbian narrative of our times [laughter]?

DI: *Now* we're getting to the real story! In a roundabout way! Many people have imposed the romance of crime narrative on this project. It makes me very angry most of the time because nobody believes my real motives. People think I'm a real do-gooder, a Mennonite missionary trying to save the poor prisoners of the world. Either that or, 'you're falling in love with him and you're going to get into trouble.' They don't believe that I'm just doing this because I'm a writer and I recognize a good story. It really bugs me because I feel I'm not being acknowledged professionally, because I'm a woman, right.

JANICE: Right.

DI: You're either a missionary or –

JANICE: – the angel of the house, or seductive, the two poles of the good girl–bad girl scenario.

DI: I don't think that's true of a woman lawyer working with inmates. I think it's because writing is such a disreputable profession to begin with. It's not properly defined for people. I had so much trouble getting permission from the administration because they don't understand the role of the writer at all. I had to make them respect me as a writer and take this project seriously. I think they gave permission because they didn't think this would really happen. I'm making them believe that it's really happening and really serious and that what they say is part of the project and is going into the book.

JANICE: Isn't part of the fear of writing someone's story the intimacy of the project, so there's anxiety about disclosure?

DI: A fear of intimacy. Yes. Sometimes when I do public readings of my poetry it happens in a different way. There is a lot of self-disclosure and it is a very intimate thing; sometimes it feels like an emotional strip-act and sometimes people fall in love with me, listening to my poetry. Afterwards they come and talk to me because they were so moved by what I gave to them as audience and they somehow took it personally. I have to explain to them the poetry reading is over now and it was an act.

JANICE: Your poet persona?

DI: It's sort of a masquerade persona, isn't it, because you can say things in poetry that you can't say to your best friend. It's not a false self; it's like your true self, more true than the one you're willing to live with in ordinary life. Once you start writing, you have to keep on doing it because you become aware of the fictional nature of identity. Identity is not static but keeps on changing. I thought in my first book I got to the very end of what I knew or the very bottom of the question, but as soon as that was finished I had to start over in another take so I didn't become stuck in the one I gave away to people. When I'm performing it, then I am in the story, reliving it.

JANICE: When you're talking about this persona that has this power of seduction for the audience, I keep thinking about the myth of male poet as lover who takes advantage of this rhetorical power. How do you resist being seduced by your own poetic voice?

DI: Well, I experience it as something I have to protect myself against as a woman, and as a person. I wouldn't want to be entirely seduced by that role because I think it would be very dangerous. Maybe in terms of tradition it's easier for men, those men who see lovemaking as the taking of power. I experience lovemaking as the sharing of power, so I don't want to make love with my audience. It would tear me apart. I want to make love to them just in language, not my body. I want a big audience, you see, and my body isn't big enough to contain the whole audience. But the body of my words is. It's displaced desire for everyone. I do want them to love me, yeah I do want them to all love me. Doesn't everyone? Don't you?

JANICE: You're in the process of writing a PHD dissertation. Certain kinds or imaginative thinking don't fit into the traditional academy. All of the messy things that are left out of 'proper' intellectual work in an academic setting become problems.

DI: They become handicaps for us. I think becoming a poet for me was first of all a way of acknowledging and then affirming that I experience my ways of knowing as handicaps in the academic world. I was trying to figure out how to make the gift of language something creative instead of a handicap, also in ordinary life.

JANICE: In your new poem about what it is to be a poet, you write about the poet as someone who sees and knows too much. I was thinking about the figure of the child, the voice inside that always asks questions, the wrong questions, and tries to have a dialogue when there is no respondent. In your poem you talk about the process of coming to consciousness as a human being and understanding yourself as an inquiring, curious, embodied mind. Is part of this process a recognition of the bright child?

DI: Yeah, it's interesting that you see it as a more general experience because I saw it as a specific role. Perhaps it isn't truly the consciousness of everybody, but it seems a lot of people can repress or put aside that questioning self. Poets have more trouble than others repressing that questioning self for the sake of an ordinary common successful life. That's why it feels like a handicap unless you can get acknowledgment for it or truly create something with it.

JANICE: You spoke about a recent deep personal crisis of identity. You teach creative writing at workshops and in schools. How much do you sense that writing itself puts the writer in crisis. Is it a dangerous activity?

DI: Yeah, I think it is particularly for women and for underprivileged people because you inevitably have to critique your oppression or your silencing, whatever it was. I think it's a very dangerous activity. Most of the people that I teach writing to have been women, and I see most of them approaching this understanding, and then they stop themselves from going very far. I'm sympathetic and I understand why they stop themselves from going further with it because it's so scary and it takes a lot of strength to get through it. I really had to put my life on the line for it at some point, and I don't think most people are willing to do that. So I push them towards it, but if they say no, which is what most of them say, I just leave it at that. I just push them as far as they want to go with it.

JANICE: When you talk about the danger writing poses for women and other underprivileged people, how do you address the question of voice as something authentic that has to be developed by particular writing? How would you feel about someone writing your Mennonite story?

DI: I do think that this thing called voice is something that needs to be protected and guarded by people. I experience this personally in teacher-student relationships where the student shows me her writing, and then we talk about it in detail. I've worked with women trying to find language for writing about abusive marriages. In helping the student to develop the language skill to express and to contain that experience, I've sometimes felt really inspired by the poetry and might be very tempted to steal stuff since once in a while there would be just a fantastic line. I would *try* to really push the student to make the rest of the poem measure up to the knowledge of this line. A lot of the time she couldn't get that far. So I was tempted to steal it and do it myself, and I was very conscious of stopping myself from doing that. It would be a very easy thing to do. There is a real discrepancy between having life knowledge and power. There are those who have power with language, that is, access to publishing and so on, and then there are people with stories that are not fully realized and that's where all the energy is, in the new stuff, that's the lifeblood. This is part of the debate on the politics of writing which is happening around the Women's Press issue – trying to find a language for what is at stake. It's taking a long time to articulate this.

JANICE: In discussions of this issue there is a temptation to glorify oppression: the more facets of one's identity located within an oppressive system, the more lifeblood there is for story. But doesn't this put women who suffer multiple oppressions in an extremely uncomfortable position because they have to carry the burden of exoticism for women?

DI: Well, writing isn't just about oppression. It's also about celebration and invention. Oppression is only one of the ways that we can talk about difference. It's perhaps the easiest one to address in terms like affirmative action, trying to give access to people who didn't have access. But this isn't all that writing's about, and surely it shouldn't be the way to measure the worth of it in the end because you lose the sense of language. Even a story of oppression has to be realized in the language; otherwise it's not working and can't be heard.

Banff, August 1989

Nicole Brossard

Certain Words

Amid the worst possible misfortunes, the most daring nights of adoration, tragic death, and the softest skin, by the shores of all seas, and clothed in a utopian body and ecstasies, we proceed along the relief of words, agile amount the sharp coral of l'Isla de las Mujeres. Dressed in a woman's body, patiently we mark time at the edge of the page; we are awaiting a feminine presence. With wet fingers, we turn the pages. We are waiting for truth to break through.

From one reading to another, words relay back and forth as though to test our endurance around an idée fixe, around the few self-images we have, images which apply to us only in the fictive space of our particular version of reality. From one reading to another, we fabulate stories from our desire, which is to identify what inspires us and what plunges us into such a state of 'indescribable' fervour.

When this fervour comes over us, we say we are captivated by our reading and we advance slowly/rapidly toward our destiny. Our destiny is like a project, a life woven into us by innumerable lines; some are called the lines of the hand holding the volume. These lines innervate our entire body, like the logic of thought derived from the senses. Engrossed in our reading, we become aware of (being) the cause and the origin of the faces and landscapes surrounding us for we make allusion to them as one does to childhood, a desire, an inclination. Engrossed in our reading, we hear murmurs, entreaties, cries; we hear our voice looking for its horizon.

In our reading, there are mauves, some indigo, terrible looks, women adorned in jewels and silence. Bodies, sorely tried. Stirring visions. We open and close our eyes on them in the hope of a sonorous sequence, or a vital discussion perhaps. Our fervour sweeps into the text in order that from the discussion, truth might break through.

Amid the rhetoric, the logic of the senses, the paradoxes, and the sensation of becoming, we advance through our intention of forms. Sometimes, in the middle of the night, we might wake to re-read a passage, to see again the women we desire. And as we read it over, in our breast is an 'indescribable' sensation which keeps us awake until dawn. At dawn, our spirit is extravagant; it wanders freely in forbidden zones and we have no choice but to explore them. I've heard that some women write at dawn, when they are in this state. I've heard that sometimes they burst into tears.

'I know the rhythms of the voice; I know how it jumps about. I know the experience and the adventure of the gaze.' Toward this we soar with each reading, incredulous before truth, which, like a memory of shadow and of fervour, bursts in on us.

The words we notice speak to us and they fill us with unrest and pleasure. These words are revelations, enigmas, address. We transform them by an unconscious method, yet our consciousness finds itself enlightened by the process. Women reading, we become the allusion and the tone of a text.

What animates us in a sentence or an expression is a decision to be it. Inclined to become one with the text in order to seize in the fire of the action the brilliant exploit of our desire, we are astonished before the unanimity forming with us. Each intense reading is a beam of action.

Amid the equations, the pivotal axes, the intoxicating audacity, and the light which criss-crosses over us, we advance in our reading the way in theory we become what we desire. We advance toward a subtle and complex woman who reflects the process of our thinking and its forms of development. Words are one way to devour the desire which devours us with comparisons, taking us to the place where we become the appetite of knowledge and the knowledge of consciousness.

When we turn the pages with our wet fingers, going from terror to ecstasy, we confront eternity; we are believers and disbelieving before the sum total of bodies, craniums, orgasms; we confront the beyond of the whole and become desire's precision in the unrecountable space of the brain.

Truly, the sensational effect of reading is a feeling we cannot express, unless we underline. *With each reading, the intimacy of eternity is an intrigue we invent.* All reading, every reading, is a desire for image, an intention to re/present, which gives us hope.

From *The Aerial Letter*, trans. Marlene Wildeman (Toronto: Women's Press 1988)

Nicole Brossard

'Before I became a feminist, I suppose I was an angel, a poet, a revolutionary ...'

JANICE: Would you reflect on a comment you made during a 1975 Quebec conference on women and writing? You said, 'For that which speaks wants at the same time to condemn the law that calls for its repression, that which is forbidden desires and that which desires writes propelled by the very law it transgresses.' What do you mean by transgression and desire?

NICOLE: The notion of transgression has always been important in my writing. In books, mainly those published in the seventies, transgressing meant taking risks, making trouble in language and the bourgeois mentality, going over the limits of what is expected in a poem or a novel. Very often, I made a connection between transgression and desire because you transgress the permissible social space in order to make space for your desire. Transgression is defiance and can also be read as an attempt at renewal. If we talk in terms of feminist transgression, it is more complicated because the goal is not to make trouble for the sake of it, but to change the law and the authority to which it refers. Therefore transgression might not be enough. If we accept that transgression marginalizes those who do it, then we must ask the question: since the feminine is already marginalized in a patriarchal society, how can we transgress the law without marginalizing ourselves more? Personally, I can say that writing a feminist consciousness – which means somehow having to sort out and rethink values, patterns of behaviour, identities, fiction and reality – brought me to shift from the word 'transgression' to the word 'vision.'

JANICE: You talk of accomplices in your project of feminist 'vision.'

Elizabeth Meese claims that because of women's marginalized relation to discourse, all women who write are in a sense 'feminist.' Does
this perspective tend to elide the differences between women and the
discursive privileges certain women enjoy?

NICOLE: I don't think so. I wish that discursive analysis would not
be considered a privilege. I believe that a feminist is a woman who
can claim this title for herself because she is convinced within and
beyond her own personal experience that this reality has to be changed
in order for women to be able to breathe without further fear and
humiliation. There is a difference between a woman complaining
about woman's destiny in a man's world and a woman fighting for
a change of values in mentality and the laws as a result of her understanding of patriarchal tricks and lies. I also believe that a feminist
consciousness changes your perspective on reality and therefore your
relation to people, to social attitudes, to morality, to art and language.

JANICE: Would you describe the development of your own feminist
consciousness?

NICOLE: Before I became a feminist, I suppose I was an angel, a
poet, a revolutionary, which I still am [laugh], but I was definitely
not identifying with women. In fact, I became a feminist when I
became a mother. Almost at the same time I fell in love with another
woman. Suddenly I was living the most common experience in a
woman's life, motherhood, and at the same time, I was living the
most marginal experience in a woman's life, lesbianism. Motherhood
made life absolutely concrete for me, and lesbianism made my life
absolute fiction in a patriarchal heterosexual world. Motherhood
shaped my solidarity with women and gave me a feminist consciousness just as lesbianism gave me new ideas about almost everything
and opened new spaces for me to explore. I read feminist and lesbian
books. I surrounded myself with other women for the pleasure of
being together but also to share some projects like the feminist magazine *Les Têtes de pioche*, the film *Some American Feminists*, and the
collective play *La Nef des sorcières*. Lesbianism has affected my writing
in the sense that it raised new questions, clarified others. It definitely
changed my *rapport d'adresse*. It multiplied my senses, energized my
body in a new way. It offered me new metaphors; for example, the
spiral and the hologram. In other words, lesbianism gave me new

feelings and new ideas about life, love, power, memory, identity. It gave another rhythm to my voice and therefore to my sentences. It stimulated me to look for the missing link between what we call fiction and reality.

JANICE: Your writing and language are anything but 'the expected.' There is a very dramatic moment when you write in L'Amèr, 'I have murdered the womb and I am writing it.' It's a passage of great violence, which is shocking to the reader.

NICOLE: It certainly is. Here you have the kind of sentence that comes out when you don't yet understand how you have been cheated. Without doubt, that phrase says that to a certain degree maternity makes women infirm. In writing that sentence, I wanted to signify how maternity in a patriarchal society makes women extremely vulnerable. The day I gave birth I became mortal and understood that it was necessary for me to stay alive in order to care for this new life. I don't know if I still agree with that sentence. It is a sentence of despair, but at the same time it communicates the information that the subject of the verb resists producing children for patriarchy. The sentence resists clichés about the docile patriarchal mother.

JANICE: You write about your disinterest in modes of 'authentic' self-expression.

NICOLE: Well, I write because I believe that there are things which can only be said or conceived because of what we encounter in the process of writing, in the act of writing. I write to discover things which cannot be thought in the natural stream of thinking or in speech. I don't write what I know; I write what through language I process of my emotions, sensations, ideas, knowledge. I would rather believe more in an authentic voice than in an authentic self-expression. In life I am authentic in my self-expression. In writing I search for my voice in the 'authenticity' of words.

JANICE: In your Journal intime, you define the journal form as 'propaganda of the everyday.' Traditionally the journal has been a significant privatized writing practice for many women.

NICOLE: Yes, well, I know I can be harsh on prose, the novel, anecdotes, journal intime. I mean the novel in general. I don't like novels because I associate them with anecdotes. I know this is unfair and that it is a very personal point of view. Yet I like my resistance to narrative prose because it has permitted me to question the novel from different angles. It is certain that there is a women's tradition in the use of *journal intime*, letters, and autobiography and even of novels if we think of it. In fact, it is interesting to notice that it is women who very often wrote influential novels like *Gone with the Wind*, *The Tale of Genji* [Murasaki Shibiku], *La Sage de Gösta Berling* [Selma Lagerlöf], *Frankenstein*, *La Princesse de Clèves*. Women are great tellers. But to come back to the *journal intime*, let's say that the more women's values and experience are socialized, the more they will be displaced into 'fiction.' If we come to think of it, journals and letters have been expressing the underground of reality. Your question reminds me of what Gertrude Stein says in the *Autobiography of Everyone*. She says that in the nineteenth century, men, when they were writing, were inventing all sorts of other men. On the other hand, women were unable to invent other women but were always creating women in their image. I think this is a great way to mock the idea of a hierarchy of inventiveness between men and women.

JANICE: You quote Monique Wittig advising us that we must invent what we don't remember. Is this the impetus for your lesbian love poems *Lovhers*, the suppressed history of lesbian writing?

NICOLE: *Lovhers* is a work of love inspired by one woman and conveying the continent of women. When I wrote that book, I invested words in a different way – words like 'memory,' 'sleep,' 'vertigo.' Lesbian love brought in a new set of feelings and knowledge which expanded words in a different way. Love has a very interesting effect on your minds. It makes us travel in our past, present, and future. That is why very often people have the impression that they have always known the loved one. Love brings, along with pleasure, a capacity to see reality in three dimensions; it brings details to our attention. In our excitement and enthusiasm we create new metaphors. I like Wittig's sentence because in fact lesbian love calls for a re-membering – the way Mary Daly uses the word – which can only be achieved by the way we invent what we know from an ancient memory which tells us about the ever so good feeling of that woman's soft keen skin.

JANICE: Memory as a strategy of writing is central to Elly Danica's 'autofiction' *Don't: A Woman's Word*. You were sent the text in manuscript form when you participated in the West Word women writers' retreat. How does memory as recovery relate to memory as environment and invention? What was your experience of working with Elly on the manuscript?

NICOLE: In 1988, at the Third International Book Fair, I gave a presentation in which I said that without an inner narrative [*un récit intérieur*], without a narrative lighting [*un éclairage sur les événements que donne tout récit*], memory is an eater of destiny. In other words, if you don't narrate the story of your life to yourself, this story might eat you from the inside. All the time I was preparing that paper, I thought of Elly Danica's book since after reading her manuscript, it became clear to me how much women's memory is occupied by males through the marks of terror and violence they have left on women's body and soul. The younger you are when men's terrorism destroys your integrity, the longer it takes you to clear your territory. When men introduce themselves in our life through physical or verbal violence, they literally break our inner clock; they stop our life, stealing both our time and energy. Narrative is a key element to bridge memory and the present. Narrative is a way to put our inner clock back to the present, and that is why a lot of women use it even in their poetic texts.

JANICE: You create character out of the urban environment in *French Kiss* where the bodies of cars are fleshy. 'Georgraphy' spatializes character. What is the significance of the city and the body in your work?

NICOLE: Especially in *French Kiss*, there is a metaphoric network among the city, the body, the streets, the veins. The city has a nervous and erotic system just as the tongue and language are movement in the kissing or speaking mouth. The pleasure given by city life is associated with the pleasure given by the complexity of language.

JANICE: I was interested in how you remapped the city so that it was no longer a space of male aggression where women are at risk on the streets. Instead of a place of potential violence and agoraphobia, it is playful, joyous, and explosively pleasurable.

NICOLE: Cities are a reservoir of differences, contrasts, contradictions. They can be monstrous as well as sumptuous. Because of their eccentricities they keep you alert in thinking. They remind you of solitude and togetherness, of fun and suffering. They offer their past, present, and their future/no-future at the same time. They make you travel. I know that I travel in Montreal just as I would in a foreign city. I rediscover my city every time I go downtown. The city makes my senses work, it makes me wonder about human species. In fact, very often cities will reverberate your feelings: if you are scared, the city will seem more dangerous; if you feel good, the city will be gorgeous; if you feel bad the city will be hell. You say that cities are a space of male aggression against women, but isn't home also a place of male aggression?

JANICE: You're right. The domestic can be dangerous. Your revision of the city tampers with the symbolic in a way which differs from other postmodern writers. Gail Scott writes about gender specific postmoderns. What is your sense of this specificity?

NICOLE: It seems to me that woman 'derives,' diverts, or shifts meaning in such a way that meaning can be curved and redirected towards her experience and to *what matters*. In other words, post-modern women writers seem to re-route words in such a way that words will provide new meaning rather than a jab in grammar or the syntax. Marcelle Desjardins, a Quebec woman poet of the sixties, writes in one of her poems: 'do I say the truth or do I write a poem?' I believe that this has been and is still at stake for a lot of women in their writing. To me this also explains why women will link narrative fragments, poetical prose, autobiographical passages, and poetry in the same piece of writing. Because women's experience is margin-alized in life as well as in literature, women's subjectivity needs all genres at the same time. The way we re-route words to our own experience opens up entire zones of unknown and unspoken dimen-sions of reality. It seems that while women re-route language, men sink into a kind of 'deroute.' On the other hand, in recent Quebec poetry I can sense that the younger women seem to 'neutralize' their writing. No more anger, utopias, great passions, just a quiet tone to talk about love, childhood, the disaster at the end of the century. But we have to wait and see what happens in the next future of women's writing. In any case, this convinces me that the work accomplished by postmodern women's writing with a feminist consciousness is the most stimulating.

JANICE: So young Quebec women write 'neutralized' texts.

NICOLE: Yes, most of them. For young women, feminism is taken for granted. They have managed their lives to be nice and cool and don't focus any more on the questions of feminist consciousness and the combat.

JANICE: Is this a positive and inevitable progression? Or is it dangerous to not continually ask how we as women are positioned in this culture? Is this 'quiet tone' a refusal to take up the class interests of impoverished women?

NICOLE: It is dangerous in the sense that we lose our focus. In a certain way, it neutralizes us again. Since feminist subjectivity is already marginalized, it seems, unfortunately, that either we keep focused on the feminine subject, risking repetition – as if men never repeated themselves – or we neutralize ourselves into the poetic subject. While I say that, I am trying to understand this horrible double bind into which the feminine gender is *enfermé*. For example, I know that, as a writer, I cannot always use the word *woman* in a poem, but I also know that when, as a reader, I see the word *woman* in a poem, it does have a positive effect on me. I still believe that to write *I am a woman* is full of consequences. I also think that patriarchal meaning cannot stand the visibility of women as a radical subject. It's like parents who accept their daughter's lesbianism as long as she doesn't use the word *lesbian*. In women's writing we are asking, 'What's reality,' and 'What's fiction?' because the reality we live in is a fiction for women since we didn't participate in creating it. Reality has been created through men's fictions, through the imaginary men projected of themselves on reality. If women had built our cities, the architecture would be totally different, because we would have projected part of our bodies as men projected their penis in military arsenals and guns. We would have projected the shapes of our bodies, our minds, and our emotions in the way we light up our cities, in architecture and painting. The question for women in playing with language is really a matter of life and death. We're not just playing for fun in a kind of game. We're finding our own voice, exploring it, and making new sense where the general sense has lost its meaning and is no longer of use. If you want to grow, you've got to be at the origin of new meaning, somehow you have to honour your gender.

JANICE: Some feminist critics have taken on the notion of authenticity in writing. Elaine Marks suggested in one essay that the more numerous the oppressions, the more 'authentic' the writing. Could you comment on this as a lesbian writer in Quebec?

NICOLE: A good writer can only be authentic in the way he or she uses language. The authenticity of a work of art is in the style, which is to say, no one other than this writer can write about the same subject in the same way. In painting, no one can draw a flower like Georgia O'Keefe. Usually the more numerous the oppressions, the more people are unable to talk about their oppression, not because of the social aspect of it, but because the suffering, the humiliation, and the negation have silenced them. I would also say that exploitation and domination call for revolt and that colonization calls for a quest of identity. You can be exploited but not colonized. You can be exploited and still be proud of what you are. But if you are colonized, you don't even know who you are because being colonized means adopting the dominant devalued perspective of yourself. Fighting exploitation is talking about the facts; finding out about your identity is talking about values, memory, and desire. Now it is certain that feminism has made space for women to testify about their lives. This is very important because previously the same testimonies have been denied their 'authenticity.' Furthermore, we now know that these testimonies have a political impact. In fact, one of the main achievements of feminism is that validating women's experience and subjectively has given women self-confidence in their own evaluation of reality as well as in their creativity. As a lesbian and a Québécoise, I belong to minorities, but I always write as if the world belonged to me, allowing my desire to shape around me the space I need to be what I am.

JANICE: As you know there have been important discussions in the community of feminist writers about racism. How do you relate to these conversations?

NICOLE: Sexism and racism can be found in little details as well as in obvious aggression and rejection. I think that Black women have made their points in showing White feminists where the subtleties of racism are hiding in everyday life, spoken or written language. Now, in terms of writing, I don't believe in such a thing as being 'politically correct.' I say that my politics have brought me as far as I could dream, but being politically correct never improved my writing. Either you question reality, language, cliché, alterity, and difference, or you don't and simply rely on what people tell you to think. The same thing applies to me as a lesbian, a feminist, or a Québécoise. On the other hand, I believe strongly in being 'politically connected,' which means – sisterhood, solidarity.

JANICE: You worked with other Quebec authors to develop a politicized analysis of aesthetics during what anglophone Canada called the FLQ crisis. You spoke of the necessity of changing discursive forms in order to communicate radical change.

NICOLE: I have always been fascinated by patterns of discursive relations developing between the dominator and the dominated. From the dominant group one can see a chain reaction that goes from 'you're talking nonsense,' to paternalistic listening, to guilt or irritability, then negotiation, then either acceptance, rejection, or neutralization of the dominated. From the dominated group: a burst of anger, followed by the shaping of an identity and solidarity, empowerment, then negotiation, then autonomy, resistance, or integration. Most of the time guns interrupt the process, and the discursive forms are simplified by a cycle of violence-revenge arguments. Most of the time dominator and dominated have their own culture, values, and traditions, but in the case of women opposing men's domination, we have to consider that, because women live in the same culture as those they oppose, most of the time they are already 'integrated' or 'neutralized' by institutions such as marriage or heterosexism. What interests me in those patterns is when the dominated responds to the dominator's 'you're talking nonsense' with 'you're lying' and from that moment starts to uncover the lies. Uncovering lies makes space for a new sense and thereby transforms meaning. This is where I believe radical change can occur because then one has to take into account that new meaning. The new meaning also starts to produce new metaphors which change the way we see things.

JANICE: In feminist discourse the notion of 'identity politics' has been criticized as having authorized only White women to speak. Do the tensions which have developed between Quebec nationalism and the Native desire for sovereignty during the Meech Lake debates and the blockade at Oka suggest a problematic effect of privileging Quebec identity over other collective identities?

NICOLE: I sense that your question has two directions: one dealing with Native interest and another about why an independent Quebec. On the first subject, a recent survey [November 1990] shows that a majority of Quebeckers would support the political and legislative autonomy of Natives in Quebec. The second direction deals with nationalism and feminism, which is actually for me a great source of questioning. In a recent text I wrote: 'The country which enters into us through the memory of arrogant winner and through the suffering of the losers is a country which divides us.' Nationalism is like heterosexuality; it makes women stick to their men. Now in a feminist context, women have to stick together, don't they? But in what language, on the ground of what tradition, what history? In our attempts to change all patriarchal forms of domination over women, the only ground where I believe we can stick together is the ground of each of our herstories and of a mutual political validation. There is a lot we can teach each other if we don't start by promoting our mutual males' traditions.

JANICE: In your work, you find risk and exploration pleasurable. Can you talk about your process of writing?

NICOLE: It is a difficult question. Risks, I take by exploring. I take risks by phrasing inner radical certitudes which can be offensive to common sense. But on a larger scale writing is full of risks because you don't know where it will take you. After all, we write with that *fragile coherent system full of contradictions* which we call the self. It is always frightening to think that a writer has no rest in dealing with a question such as the meaning of life. It is also difficult for me to answer your question because poetry calls for one process while prose as well as a 'text' calls for another process. Writing poetry, you need to hear an inner voice; writing a 'text' you simply need words + words; writing a novel you need time, patience, and a story. Sometimes I see words in a very material way (sounds, etymology, shape of letters), sometimes I see words through tears, sometimes they are flat, sometimes in 3-D. I have written texts in cold blood, others with a lot of tears, others out of pure sexual energy. Most of them with the dictionaries beside me, some of them on a café, most of them believing that they were worth sharing because something was happening in language.

JANICE: Could you describe a politics of reading your texts?

NICOLE: When you read a book, it is always a very serious thing. A book should always bring you more consciousness about life and about yourself. It should make you ask questions. I write to explore, to understand more, and to discover. And I want the reader to do the same – to stop, to question, to explore with me while reading the text. If my writing is elliptical and full of rupture, it is not because I want to be nasty to the reader. It is my way of creating new spaces for new meaning which would not appear if I wrote in a linear way.

JANICE: In making these new textual spaces for the reader's pleasure, how do you deal with criticism about inaccessibility or élitism?

NICOLE: I don't believe in élitist writing. When you read a book, you have the choice of whether to take it or leave it. If you take it, you have to be willing to do some work on your own part as a reader. You also have to develop a habit of reading. With experience you can read 'difficult' books more easily. Through le nouveau roman and postmodernism there has been a kind of education in reading. The more you are able to follow what the writer has been doing with language, the more you enjoy your reading, because you also are playing and recreating the game which gives you pleasure. The more a text has layers of reading, the more it is exciting. There are two kinds of pleasure in reading. One is the pleasure of recognizing. For example, if I write a novel in which the action takes place in cities which you, the reader, have lived in, it will give you a kind of pleasure to recognize those places. That pleasure reinforces your identification with characters and your interest in the story. The other kind of pleasure comes strictly from the writing itself. Because of the way language is being used, you have to wander between the meanings even though you may intuit what the sentence means. This is both intellectual and mental pleasure, while the first example is about emotional pleasure.

JANICE: How do you distinguish between 'mental' and 'intellectual' inquiry?

NICOLE: For me, the mental recognizes shapes, patterns, abstraction, lines. The intellectual deals with value, knowledge, morals, discursive posture. The mental is visual – it intuits patterns; the intellectual is verbal – it searches meaning and 'truth' among words.

JANICE: In Dorothy Hénault's NFB film on your writing in the *Firewords* trilogy, she develops an interesting reading of your work which emphasizes the intellectual and, except in one scene, tends to diminish the sensual, erotic, visceral quality of your writing.

NICOLE: It's hard for me to tell. I only know that I cannot think properly without emotions and that I would hate to be just a garden of emotions. The best moments of writing are when memory, emotions, desire, thought, sensations, and knowledge all synchronize in the act of writing. In *Firewords* I believe that Dorothy saw what she needed to see in my writing. This process is about reading. A reader always focuses on what she or he needs. This is usually the part that we underline as if the writing belongs to us from now on. It would be an interesting experience to give a book to one hundred readers, see all the passages they underline (take with them), and see what's left for the author, which indeed would be the part where the author's subjectivity did not encounter the reader's subjectivity.

JANICE: Your work has been translated and made available to anglophone readers, and you have worked very closely with your translators. How does the translation process vary with each book?

NICOLE: First, I have to say that I have been very lucky in having as translators women like Barbara Godard, Patricia Claxton, Marlene Wildeman, and Susanne de Lotbinière-Harwood for two reasons: these women are familiar with my writing, and most of all they are creative in their way of approaching translation. Indeed, the translation process varies with each book. Translating *French Kiss* or *Picture Theory* calls for different approaches because of the writing. *Mauve Desert* calls for rhythm and sensuality; *French Kiss* obliges the translator to shift very quickly from one pun to another, etc. Personally, I have always been fascinated by translation, as I am usually writing about acts of passage, whether it is passage from fiction to reality, from reality to fiction, or from one language to another. I wrote *Mauve Desert* because it blows my mind to think that someone can conceive a reality in their language while I can't in mine and vice-versa. I remember one day Patricia Claxton was asking me about the word *sapin*. I asked her to draw what a *sapin* was for her, so she drew 🌲; while I drew mine, which was 🌲. One meaning, two images in the back of the mind. I like to work with translators because it keeps me alert in my own language, for which my fascination has no rest, as well as alerting me to other languages. The way we see and construct reality depends so much on the language which we are given at our birth.

JANICE: Daphne Marlatt writes language-centred poetry and prose. Was this an advantage in working on the 'trance-formation' of each other's work? What affinities and differences did you encounter?

NICOLE: Working and speaking with Daphne is always a great pleasure for many reasons. I like the way Daphne thinks, feels, and writes. I am curious about her language (English and the poetic tradition that comes with it), and she is also curious about mine. Both of us know the weight of language. Both of us were, in the sixties, the only woman poet among male poets. As for our differences, there are just enough differences that we can recognize ourselves in them and be curious to know more about the part that we don't recognize. To be honest with you, I would say that I take Daphne and her writing for granted. There are people to whom you know that you will always be faithful. Daphne is one of them for me.

JANICE: You take pleasure in the slipperiness of language.

NICOLE: Yes. Because changing the course of meaning is one of the greatest pleasures in writing. I like to be surprised by language. Sometimes the surprise pops out haphazardly. Sometimes it is the result of a difficult crafting; sometimes it is the result of a 'coherent contradiction.' Slipperiness has also to do with the aura of the words, their connotations. In fact, the life of a language takes place with the aura of words – their connotations; it is there that the meaning displays and renews itself. I also believe that there is a memory in language which leads to reconstituting patterns of ancient meaning. Once I wrote a text with the words *star, mirror,* and *speculum.* I went to look up the word *speculum* in order to be certain of its meaning, and there I found that the speculum was in earlier times a small mirror used to look at the stars. Without knowing, I had reconstituted a memory already at work in the language. This is exciting. Some writers say that writing is painful for them. I know sometimes it can be difficult, but writing definitely brings its own pleasure, even physically.

JANICE: What is your fascination with the multi-dimensions of holograms, which figure in *French Kiss* and are made central in *Picture Theory*?

NICOLE: When I wrote *Picture Theory*, I had completely forgotten that the hologram was already there in *French Kiss*. So it means that for almost ten years I had been bearing this word in my mind. But why was it only explored ten years later? As well, Arizona and the desert, which are central in *Mauve Desert*, are already present in *Picture Theory*. But why the hologram in *Picture Theory*? Well, I think that my questioning about woman, women, the real, the symbolic, the imaginary, and the notion of fiction versus reality, all came together in such a way that only the metaphor of the hologram could account for them. The hologram deals with a 'real' object, which through 'virtual' image produces a 'fictive' image. It is as if using 'real' characters through imagination – which is the virtual part of the real – I wanted to envision a symbolic woman, fictive but yet changing the perception of womanhood. I have often said that writing *Picture Theory* was making a synthesis of my world, a synthesis like a conclusion which simultaneously opens up on a new horizon. It is hard for me to talk about the state of mind I was in when I wrote *Picture Theory*, but I know that this is the state of mind which I value most. Probably because it embodies certitudes, questions, and utopias in an enigmatic encounter of fiction and reality.

Toronto, February 1986 – Montreal, December 1990

Elly Danica

Excerpt from *Don't: A Woman's Word*

1.19 I lose hope. Nobody believes me. Thirty. It's now or never. I learn to live with never. Never again. I don't remember. I don't want to remember. Memory pursues me. Memory uses a pen to pursue me. Memory runs out the ends of my fingers and makes marks on paper. I don't have to read this. This is useless. What does this mean? Indulgence. Sin. No right to write of how I feel. Bitter. Indulgence. Bitter, but hold on. Don't let it go. Don't let the tears come. Indulgence. A sin. The sin of the women to live only in their pain. The sin of the women never to see the universal. Stuck in the mundane. You'll never be spiritually evolved. Stuck. Making marks on paper. I never stop. I scream in frustration. I live alone. Now I can scream. And again. And again. I don't remember. Don't make me remember. You never forget. Hate has a purpose. Hate serves memory's purpose. The marks on paper weigh fifty pounds. I can't carry this weight anymore.

1.20 Nightmare. I'm awake. How can this be a dream? I wish it was a dream. I could forget if it was a dream. Please tell me this was a dream. Tell me I'm wrong. Tell me I can't remember it. Tell me it was too long ago. Tell me kids get it wrong. Tell me I don't have to remember.

1.21 Forty. The Year of the Hare. The year of light in darkness. Rebirth. Memory as talisman. The dawn of hope. Somebody believes me. I can't keep the secret anymore. The secret is killing me. Hands around my throat. Forty. Nightmares. Gray skies. March hare. Madness. I need rage. I only know how to rage at myself.

1.22 Descent again. Follow the March hare. The Goddess Inanna on a meat-hook in hell. Dead meat. Spread your legs, dog meat. Dead dog meat.

1.23 There is still hate. There is more. Always more. I find one shard implanted under my skin. I rejoice. I remove it with care. I try not to leave scars. I don't use a pocket knife. I try to heal the wound. Why no relief? There are two? I will remove the second then. Still no relief. There are more? Still more?

1.24 The woman made of potshards. Pieces. Not herself. Never herself. Who is herself? Only broken pieces. Each one removed grows a new piece in its place. The wounds fester. There is no healing. The bleeding cannot be staunched. There is no healing. Fear again. The pieces cannot be removed.

Can't cut out your soul. What soul? Remember the star search? No. Only the pieces. Only the pain.

1.25 Inanna had insurance. If I'm gone too long, come for me. Who will be my insurance? Who will bribe the guardians of darkness and bring me back to the light? Who could find all the pieces? How can this be done? How can this not be done? Faith in the process. Descend. Enter. Memory.

From *Don't: A Woman's Word* (Charlottetown: Gynergy Books 1988; reprint, Toronto: McClelland and Stewart 1990)

Elly Danica

'an enormous risk, but it's got to be done'

JANICE: Autobiographical accounts by women about their incest experiences have produced very different forms of writing. For instance, Sylvia Fraser's book ends with a discussion about forgiveness. Would you talk about how forgiveness isn't part of your story?

ELLY: I think there are things that human beings do to each other that are not forgivable, and I put child abuse in that category. I absolutely do *not* think forgiveness is appropriate. I get criticized for it a lot.

JANICE: Sylvia Fraser talks about forgiveness as part of her healing process.

ELLY: I have problems with the way Sylvia Fraser has written her book. She sees herself and her father as co-victims. I cannot accept that at all. If you consider power imbalances, as you *must* in this issue, there's no such thing as adults and children being co-victims in this scenario.

JANICE: The sexual abuse of children is widespread. Statistics suggest 54 per cent of all girls under the age of eighteen have been abused, as have about 33 per cent of boys. We know this is a cross-cultural, cross-class phenomenon, but how can we discuss the specifics of cultural attitudes? Di Brandt, the Mennonite poet, has recently published a poem 'nonresistance or, love Mennonite style.' In it she depicts a philosophy of non-resistance that makes it very difficult for the women inside her community to object to their abuse. At the end of the poem a man sexually abuses his granddaughter, who remains completely passive. In conversation Di wondered whether the passivity on the part of the mother in your *Don't* story is cultural. There are passive women in many cultures, but does the particularity of your story arise out of a Dutch culture?

ELLY: In fact I want to do some thinking and reading about this. I have some serious questions because both my parents were teenagers during the Second World War occupation of Holland. I wonder if history determined their respective ways of dealing with authority – my father's abuse of it, my mother backing down in the face of my father's authority. My mother also was unable to trust that any authority outside of the family would in any way protect her from her husband.

JANICE: You're suggesting that the historical culture experience of fascism socialized your family.

ELLY: Yes, I think patriarchy is at its root a fascistic ideology. As well, women are socialized into passivity; any other response to 'authority' is considered deviant or an over-reaction in women. In my teens, not earlier, I challenged my mother about what was going on, and she said, well look, I married him, this is the way it is, and it can't be changed. She still feels that way, which is really horrifying. This was a lesson she expected I would learn too – not to challenge but to accept the world as defined by my father and other men.

JANICE: It is horrifying. Have you ever talked to her about the book?

ELLY: No. I don't have access to my mother because my father, as one of my sisters-in-law has told me recently, is keeping her virtually a prisoner. And she's dying, so it makes it even more awful – I mean, it's really creepy. And he defines what intervention or non-intervention will happen in terms of the treatment she's supposed to get for the cancer. When I did talk to her a number of years ago, she claimed the reason she has cancer at all is because he insisted she go on estrogen replacement therapy, which she was on for twenty years. I started reading about hormones when I was at university in the seventies, and I tried to explain the dangers to her, but she said, yeah well, that may be so, but he won't let me stop taking them. This was a woman in her fifties. She wasn't allowed to age in an appropriate way, because *he* couldn't live with that. My mother's story is another whole chapter in this tyranny.

JANICE: Just as the incest narratives of survivors have escaped publication and public discussion until recently, the figure of the mother escapes many of these incest narratives. The horror for me is thinking about the absent mother in your story, without falling into the mother-blaming which has prevailed in so much social theory.

ELLY: I haven't had a mother since I was four years old. I listen to other people and watch women who are my peers interact with their mothers. For most of them, interacting is fraught with all kinds of difficulty and ancient scenarios that are replayed. This summer, one woman told me, 'I can't deal with my mother.' I said, yes, but you *at least* have an interaction with your mother, no matter how difficult it is.

JANICE: One can consider incest morally, as evil. Or we can think about this non-consenting defilement of another's body as a shattering of boundaries. The voice in *Don't* writes herself as 'The woman made of potshards. Pieces. Not herself. Never herself. Who is herself? Only broken pieces.' What are the effects of this dissociation and the exploding boundaries?

ELLY: I had a lot of trouble establishing boundaries because I had no sense of myself as an adult and because as a child every time I tried to set up boundaries, they were viciously quashed to make it clear I had no right to personal boundaries. One of the most difficult things I had to do from my late twenties to my late thirties was to discover that I did have boundaries. Earlier I took on everybody else's *stuff*, because I couldn't set clear boundaries. As a child, you learn there is a you and not you. Your personal, physical, emotional integrity ought to be respected. And I didn't have that.

JANICE: Your book deeply disturbed me. The writing itself violates the reader's boundaries, which break down. It's as though the reader symptomatically experiences the pain.

ELLY: I very much wanted to see a change in how society looks at incest. I wanted to present on paper the pain of this experience with no space between the text and the reader. No distance. When we're faced with pain or horror, we often make a distancing manoeuvre – well, at least that's not me. There are people who read a genre of horrible stories because the stories scare them or make them feel creepy and they get a rush out of it. I didn't want my work to fit into that category; I didn't want it to be picked up and used in any pornographic sense. So I tried to write about pain in a way which had to be experienced by the reader and very carefully weighed. We have lots of straight-up narrative that says this happened, that happened, that happened. These are important, but they don't seem to have been enough to get the culture as a whole to look at what it is we are doing when kids have to survive this kind of pain and trauma, or to consider how we disempower not only those children but the adult women and young men these people become. When you're traumatized on that order, you're not a functioning or an appropriately functioning adult by the time you're twenty-five years old. You have too much garbage you still have to deal with. And so we who were taught as children that we are victims ask as adults less of our society. I see abuse of children as a way that patriarchy maintains its power by making large numbers of people unwilling or unable to challenge their learned powerlessness. There is rhetoric on the surface which says in a very vague way that abuse ought not to be done, but, in fact, patriarchy also gives very clear permission for males to abuse.

JANICE: So you see your writing as a feminist political practice?

ELLY: Oh, absolutely. I grew up and went to university in the era when we talked about the personal being political, and that's the basis on which I made a commitment to write this book as an adult. I made a commitment to write it as a kid, not having any idea what it was I had to write – just saying that some day I was going to tell this story and I was going to tell it in some way that would make a difference. I had to do an *awful* lot of reading and an *awful* lot of thinking, an awful lot of personal growing before I got to the place where I could do this. It happened as political practice.

JANICE: Your writing intersects with the work of feminist therapists who encourage survivors to speak and acknowledge their voices. It also intervenes in a personal way for individual readers who have their own stories to tell.

ELLY: That's what I hear. Women tell me that quite consistently. Many women tell me that they are writing journals in an effort to come to terms with the abuse. I used my extensive journal writing to search for a voice, for an 'I' who could speak with authority about the Self. For me, the daily writing was where and how I worked

towards a re-integration of the aspects of Self which had been fragmented. So it was a search, a quest, to find the pieces and then a
long process of writing them into a *whole* I could live with. I sometimes
think that I wrote myself as a character called 'Self,' and as new
insights were gained I had to find ways to re-vision the 'Self' to allow
for what I learned.

JANICE: Your writing telegraphs pain and is difficult to read. But
graphically, your writing on the page offers a certain distance from
the pain because each paragraph is numbered like a biblical verse or
philosophical argument. When I first read *Don't*, I thought it was a
response to Wittgenstein's numbered paragraphs, where he says,
'Where man cannot speak, there must he be silent.' Your 'woman's
word' appeared to me as the beginning of a woman's speech in that
space where men have to be silent. Can you talk about your innovative form?

ELLY: I had to find a structure that would function on more than
one level because I didn't want to eliminate a whole group of readers
who weren't interested in experimental writing. I had to make it clear
enough for that group, but interesting enough for women who read
it on more than one level. It took a hell of a long time to sort out
that structure. Because I've been very, very isolated in rural Saskatchewan for most of the last fifteen years, I didn't have access to very
much experimental writing. I tried different ways until it worked for
me. Now I do read theory when I can get my hands on it, but at that
point I still hadn't read a lot of what was happening in Quebec feminist writing. I was quite amazed at what I managed to do without
that context.

JANICE: You discovered, in Virginia Woolf's words, a formal 'vehicle
for your use.'

ELLY: Yes, but it took me fifteen years of just slugging away at it.

JANICE: Can you define your book as autobiography or fiction?

ELLY: That's always been really difficult; I wrote it because I basically
had no choice. I was trying to write other things, and it kept leaking
through. After it was written, I didn't know what to call it. When I
went to Vancouver with the manuscript, I thought I had only some
notes, but the West Word workshop leader, Nicole Brossard, recognized that this manuscript could stand on its own and didn't need

tampering with. In fact, when I tried to change how it looked on the page, she was quite upset and said, no, that's a different book.

JANICE: That must have been wonderfully affirming for you after your initial pre-writing of thousands of pages.

ELLY: It *was* really wonderful. But it took me almost a year before I even believed it. I didn't have a context for Nicole's comments. She was reading something quite different from what I thought I had written. She mentioned some theoretical writers and the concept of postmodernism, which I didn't know about. I had to read postmodernist writing to get some sense of where people felt my narrative belonged. For twenty years I had been reading other theoretical essays on life-writing, women's autobiography, and feminist writers, but I hadn't discovered postmodernist fiction, and certainly nothing that was feminist.

JANICE: As well as thinking about *Don't* in relation to literary theory, we can find a context for it in legal discourses. When you published it, were you concerned about being sued?

ELLY: Yes I was mostly concerned because I don't want my father to get his hands on any of this pittance that I'm going to make. I've always been *desperately* poor. Now I want whatever resources come from this book to be mine. I was concerned that there be nothing actionable in this text, so Libby Oughton, my publisher, did get a legal opinion from the Writer's Union and she was told that it should be all right, particularly because the decision had been made to publish it as fiction.

JANICE: Did you do advance publicity before you published *Don't*?

ELLY: No, that was a decision Libby made, because she was also afraid that I'd be put under a great deal of pressure not to publish it. At that point I wasn't strong enough to have withstood pressure. We did no advance publicity and in fact did very little the first year the book was out, because I was really afraid. I didn't know what was going to happen to me on publishing this book, and I wanted to take very small steps.

JANICE: Have you had abusive things happen to you as a result?

ELLY: No. The responses have been wonderfully affirming. The kind of warmth and caring that I get from audiences has been very very empowering for me. I always do a question and answer session after the reading, and I hear that these are very empowering for the people in the audience. I think it's a fair exchange.

JANICE: After I read your book, I felt strangely violated. I began to have memories that were really body memories of being abused when I was a child, memories which were both vague and precise but completely insistent. Although I couldn't absolutely identify the abuser, I finally assumed the experience of abuse must be true because I couldn't not believe the memories and bodily sensations.

ELLY: It takes an awful lot of energy to finally recognize the memories for what they are. That's hard work.

JANICE: Perhaps I'll never remember the story. Do a lot of women remember, not the story, but just the sensations?

ELLY: Some do. It depends on different personal situations and different times in one's life because its a process. You may have recovered certain material, incidents or memories. They may not connect holistically for some time until you do whatever work you need to get to the place where it's either safe or possible to remember.

JANICE: Nicole Brossard told me that a number of women she knew had, like me, olfactory memories. It's as though our intellects and our voices can forget, but not our bodies.

ELLY: I'm convinced of this. Look at the absolute celebration in literature of those sensory memories, for instance, in the beginning of the *Remembrance of Things Past*.

JANICE: Proust's 'madeleine'!

ELLY: Different women I've talked to have different sorts of body memories. Not all of them have to do with pressure or sensations of the body; some are images that don't make sense, some are smells, some, sounds. The physical body seems to have a life of its own, separate from the intellect. I want to do more work with that because I wasn't really conscious of what I was saying when I wrote; I just put it into the narrative because that's where it fit.

JANICE: Your bodily memories guided you through your remembering.

ELLY: Yes. But I've been thinking about what this says about our physical bodies and their lives.

JANICE: Are these memories extra-linguistic when they come back as smells or in purely visual terms? My own memories suggest the

experience occurred before I had any language. I think it was a ba-
bysitter outside my family who abused me when I was a very young
child. So the memory is literally pre-linguistic and infantile. Perhaps
there is no story.

ELLY: Yes, there is a story, but you may need more tools or more
time before you can interpret it.

JANICE: In *The Body in Pain: The Making and Unmaking of Language*
Elaine Scarry analyses pain's relation to language. She identifies pain
as existing at the edges of language, resisting articulation.

ELLY: Yes, when I tried to write in what I thought were appropriate
ways – how I'd been *taught* language – the writing was *awful*, almost
sentimental, because when you try to put the story into 'normal'
narrative structure, the pain is not there. The language we are obliged
to use works to obliterate or minimalize our pain. In patriarchal language we're not supposed to tell the truth about our lives and our
pain. I'm looking at the dictionary with a new project in mind, and
it is clear to me that women are written *out* of the dictionary. If words
are not gender-neutral but gender-male, how can that language be
used to tell *our* stories? None of the resonances that apply to any of
those words or phrases refer to us as women, except perhaps in a
negative or derogatory way.

JANICE: Is this research in preparation for new autobiographical or
fictive work?

ELLY: It's much more fictive.

JANICE: And that's a different process.

ELLY: Yes, because it's not specifically self-referential. Some of the
political analysis I've been looking at over the last years is considered
in relation to the place of women in this larger world.

JANICE: Your first book had the mythological structure of *The Book
of Inanna*. Do mythological structures or patterns play a role in your
fiction too?

ELLY: Yes. I'm interested in recovering mythological structures with
women at their centre because those myths have either been hidden
or retold from a masculine perspective where we're erased or marginalized. I've also been very interested in archaeology since I was
very young. In the next text I'm working on, there will be references
to archeology and a further uncovering of the past of women.

JANICE: Your painting at the end of *Don't* is a sign of healing and making yourself whole again. Do you continue to paint?

ELLY: Oh, yes. In fact I was painting this afternoon because it's a way that I can think. I enjoy doodling with colour very, very much. The colours are healing, though unfortunately the painting in the book is reproduced in black and white. I use a lot of pastels, pale pinks, and peaches and lavenders, which are quite lovely.

JANICE: What's the relationship between your painting and your writing? Do they come from different places?

ELLY: They seem to because there are no references in the painting to the past or pain, even though my writing has been focused on this for a number of years. Painting and writing seem to come from different parts of my being, but they balance each other. When I'm frustrated and can't get to where I want to go in my writing, I paint for relief from words.

JANICE: Is there something else you would like to talk about in this interview?

ELLY: Well, it's difficult because you're asking questions from a theoretical background, and you have very definite ideas of what you want. I'm not sure I have a base from which to answer your questions.

JANICE: I'm in the middle of writing a paper on *Don't*, so I'm probably overly engaged with my own interpretation of your work. Also because I've experienced my own memories of child sexual abuse, it's actually quite hard for me to talk to you. Maybe I disappear behind theoretical questions in order to hide the tension that *I* feel. When I was writing my paper, I tried to reread your book. I started it again and again but was unable to continue. As a reader and literary critic, I couldn't get hold of your book. So in this interview, maybe I'm framing my questions in a theoretical way in part to protect myself.

ELLY: I just read a really interesting first chapter of a thesis where the woman was trying to do a very theoretical piece on the problems that battered women have. She had been battling with this for months and months and finally realized that what she wanted to write about was her own experience and make a more personal connection between the content and the work that she had to do with it. It was only when she made that connection and used a more personal approach that it really started to flow for her. Your academic training teaches you that the personal is hardly relevant. The writing that I have done in this book makes it very clear that I think the personal is *absolutely* relevant. For too long we've been trying to fit into a male academic paradigm of what it is we should be saying and how we should be saying it. But personal engagement is very, very difficult and very painful and very risky in an academic environment.

JANICE: It is risky. I was having lunch with some feminist academic women and telling them I was working on this paper. I started to talk about it and really couldn't stop myself. A woman sitting beside me whom I'd just met was listening and very supportive, but a couple of other women said they didn't want to talk about it. So I said I was really sorry if I'd offended them, but they wouldn't tell me *why* they didn't want to talk about it. I realized afterwards I was just furious at being silenced, and then I felt guilty because they might have experienced some form of abuse themselves and their pain might have surfaced in response to my words. But it also felt like I was being censored in a WASP family, where one was often told what were appropriate topics of conversation.

ELLY: I think that we're not at a point where we have such large women's studies departments in universities across this country that we really have our own place yet. We're still on the outside trying to get a bigger chunk of the pie, and that's taking a lot of women's energy. More and more women are going to look at what it is we're doing and decide that what we have to say is much more important than the context in which we're allowed to say it. That's an *enormous* risk, but it's got to be done.

rural Saskatchewan–Edmonton, November 1989

'... once I remembered ... all of the rest of it was there.'

JANICE: It's been a few months since we've spoken, and we've had an opportunity to look at the first interview and talk about it. For me, it works as a kind of protection in that I begin speaking in the voice of the feminist literary critic, and then something, as you say, bleeds through or interrupts that particular authorial voice and I'm left with how my own experience becomes a critical strategy in my work.

ELLY: From looking at what happened to you and then reading it as text, I think that's really exciting, because what you're doing is you're not blocking off your real self into this little box the academy really would like you to be in, so I find that really exciting. For me, your interview was the first time I'd had to deal with my text having any kind of authority in the context of the academy, and so to be examined with critical tools. I found it really terrifying. I came away from the conversation we had over the telephone really depressed, thinking my text wasn't going to measure up, I wasn't going to measure up and there was really nothing for it, that I was terribly stupid and that's how I felt. I didn't get that from you personally; I got that from the vocabulary that was used in the interview.

JANICE: That's one of the very sticky problems of a feminist critic – you need to speak out of both sides of your mouth; you have this particular vocabulary which comes from your intellectual work and deals with a certain body of knowledge you work within, and you also have another way of speaking to issues and to texts which derives from a longer history, your own long history as a woman and in connection with women in the community and your friends outside your academic disciplining. The question of language is interesting for feminists since we have to develop a fluid discourse, so that we can translate easily from one language sphere to another.

ELLY: I can remember when I was at university talking once to a couple of women in a rooming-house that I lived in. I thought I was speaking English, and I thought that it was very simple because I didn't consider myself an academic or even an intellectual and as I talked – I can't even remember what the issue was, but it wasn't anything too rarefied – they became more and more uncomfortable and more and more puzzled, until finally they basically dismissed me and said, 'You don't speak our language, so go away.' That's always stayed with me because I worry that because we talk to each other in this language, which becomes a shorthand for a whole lot of concepts and ideas that we carry, we're not speaking directly enough or clearly enough to the larger community. Maybe it's one of the things that as feminists we should be aware of because I don't feel that as feminists we're getting our beliefs and our values out into the community, and perhaps it's language that is making that impossible.

JANICE: I don't know how to answer that because I think it's one of the central issues in contemporary feminist work.

ELLY: The issue really is, whose language are we speaking here.

JANICE: I don't like to think we're speaking someone else's language, like some monolithic male theoretical language, because I don't think that's it, I think –

ELLY: Maybe it's just an issue around a theoretical language at all.

JANICE: Yes, it's an issue around theoretical language.

ELLY: But I was surprised that it made me so uncomfortable because I've been increasingly looking at feminist literary criticism, and I guess because I wasn't in a place where I had an opportunity to discuss this with my peers, I really felt I was in a great big pond and drowning when I had to address it in terms of my own writing. And it was very scary for me.

JANICE: Many of us do feel quite excluded from the academy for a whole bunch of different reasons. Working-class students feel excluded, practically, and also in terms of what they imagine an intellectual life to be, how it's represented in terms of a particular class formation. For women it's more complicated because many of us are first-generation women in university and we feel excluded psychologically; for me, to spend time thinking is to not be doing 'useful' work. There's that kind of work ethic coming from some families that intellectual work is not 'real work.' So when you talk about the questions of 'real' self and losing a sense of your 'real self,' what I feel within the context of feminist theorizing and feminist thinking about literature is that my real self is not – homogeneous. She's split and splintered and feels comfortable and uncomfortable in a lot of different ways and different contexts and with different languages. Rather than seeing that fragmentation as negative, I want to swim a number of different strokes in different waters. It feels quite liberating and I don't want to give any of the different voices or conversations up. This split between community women and feminist academic theorists in some ways is a very artificial one dependent on the ideal of the cloistered scholar. At the same time, the whole notion of being an intellectual in a sometimes anti-intellectual culture can be intimidating. We're made into monsters. We can work to break down the stereotypes, and still acknowledge these contradictions.

ELLY: Certainly in my life I've found that the people in my community said I don't do any work, not *any* work at all, because reading and thinking are certainly not work. I'm not in an academic context, so I couldn't get any validation at all for my work, but I was again really surprised that I couldn't even give it to *myself* when I had to look at my work in these theoretical ways and I'm just wondering where that all comes from.

JANICE: In your book your process of survival in an abusive family requires a kind of internal displacement where you're able to shift ground and see part as abused and this other part of yourself as whole and thinking and feeling. Can you describe this position of analysis and thinking?

ELLY: Well then you have authority. What that seems to have brought up, when I looked at my text from a theoretical perspective, is all kinds of fear, and that fear is related to my history. *That* was what was so terrifying; and *that* was at the same time very fascinating.

JANICE: It's also really interesting because while one wouldn't like to think in absolute terms of the academy as an abusive father, the university does in fact embody a history of patriarchy, and the structures are organized in ways which make it very difficult for women to work in women-defined ways around women's issues.

ELLY: When I was at university, I tried to feel comfortable in three different areas. I took the core classes in anthropology, political science, and sociology. I felt them all to have a secret language. I was on the outside, and there was nothing that referred to my life. So when this theoretical vocabulary was used in terms of my work, it was like it brought all that up again and I wanted to push against it – *no*, don't use that around me, don't make me have to *think* about this kind of stuff. It really is a fascinating experience, and I've thought a lot about it since we talked and I need to look at all these reasons why I feel so uncomfortable with it.

JANICE: This also makes me recognize my need to look at the relationship between my writerly and my academic identities.

ELLY: And we need to find ways that we're not boxed in either one. I don't think that we should become anti-intellectual and stop making theory around the work we're doing because theory brings forth incredible insights and I love to read it. But then again, seeing it in terms of my own work is like, wait a minute! What does this mean?

JANICE: The other question I have has to do with the fact that you are here right now as part of an amazing six-month whistle-stop tour across Canada, and you toured again just last fall. Many authors do this kind of tour, but yours reminds me of Pauline Johnson, that sense of the whole town coming out. You have two and three hundred people coming to your readings where discussion ranges from child sexual abuse to literary questions and back again. In some ways, moving across the country, you're creating a thinking-feeling space, an embodied intellectual conversation and analysis of important feminist questions about violence against women and children.

ELLY: It seems to be really really important, both to me and to the audiences, that I appear in person. They want to see that I'm all right. They want to see how I function in the real world because often the text leaves them devastated, and they really want to connect with me. One of the things that happens – and the first few times it happened I was really uncomfortable. Now I understand it a little more, although I don't claim to understand it all the way – people want to hold my hand and both thank me and tell me snippets of their own stories. They want to connect with me. They want eye contact, they want to have a verbal contact, and they want to hold my hand while they do this. And it's very beautiful, and people come up to me quite often and say, 'Your book changed my life.' And I don't think as a writer that it gets any better than that, to have that kind of impact, even in one life, never mind hearing that several times across the country. I think part of my commitment to this book is to try to get people to realize both that our telling can be very very powerful because obviously it's powerful in others' lives, because they stand before me really affected by what this book has done and said. And I want to encourage them to also tell their stories, because I think we need a body of this work if we're going to make a change. I do a question-and-answer period after I do a very long reading, and try to tell each person in the audience that I don't have any corner on this, that it's not me alone who can make these changes in anyone's life, who can stand in front of an audience and talk about this as an issue. We need many many other women and men to do this work because it will create change, not necessarily just one or two of us. The people want to hold my hand and tell me their stories! How many other writers with a fiction or a non-fiction book experience this? Maybe I'm being naïve and maybe this happens on a regular basis after readings, but I don't think so, because I've been to readings where I didn't see this happen.

JANICE: Some writers would say what you're experiencing – they would say there is literary work and then there are other kinds of writing which connect with different parts of people's beings and don't have that pristine quality of literary work – I'm making up some abstract bogeyman –

ELLY: Yes, I can understand this because there's that whole thing that if it relates to our personal pain and our stories it's not high art, and I think that if the written word connects with the real lives of real people then it is everything it ought to be and it doesn't need to be justified in any other way. But I'm continually amazed at the response and at the warmth. People feel they know me *very* well. When they tell me about themselves, it's a kind of sharing with a friend about something that has happened. It's very intimate and I find it – although it's often great pain – a very beautiful kind of experience because it's empowering. It's like my speaking and my reading are empowering for me and also empowering for others. But their speaking back to me their stories is empowering both for them and for me, so I feel it's a very fair exchange and very very beautiful.

JANICE: When you say your readers know you very well, how well do they know you? When you wrote what you called 'autofiction,' *Don't,* you were a particular person, and now from all accounts you've changed and grown and opened in all kinds of ways just because of the very powerful experience and process of finishing the book. So how well do they know you, if writing itself is a process of both exploration and self-transformation?

ELLY: I think they know the self that is described in the book. So that's the part they know through the text. They're probably as amazed as I am in the woman who stands in front of them and delivers this text from a podium. I think they would know an aspect of myself that I've called up, probably the child selves within themselves, and so we can connect on that level, but of course there's much more to me that's not in that text. That text is primarily about the wounded self trying to dig her way out of the pit, so that there are whole other parts of my life – and certainly my intellectual life – that absolutely don't show up in that book. But for a certain part of who I am, they certainly do know me because I tried to be as honest as I possibly could, and so they ask for clarification, they ask for reassurance that I'm well, that I'm happy, and putting those two things together, I think they know me quite well.

JANICE: One of the questions you were interested in is the whole problem of authorial voice and how women find a voice to speak.

ELLY: The quote that goes through my mind from Alice Walker is that you've got to get man off your eyeball before you can see anything at all, and I wonder how you get patriarchy and patriarchal agendas out of your head so you can speak from the centred place of your true self. First you have to find who that true self *is*, and then you've go to learn to speak from there. I've been looking for a number of months for essays or anything about this because I'm very very interested in the process of arriving at that place. Do we speak differently when we arrive there? Where does the authority for our own voices come from? Is it engendered in our bodies? Is it engendered in our intellectual processes, so that it's arrived at after many years of reading and research? Or is it more – direct from the body when you arrive at a certain age perhaps? I don't know. And I've got all these questions about where the voice might come from, and I'm looking for someone to dialogue with around this and hoping I could find essays or a book and I can't find anything. But it fascinates me because it's a real struggle for me. When I write, the first thing I want to know is: who's speaking? And in my book I wrote both from my father's voice and my own voice; and I find it very wrenching when I read aloud to have to go into his voice and speak from his voice, yet I remember his dialogue very very clearly; so it's not an issue of wondering if I've got it right – it's just having to take that voice into my body is really difficult. Especially since this other part of me in my next book is trying to struggle with getting that voice out of my body, out of my head. Yet I'm very uncomfortable because I don't know what will replace it. And so I've got all of these characters in this new work basically trying to help the writer find out where her voice is, where it comes from, and what she should use it for, because I think that's really important as well. It's not only how we say what we say, but very much *what* we say. I feel an enormous responsibility in terms of my readers to say something that is meaningful. Part of me would very much like to be flippant now because this was *so* hard and reading from it's so hard; so I've made a pact with myself that yes, I can say some things in a flippant way, but I've got to have a commitment to a serious sub-text.

JANICE: How old were you when you began remembering and writing?

ELLY: I started seriously writing in 1976, which was the first year I was in my old church, and it was why I moved to this old church, so that I could write. I wrote every day. I wrote about what was happening, what I was thinking about, and what I was reading. Every once in a while I would get to a point in great despair where I would say I've got to write about whatever it is that's causing me all this pain. And then I would turn on myself and become very self-abusive, because it was so scary to even look at this. I did that for all those years until I turned about thirty-eight, I think, and that spring I had a health crisis that got me to realize I had to quit jerking my body around, quit punishing my body. I had to really face what it was that was causing me all this pain. I didn't know what it was, but I felt I had access to a couple of things that had been coming to the surface over the last couple of years, and they were both physical sensations and visual images. What I was finally able to do was make a commitment to start from a visual image, the image that I've talked about of the door with a very high clearance, and so I created a safe space for myself emotionally and physically; I talked to friends and said I'm going to try and see what's going on, but can I call you if it goes wrong, like if I get really frightened, or if I become so terrified that I'm going to do damage to myself. So once I had those assurances from my friends that they were available by phone day or night, I sat down and started to write everything I remembered about that one visual image, tried to address the visual image, tried to look at it ... I talked about light, I talked about doors, I talked about everything I could think of around the image until it began to open up for me. Then once it opened up, it was a very very rapid process, and I remembered where that door was, which I hadn't remembered until then; I remembered very suddenly that the only way I could have seen that light and that door from that angle would be if I'd been on my back and what did that mean? As soon as I remembered *on my back,* I got a sensation of cold and roughness against my back and remembered *where* in the house I would have been on a floor that would have been that cold because it was really really bitterly cold and remembered it was a concrete floor. That drew me into looking *where* in my house was a concrete floor. There was *enormous* resistance right then because I knew I was on very dangerous turf and had to talk myself into going further with it. By that time it was very late at night, I really wanted to sleep, but I said no, you've got to look at this, it's here, you've got to look at it. And I recognized that that floor was in a room in the basement which I had not remembered for almost twenty years. I remembered all kinds of places and details about the rest of the house I grew up in, but I had not remembered there was a basement with a photography studio, with photo labs, with cameras, with men, and once I remembered that, then all of the rest of it was there.

Edmonton, January 1990

Kristjana Gunnars

Excerpt from *The Prowler*

101

It is possible to be so full of love that the voice that is inundated with words is unable to speak.

The simplest words clamour to get out, but all that emerges is silence.

This is the voice that sits beside hospital beds. The voice that cannot see clearly which configuration of words will be the one to remove all the rolls of barbed wire.

Love seeks refuge in figurative language. Love is ashamed of itself, of its own transparency. It is vulnerable territory. A people without its own army, easily occupied by armed forces of other nations.

Love turns itself out.

102

The problem of Dr Patel, who came from India, was never resolved. I worried that he might find it offensive watching us eat the meat of a whale. If I had been allowed to speak, I would have said: the white Inuit take what comes in its own season.

103

There is a reason for the scarcity of stories. Of cards in the deck. Aside from the tendency stories have to repress themselves in their desire to fall in with dogma.

There was much illness. Large patches of months and years were blotched out. A kind of ink stain appeared in the text, where the consciousness became obliterated. It was not exactly unconsciousness that took over, but a state of exhausted ennui. A desire to forget.

The ink stains did not always have names. Often they were called the flu, or they bore the titles of common childhood illnesses. On one occasion it was a form of typhoid fever. On another occasion it was suspected of being polio. But most of them were just there, frequent collapses, a way of life.

They were times when I lay semiconscious, vaguely aware that an unknown hand was examining glands or listening to heartbeats with a stethoscope. Voices of the doctor and my mother could be heard above me, coming as if from a great distance. When I opened my eyes there would be faces bent over me, usually bearing an expression of helpless concern.

Times when I found myself on a cold floor in the middle of the night. The familiar ring in my ears, announcing the appearance of some alien force arriving to retrieve me. Slowly I knew I was disappearing. It did not cause me much concern. Everyone else was far too fussy, I thought.

Those who are disappearing are far wiser than those who sit by the bedside. There were times I wanted to reassure the faces that I was simply taking a break. But I was not always able to fetch my voice from that great distance. It seemed like a phenomenally long way to go, down somewhere in an area of wet ocean caverns, where my voice was lodged for a while.

That is an area where there is a cessation of stories. If death is another play after the one about life, it must like all good plays have rehearsals. The consciousness rehearses an existence without stories.

It is in the nature of writing to contain a note of defiance. To confront its opposite, to stare it down. To make a certain claim for life.

It is also a confrontation that looks in, for what is being defied is located inside writing. A form of cold war, where the ink that is directed into patterns is carefully watched so it will not spill over and spread out, uncontrolled.

From *The Prowler* (Red Deer, Alberta: Red Deer College Press 1989)

Kristjana Gunnars

'In that gap where one searches, the muse hangs around ...'

JANICE: I'm drawn to your work because it is propelled by a certain melancholia. Julia Kristeva wrote, that 'there is no writing other than the amorous, there is no imagination that is not overtly or secretly melancholy.'

KRISTJANA: That may be a true statement for me. What propels me to write in the first place is sadness. When I'm very happy, I see less reason to write. When one is unhappy, it is because one doesn't have what one wants or desires, so there is a gap. In that gap where one searches, the muse hangs around, for me anyway. Also, when I started to write, I felt like I was in a hole of some kind, but I wasn't sure what kind of hole it was. I was doing the bourgeois married thing – raising a child and living in a bungalow in the suburbs and just being married. I felt I had to do something to become a person because I didn't feel I was one. Something was seriously missing in my life. I tried to write myself out of my non-existent state. I wasn't acknowledged. It's no specific person's fault, I just wasn't acknowledged.

As a writer there is a kind of power in that weakness. It's like the whole world is a stage and everybody's playing a part. You come on the scene, and you're really not a very good actor. You don't carry your costume very well, you can't hold a sword for the life of you, you can't do the dance, and you really wonder what you should be doing if you can't play the part well. That's how I felt. And that's part of being an immigrant. It's also part of being a disassociated personality, which you are sometimes when you are a woman at home. You're sort of dislocated. You see everybody else parading around, and you're looking at them and thinking – it can't possibly be that the world extends to where my front lawn begins and then it stops. The realm I'm in is not the world, it's something else. So you write to incorporate your own life into the world out there, but in a very arrogant fashion you also write to bring the world to its knees, so that it will accept where you are as a place worth being.

I think it's a very profound motive that makes people like us *carry* on and just *go* and try to accomplish things. It's the worst thing to be alive and feel you might as well not be because it makes no difference to anybody. So, I guess there is a sadness in the anxiety that you are always in danger of being obliterated.

JANICE: How much of this sadness is derived from your experience as an immigrant? In 'The Night Workers of Ragnorök' you write that your immigrant experience is one of absence – 'the sense that you are always without something essential: a fear that you have forgotten something important, or left a part of you behind.'

KRISTJANA: All those feelings of possible non-entity or non-existence are magnified for the immigrant, who can't relate to the surrounding countryside or to any small town or urban centre with any childhood memories. To be an immigrant means you have no relation to what's around you, no history, and no family. So you have no standing, except for what you create yourself out of the air. Sometimes to be a woman also means those things. You have no standing because you're holed up at home, not *participating* in the working world. In spite of this fact, I've always had this one project, to raise a kid. To me, that has been my life. That has given it meaning, substance, direction, and I've given up an awful lot of other things to do it. I've been able to raise my child and write. I've not been able to do that and become minister of culture and work my way up through the political bureaucracy and go to parties and ... Still I felt that I had a lot of work to do to create a whole world here. Creating a space is like clearing the bush, so that there is a space for you. That's why I started writing all this Icelandic stuff.

JANICE: Your image of cultural homesteading has another side in that you are very committed to maintaining and developing readings of Icelandic and Icelandic-Canadian culture.

KRISTJANA: Iceland is so small, 250,000 people, and it's so threat-

ened that I actually have an expansion of my own neurosis happening
where my paranoia about becoming extinct, personally extinct, extends to all my people and my entire culture. If people like me don't
work to make sure that they do not become extinct, then you have
to incorporate or sort of *graft* that culture onto North American culture. It's the linguistic equivalent of establishing a grand library of
Icelandic books in this country, just in case someone puts an atom
bomb in the old country and all that stuff perishes. There might still
be something *here*, so that it would exist here. I hope that there are
some Icelanders in Australia and England doing the same thing, because it's important when you have a distinct culture. I empathize
with Native people for the same reason. If they're not writing or
committing their culture to some permanent form so that it can be
absorbed onto this one, grafted onto it or somehow shared or made
part of this one, then it might disappear. The verbal, the oral tradition
is wonderful, of course, but every time there is a new transference
of cultural information orally it gets changed.

JANICE: *Unexpected Fictions*, the collection of Icelandic-Canadian
stories you edited, illustrates this grafting process. But you claim that
a number of the authors don't know that much about Iceland and
the stories actually enact Western Canada.

KRISTJANA: You're kind of a cultural archaeologist when you edit
a book like that. Or perhaps just a student. I set out simply, as editor,
as student, to find out where we are at, and who of our writers are
sharing with the rest of Canada whatever Icelandic thing they are
and know and happen to have inside them. But not very many of
them are doing that, so that's where you are. It's more or less completely gone. When I was assigned this job, the Icelandic community
thought that there would be a nice showcase of accomplished Icelandic writers. What they got, instead, and they may not realize it
until some scholar comes along and points this out, is a showcase of
how little there is left. There's really nothing left. I know all these
people personally, and I wouldn't rely on any of them to hand over
the Icelandic culture to the next generation. Also, the Icelandic culture
in Canada is *different* from the Icelandic one that I know. Not only
is the old one disappearing, but we don't know what the new one
looks like yet. It's not Canadian mainstream or anything like that,

it's just a new *thing*. Not until people come around and edit books like this to show us, or unless enough of them provide us with cultural information, art works, and so forth, will we know. We owe it to ourselves to find out what it's like.

JANICE: You quote Rousseau in the introduction to 'The Night Workers,' and you insist that your information is to tell the truth, not to make people believe it. How, then, do you justify your political writing. Some of your poetry about Iceland is a critique of militarism. The invasive violation of the American military bases on Icelandic terrain figures centrally in *The Prowler*. How do you resist the impulse to make people believe?

KRISTJANA: This goes back to telling the truth. That is such a tacky thing to say, but as a matter of fact I don't know how else to put it because we don't really know what the truth is. But supposing you were determined not to make anything up. Supposing we simply *admit* things, regardless of the ethics involved, regardless of how we would have to justify it, or regardless of the morality of it, or the embarrassment of it, or the wickedness of it, or *any* thing. What if we just admit the way things are. I think we're much better off doing that. So what I've been writing in relation to political scenarios is a kind of a 'let's not kid ourselves. This is the way it is.' So I think also in an emotional arena, supposing we simply admit how we feel. If I paint a culture that has all kinds of strange things in it or has garbage in it, I think that's *good*. It's a good move because that's my truth. Once we share that, at least I think we're further along. Further along, I mean, assuming there is progress in these matters.

JANICE: Do you call yourself an 'ethnic' writer?

KRISTJANA: *Never!*

JANICE: Why not?

KRISTJANA: Only when I get paid a lot of money. Sometimes it happens that people pay me for doing that, but I don't ever call myself an ethnic writer.

JANICE: How do you feel when you perform as the ethnic writer you don't believe you are?

KRISTJANA: I think all of this falsifies what we're experiencing. It's unfortunate because the term 'ethnic' has an ingredient which, for me, separates the ethnic person from the supposedly mainstream person. When people call you an ethnic writer, they're saying, you *may* be here and OK. I accept that you're here, but you come from somewhere else, don't really belong, and you're no doubt going back somewhere else. It's the visitor impulse. I don't want to be a visitor! All this work I've been trying to do, which is to create a place for *my* culture in Canada, just gets erased all the time by this ethnic label. The Icelandic-Canadian culture has influenced Canada in remarkable ways. Large parts of the northern hemisphere were put under the Canadian flag by an Icelander. Many of these people have been governing the country, in the provincial legislatures and in the federal government. Many are very dynamic and successful members of society. And they have brought their cultural attitude into all this. The women's vote in Manitoba is to a large extent the work of Icelandic women. Only Icelandic women in Canada were doing feminist work before Nellie McClung. They had the first feminist magazine in the country and went around lobbying and giving speeches. They helped create the culture we are. It seems to me unfair and unreasonable to say that this is ethnic. And this doesn't just go for the Icelandic group; they're contributing in ways that Canadians don't necessarily want to *see*. What would Canadian commerce *be* without some of these Asian cultures making it happen in certain ways? We're foolish if we don't accept this. Things don't just happen out of the blue.

JANICE: Some literary criticism, in defining certain kinds of writing as 'ethnic,' makes it exotic and 'other.' How does this reading and analysis affect how and what you write?

KRISTJANA: I think 'exotic' is at the heart of writing. No matter who you are or where you're coming from, that's what you look for, simply because otherwise you're boring. Everyone has something exotic or 'other' to tell, because every life is different. Ideas about making strange and creating surprise and so forth are what writing is. Catching people's attention. Even if you're talking about apparently very ordinary things, you can't catch people's attention unless you do something that's somehow strange or different. To me, Margaret Laurence's stories are really exotic – not because she's found some unusual African tribe a hundred years ago to tell me about but because she is honest about what is going on in this place with these people she's writing about.

JANICE: The epigraph to *The Prowler* is from Marguerite Duras's autobiographical novel *The Lover*: 'The story of my life doesn't exist, does not exist, there's never any centre to it. No path, no line. There are great spaces where you pretend there used to be someone, but it's not true, there was no one.' How does this sense of erasure and impossible recuperation inform *The Prowler*?

KRISTJANA: Well, that is a very complicated issue which has a lot to do again with living as an adult in a country you didn't grow up in. When I came to North America, my entire past life to the age of sixteen was cut off. There was nothing around me that related to anything I had experienced up till then. Everything was different: the people, the place, the smells, the colours, the culture, the language – you name it. It was just like a sharp drop. So for fourteen years, between sixteen and thirty, I felt like I didn't exist before the age of sixteen. Seriously. I felt like it was all a story told to me by somebody. And this was a very serious psychological thing. I didn't see it as a problem or as significant until much later, but I just experienced it as sadness. I was really behind because at the age of sixteen I had to start learning everything everybody else around me already knew; all that cultural baggage that everyone had, I had to learn from the beginning – from the language to modes of behaviour to finances. I didn't even know how to operate a bank account until I was in my late twenties because this whole system of doing things was foreign to me. I didn't know what the word *mortgage* meant until I was well over thirty. This may sound rather odd to you, but at that time in Iceland, we washed our clothes by hand and put them on the bushes to dry. Icelandic culture is not a commerce culture. There is no history of commerce there, and so we don't get it with out mother's milk. English people have a long history of commerce – all you have to do is read a Charles Dickens novel to see how the whole economic operation of society is incorporated. So this was a serious cultural difference. I had to overcome my ignorance as well as my lack of confidence about simply being able to operate as a normal person around here. So Marguerite Duras's quote was really true for me. Someone was supposed to exist, but it's really just a story. I never saw people from my past, I never heard from them; no one ever spoke like them, and so I had a real shock to my system when I went back at the age of twenty-five and looked at Iceland again.

JANICE: Does this absence, this amnesia, manifest itself formally in *The Prowler*? It isn't organized in chapters but in very small numbered fragments.

KRISTJANA: When I wrote *The Prowler*, enough time had passed and enough education had taken place that I could sit down and say, OK, I'm going to try to recover this past and act as if it was a real past, not just a movie, but a dimension of experience that can be shared by other Canadians. And I really wanted to write this book because I felt that if I pulled it off, then I could convince people *here* that my reality does exist. I could say to my friends in North America, well, I spent a lot of time on a ship when I was growing up, but to them it would just be a story. They would have no sense of how it felt, the smell of the oil, and the smell of the saltwater and the seabirds and the noise. In order to make it real, you have to be able to convey that. That's where creative writing comes in, and I at least wanted to try.

JANICE: The narrator of your novel is reluctant to assume her authority. She says if she believed in a god, *The Prowler* would be God's story. Why this reluctance, this narrative self-distancing?

KRISTJANA: Well, it's part of the complication of disbelief. You may want to make something real that has been erased from you, but you may not really believe that it is real. So part of the reluctance is that you're overcoming your own sense of disbelief. Somehow you too have been brainwashed into thinking that this isn't a real world, that Iceland doesn't exist. You imagined it and it's just a shared story. The other part is you might dislike the arrogance that is involved in sitting down to write your own story.

JANICE: The other side of the arrogance though is personal vulnerability.

KRISTJANA: Well absolutely. And so I tried to be as forthright as I could. That is a vulnerable thing to do. I tried to incorporate all my feelings about the project into the project, so that it wouldn't come off as a show. I'm not trying to entertain anyone, though it's good if they are. I wanted to approach it as part of a process rather than a product – here's a book which will keep you awake for an hour.

JANICE: This 'process experience' demands a very active reader because we're constantly shifting ground.

KRISTJANA: In a project like this you have to activate the reader.

The reader can't be passive, she *has* to care; otherwise the project fails. Because you are trying to make real something you fear might be imaginary, only the power of your conveyance is going to make it real. As soon as the reader *feels* it, or has a strong sense of it or gets involved or engaged in it, then it's real. If there is no engagement, there's no element of fascination, and then it's not real and you have to admit that yes, in fact it wasn't a real life, you really didn't exist until after you came here.

JANICE: So reading has to do with proximity and desire.

KRISTJANA: Sure. The reader has to be seduced into an engagement.

JANICE: *The Prowler* is a text of extreme pain. There is a split in the women characters; the anorexic sister is an emblem of the lived experience of poverty as well as the female body's impoverishment.

KRISTJANA: The anorexic parallel figure is an example of how important the narrator's project is. She'll go through the whole disappearance routine if this project doesn't succeed. I'm writing something into existence, and it has to succeed or else I'm going to turn into a pile of ashes like this other figure who isn't writing. That figure in real life struck me as a horror story because it had a lot to do with my own deepest fears about simply not existing.

JANICE: Do things get out of control in your writing?

KRISTJANA: Hm. I think I've tried to control them the way I've tried to control my own life and my own emotions. I think I really do have a mind that goes on automatic shut-down if something is too terrible to face.

JANICE: As a writer you are out of control in the sense that you can't control how the work is going to be received. In *Carnival of Longing* you write, 'All my words may speak another story / depending on the reading / Freudian story, Jungian / Lacanian, Barthesian, auto-biographical story / when I had not intended to tell / any story.'

KRISTJANA: That's the writer's paranoia. You write something, you think you've written something, but as a matter of fact, a hundred readers know that you've written a hundred other things, and a lot of other things show in what you've done and you are naked. You can't take off your clothes in public without people seeing your body. And there you are. And you may try to tell yourself that your body has certain qualities, but anybody can see what there is to see. So when you write a book, especially like the *Carnival of Longing* and then *The Prowler*, I guess you really are naked. The *Carnival of Longing* admits all of this.

JANICE: How is *Carnival of Longing* different from confessional poetry?

KRISTJANA: A lot of the propelling force of actually sitting down to write is a sense that things here are not what I think they are. I'd like to be able to name what they are as opposed to what I think they are. I'd like to surprise myself too. It's different from confessional poetry in that all these poems acknowledge that there may not be anything to confess. Traditional confessional poetry is I've got a secret, or I've got something I'm going to tell you about, and this is my confession. But the whole milieu where *Carnival* is coming from, theoretically and creatively, supposes that the confession itself is another lie. You only told the confession in order to impress, and so when you really get down to things you find there's a great gap and perhaps you have no feelings about this, perhaps you never *did* anything. Perhaps again, as in *The Prowler*, there is nothing, except it's opposite in the sense that *The Prowler* tries to recover something out of the fear of nothingness. *Carnival of Longing* tries to get through all those somethings into an area of nothingness. It tries to obliterate itself actually because the poems are written in a state of discomfort. It's all the discomforts that we know so well and all the discomforts we live for, such as love and things like that. It's uncomfortable to love. The poems try to obliterate those feelings until you're left with just the pleasant relief of having no more feelings.

JANICE: This seems to run against the grain of popular romance – against love as plenitude and merging and the bliss of a certain loss of identity.

KRISTJANA: Yeah, I dislike all popular conceptions of the love between two people and seriously doubt whether we know what it's all about in popular culture or in the way we even talk about it. I fear that two people loving each other and being together is full of so much that we hate and loathe at the same time, that the perfect state is to be away from all that!

JANICE: How does your poetry compensate you for this loss?

KRISTJANA: It doesn't compensate at all. It doesn't. It's just a way of reflecting because you have to reflect on things. Perhaps it provides another kind of plenitude, but I don't think it's of a similar enough order to say that it could possibly compensate.

You know how I feel about being a Canadian writer. I have a very high regard for the activity of literature and writing, and it's also very much part of my culture. It's one of the noblest things a person can do. On the other hand, to be a really good writer, you have to take risks to say and show things that are in the depths of your knowledge, your consciousness, your emotions.

JANICE: Or of everyday experience, which is sometimes risky or scandalous.

KRISTJANA: It's not necessarily confessing in the sense that you're telling about your own life. I have never told about my own life. You could read my books as many times as you want. You'll never find out how I live my life or what I do. It's not there. But if you are operating at a certain depth, everything you write reveals things about what you know, how you think, what kind of attitude you have, what kind of metaphors you choose to use, what kind of things are powerful to you. It reveals an awful lot of you even though you say nothing about yourself.

JANICE: You wouldn't consider the self-reflexiveness in *The Prowler* symptomatic of cross-genre writing, as fiction-theory rather than 'fiction'?

KRISTJANA: The distinctions we are making between theory and fiction are to some extent more academic than actual. If what you mean by your question is that *The Prowler* is something other than fiction as well as being a story, then I'm not sure you couldn't simply say it is fiction, but the kind of fiction that allows for the incorporation of cross-genre writing. There are hundreds of works of fiction out there where the text discusses its own genesis and process, which people have no trouble discussing as fiction. Sometimes the process itself is fictionalized, and sometimes it is actual. In my case, the process is actual. When I wrote *The Prowler*, I did not intend to write a novel. I had no pre-designed notion of what I was going to do, and that was the project. I was going to simply write. I took the idea of allowing myself total liberation from everything I had learned from many sources, but especially James Joyce and Roland Barthes, and a number of articles on feminist writing that pointed out the need for charting new territory in literature and of learning from yourself. I believe the answer to this kind of question is in the book. *The Prowler* is worked out of the notion that the author plays no games. Instead the text divulges its own influences – perhaps to relieve the anxiety of influence. All of the sources for that book are named in the text, with the understanding that all texts build on each other and take part in literary gene pools, if you like.

Edmonton, May 1990

Claire Harris

A Question of Joy

Incredibly the poem leaps   a grey
whine and snuffle at the door desperate
to escape I stroke its lines   'It'll be
all right little one'   but *poem* snaps at me
I'm not good at ingratitude   I seal
it in brown paper   put insufficient
postage   toss it to Canada post
I believe when *poem* gets back lessons will
have been learned   poverty/mockery/failure
In other words   a winter of the heart
by then it will lick my hands   be willing
to endure any constraint or so I
thought   Instead poem returns pit-bull angry
goes for my throat   all night we wrestle   but
I'm no Jacob   this is no angel
Come bloody morning we talk
'In the beginning was the word and the ...'
But *poem* interrupts ... 'Look you're no Yahweh
'The effing World is vexatious enough'
said the editor   'write Canadian   or
point no finger   lay no blame   write private
miasma-claim rock tree sky   write joy'
and threw me back into exterior
darkness   'Now fix me' it barks   fangs drip
There's no living with a wild thing that tastes
flesh   I begin to fashion offerings
lovers   holding the first book in my hand
friends   twelve-year-old hours spent searching through
Father's bookshelves finding Byron   Keats   Yeats
What Every Young Husband Should Know about
Sex   but *poem* snarls   growls 'You ain't a comic'
and it's true   I ain't   not vicious enough

That night I lie on the study couch wrapped
in Bay blankets   hearing restless pad and
scrape of nails at the door   wondering   Joy
its deep untainted wells   how innocence

is bound to exaltation   without thought
This I know that what of joy I've had came
before at seven I left home alone
left unknowing for school far from Mother's
voice   her stories   far from my father's laugh
his strong arms   into the company of
stranger aunts   sky dissolved   earth trembling
for my own good and proper education   Though
I have been wildly happy since   sometimes
gladness sneaks up swells into euphoria
for living   even if among distant
glowing peaks frozen in the attitudes
of serrated gods   hoar frost inscribing
trees   ice scaling the Bow   my whole world held
in shimmering faerie beauty of dawn
and ice crystals   but not joy in its pure
radiance   I suspect *poem*   because
of its savage's clarity   understands
this   know he would prefer the day Father
came back from the States to where I played some
secret game in Wind Flower fields edging
savannah beyond the chicken run   and
I ran   ran shouting leapt into his arms
while the world swirled   righted itself   I
was joyous   rooted in black earth in fable
unaware of the world outside his smile

I take up pen   pad   Three a.m. assured by
silence   felt peace   I stand above the Bow:
midnight blue   huge slow moon   sodium lights
staining snow orange on Memorial   blue
on side streets   a lone car gears down
relief surges among books   masks   comforts
these rooms   *poem* inert upon a side
table nevertheless glows   I am at ease   I am glad

Claire Harris

'I dream of a new naming ...'

JANICE: The conservative mainstream 'national' newspaper the *Globe and Mail* is not usually interested in feminist issues, and yet a controversy about the split that's occurred in Women's Press has been featured in its pages. The collective has now divided, and a group of women has accused other women of racism. As a writer and editor, would you comment on the politics of publishing in relation to this issue?

CLAIRE: I think that structural racism is really the problem with publishing here: an unspoken but bedrock determination to keep Canada Euro-centric. This is perceived by the rest of the society as simply common sense ... the *myths of those who are not European have nothing to do with Canada* ... There is no need to take even their point of view on things Canadian into account. At the heart of this is the pernicious reworking of history to leave out both the presence and the contributions of Africans and Asians, and the racism with which these groups live. As a result most people believe 'new' immigrants ... should wait a hundred years or so ... this lies behind the difficulties mainstream publishers experience with 'new' writing. Well, the *Globe and Mail* interprets *conservative, mainstream,* and *national* to mean 'no power shifts in population, culture, or access.' This issue was a bonanza for them. They could subtly highlight a 'cat' fight (feminism) and, at the same time, maintain their position on race, class, and privilege: see how much trouble these Black people cause; see how they don't understand our most important values; they want to deny freedom! Now for the Women's Press. They had never published a

Black writer, partly because here you have a bunch of middle-class White 'sisters' who know in their gut that Black writers are 'culturally disadvantaged' – in spite of their postgraduate degrees. It's well to remember, the unpublished, the unreviewed, are *not* silenced. The Schomburg Center for Research in Black Culture has more than five million items, including over one hundred thousand bound volumes. I use the word silenced here to mean that the only images/facts/ views offered for consumption are the views/images/facts chosen by others ... I am afraid there's no real way of looking at these relationships except in historical terms: colonized and colonizer ... The Women's Press episode was a political struggle between two groups of White women, both aware that it's bad for the image, not *ladylike*, to engage in a 'no holds barred' power struggle. Time for a motherhood issue ... OK? 'Racism!' Not in Canada! Miscalculation. Other side grabs 'Censorship!' ... now there's the privileged discourse ... In this country we wallow in myth ... Black women were simply used, and some of them fell for it ... It's interesting ... The politics of publishing in this country have moved from the 'standards' issue (since we began to win regional, national, and international prizes) to the 'foreign matter in the body politic' issue: *it's not in character for our house ... doesn't fit into our philosophy* line. Now, Graeme Gibson informs us we are 'non-commercial minorities' ... The effect is the censorship of a new vision of Canada ... one that includes all its people as full and legitimate citizens.

JANICE: We've moved to the topic of general publishing. Where do you place the alternative presses in this?

CLAIRE: Assuming by the alternative press you don't mean small but important shops like Goose Lane, Williams-Wallace, Red Deer College Press, etc, it seems to me that if Africans and Asians are ever going to be legitimately Canadian, anthologies of 'New Immigrant' writers, alternative magazines and publishing houses, while important, are, *in these circumstances*, simply a bridge solution. They can become just another kind of ghettoization. We ought to be included in anthologies of Canadian writers who are doing the same sorts of thing we're doing; we should be invited to what Bowering in the *Globe and Mail* quaintly calls 'upper Canada meetings.' Apart from the fact that we've paid our dues, let's call a spade a spade ... wen de wite folks an dem haul meetin up in de big house ... if we share de same interes an on paper too, ent ha no reason cept race or ignorance why i ent invite ... ent we wukin de same plantashun? Singing de same blues? Ent we pay de same tax? Ent dis so ole it ha shame? Since I'm writing on the prairies, it seems to me I have a place in books on Prairie writing. Whether mine is the received wisdom on the Prairies or not! If you're putting out an anthology on 'work,' I don't write 'work' poems; it would be insulting to be asked *simply to ensure the 'correct' political stance.*

JANICE: All right ... do you have more to say on the Women's Press issue?

CLAIRE: Yes. Back to the Women's Press / Second Story fiasco ... there are dangerously naïve assumptions which cloud the question of creative 'property.' There are two things going on here among others: one is the uninformed somewhat racist belief that anybody who does not live in the North needs 'protection by the patron.' The Third World exists everywhere ... as many Newfoundlanders, First Nations persons, and others could easily point out. Somebody who lives in Latin American is not necessarily poor or 'third world.' The Latin American men who write in the surrealistic form popularized by [Gabriel García] Marquez and others are in fact using a European form ...

JANICE: Borges as Kafkaesque. Kafka as Borgesian.

CLAIRE: Exactly. From the 1890s and on they have translated it into their own culture. These are men who consider themselves European; most of them have little or no Indian blood. Most of them are descendants of the conquering, colonizing Europeans, and live as if they are. These Latin Americans would be insulted at the idea that their forms should not be considered part of the normal history of European literature. The idea that one can *own* a form is ridiculous on any count; assuming consistency, what are they one day going to turn around and say to me? That the only forms I can use are oral? If I can use 'European' forms which history has forced on me, why cannot European women use cultural forms which wider reading, thank God, has forced on them? The idea of creative form as the property of a racial group ... not of species ... but of a group is beyond belief. Think of science.

JANICE: I had a discussion with a member of the Women's Press the other day; one response to this argument was, 'It's a structural problem wherein the oppressed have a double consciousness and understand their own cultural forms as well as the cultural forms of the oppressor, who is less knowledgable about the oppressed.'

CLAIRE: True enough – but I don't think that can be allowed to limit any writer ... we are trying to define the limits of empathy ... to Pine Sol the development of an art / a literature which reflects the variety and sentiments of the country ... we're afraid of truth ... What's interesting ... the writer takes a form ... uses it in her own way ... satisfies her own needs in her own society ... an important signpost of the truth of human relations here. Anyhow cross-fertilization of art/culture is normal. Think of Black Egypt and the Greeks ... of Africa and modern music/dance/art. It's naïve ... worse, it opens the door to a dangerous, power-grabbing, fascist sort of behaviour.

JANICE: The issue of appropriation was raised during the Montreal Third International Feminist Book Fair. British Columbia writer Anne Cameron announced her decision at this point in her writing career to give up her work on Native subjects and explore her own Anglo-Celt heritage. Cameron wanted to leave space open for Native women to write out of their own heritage.

CLAIRE: While I'm touched, I nevertheless find it very patronizing. The implication is that Cameron can write on First Nations subjects in a manner which *truly* reveals something about the nations. In fact *all* that she can finally reveal is how she and her culture view the First Nations and their myths. If we really want to understand aboriginal America, we must read First Nations writers. We would do better to support the En'owkin International School of Writing, to publish and distribute the work of such writers, to see that they get their fair share of invitations to read. We live in this 'global village,' this 'multicultural nation'; one of the things that would make life better is if we could at least try to understand each other's cultures ... view each other as one views equals. In any case I doubt that any 'outsider' can use a myth with the same degree of realization as the originators of the myth. All this is a smokescreen. The real problem is the Euro-centric approach of the Canadian literary establishment.

JANICE: Could you describe your own writing history?

CLAIRE: I started writing in Nigeria. I had been working in Canada for eight years, went on leave of absence in Nigeria, and luckily hit on the University of Lagos, where I began writing. I am one of those people who always knew they were going to be a writer,and I knew it was time to start. I mean, I was thirty-seven at that point in the game. At Lagos I met John Pepper Clark, who is one of the very well-known and very good Nigerian poets. He generously told me he would look at anything I wrote every two weeks. In December 1974 I began writing a poem – bits and pieces of stuff would come to me and I would write them down. By the end of the month I had written my first long poem. Clark looked at it, made a couple of suggestions. It was published in *Oduma*, an academic magazine distributed from the U.S. but originating in Nigeria and partly edited in Nigeria. Then some of my shorter poems were also published in *Nigeria Magazine*, a national magazine. So I knew that I was doing publishable work. Then I came back to Canada and three years passed before I could get anything published. I am one of those very stubborn people. I thought I would continue to write, continue to send it out. But I also wanted to be sure this was racism as I view racism, so I began writing stuff that could be written by anybody, because with a name like Claire Harris, there's no way anybody knows. Sure enough, I started getting work published. But unless they were publishing special editions, 'new immigrant writers' kind of stuff, they would not publish work which examined the world from the point of view of 'the powerless' *and* challenged the bedrock assumptions of this society. They would publish work written by a political naïf, or a mole. Work which ignores the pressure of power on our lives, our languages. Work that could be considered politically correct. Because the West Indies has been so deeply, so completely colonized, we are, in fact, Black Westerners. We grew up on the language and mythologies of the West, because our major religions came from the East and/or are influenced by the West. When I was at school in the West Indies, all major exams were set and marked in England, and we studied exactly the same stuff done in British schools. When I went to university in Ireland, I knew nothing about Black literature. My only forms were the forms of Europe. Our society is much the same: we have cultural content of our own, of course, and this is a major importance because it provides a subversive comment on the reality pushed by the colon-ialists. And our history, its very marginalized status, forces us to challenge Euro-content. Also many local religions like the Shango cult, for example, and many basic attitudes have retained their African roots and influence, or have been forged in the fire that was/is the Caribbean. But the West Indies is as different from Britain as Southern Italy is from Norway. ... You know the very British notion ... 'the wogs begin at Calais' ... This is not a popular idea, but it's a fact. And this is important because it means that what was 'UnCanadian' was the critical stance I took to the society ... to the peculiarly Euro-Canadian myths as they touched me.

I couldn't get my first book published. I changed the name and sent it to four publishers. One publisher wrote and said this was exactly what they wanted, but couldn't they get more poems set in Canada? Williams-Wallace asked me for the book which became *Fables from the Women's Quarters*. I promised to send it to them, but not until I had another book taken by a well-known White publisher, because I did not intend to be ghettoized. I sat down and wrote *Translation into Fiction* in about eight months, just to see what was going to happen. In the middle of the book I put poems from that first manuscript and sent it off to *Fiddlehead* ... I wanted anybody who could read to realize this was written by a Black writer. I had someone say again to me recently: 'I don't care how you write, but the book has to be set in Canada.' Brian Moore, who has won Gov-ernor General's Awards, two of them I think, has published books which are set in Ireland; Josef Skvorecky's work, which is set in Czechoslovakia and written in Czech, also wins a Governor General's Award. So when my work cannot be published here, I find it difficult to believe that we are not talking about racism. Particularly work like mine, which is both analytic and empathetic. I'm too cool when I write.

JANICE: Some of your work is enraged and moves the reader to relive imaginatively the violence of intolerance. I'm thinking of 'Po-liceman Cleared in Jaywalking Case,' which shifts from the Edmonton sidewalk to your own Caribbean childhood. But that powerful poetry deserves wide distribution, not suppression.

CLAIRE: True, but that was such a blatant incident I thought it was time for unvarnished truth ... and it is precisely the sort of issue that gets no time in Canadian poetry ... no time in Canadian history. Can I get back to publishing? Lots of other presses along with Women's Press should be asking why they have never published a Black writer. Let writers be responsible for their own work, for their own moralities. But consider: a writer writes work which shows he despises himself, but in his self-despising he picks up on Canadian myths about Indians, about Africans, or whatever – his work is headlined. In spite of his history, his work asks no questions about the relationship between the North and the South. He becomes a 'writer about town.' While it is useful to the 'mainstream,' his opinion counts. This same work is reviewed in the *London Review of Books* in ten lines,where the racism and classism are pointed out. Here it is given a full-page *Globe and Mail* review by William French, a review without any recognition of what is going on in the work. Now, it seems to me that here you've got something that's very interesting. In *How to Make Love to a Negro* the wickedly farcical look at the myth of the Black man dreaming about sexual exploits with White women fits right into the image. A great deal is made of this book, whereas important texts that need translation from French into English are not being translated. Now that's Canadian racism. Racism is the common sense of this society.

JANICE: We both heard Edmund Braithwaite talk about how the sands of the North African desert wind blow across the Atlantic to the Caribbean. He noted how this desert wind was never acknowledged until suddenly it blew north to London; the English touched the dust on their windowsills and realized, aha! maybe there is an African connection to the Caribbean climate.

CLAIRE: A classic example of the 'ownership' of knowledge ... Foucault in action ... We knew the wind was from the Sahara. Until they know it, it isn't 'knowledge.'

JANICE: Your own travels and thinking about Africa and the Caribbean offer you a double community of writers and readers. How does this locate you in Canadian writing?

CLAIRE: It interrupts and moves beyond Canadian literature as it has been defined, as in Anglo-Saxon, male. Canadian literature is not defined along the lines of the population. Multiculturalism is a male

Anglo-Saxon sun around which lesser planets circle – the African Caribbean writer is definitely in the far reaches of outer space. The advantage of being an immigrant is that you know there are other realities, because you've just come from another one. Therefore you can view this reality from a distance and with a quality of clarity. You see things that people without real experience of other possibilities cannot. One ought to be central, but in every society such people are marginalized. I arrived here in 1966. When I write about the West Indies, I now see it with the same distance as I see Canadian society. Standing outside, you can see what is really happening. At the same time that British education, and the version of British society created in the West Indies, makes Canadian society familiar.

JANICE: In your article 'Writing without a Net' you pointed out the regional differences between Black women writers in Canada; for instance, many Black Prairie dwellers do not speak a non-Canadian dialect. You want to find a new language. You 'dream of a new naming, new words, new lines shaping a new world.' How do you think through your own language and writing?

CLAIRE: What I try to do is to take the word and cleanse it. Herodotus writes about travelling through Ethiopia and encountering 'as everyone knows the most beautiful people in the world.' Two thousand years later, everyone knows the exact opposite. I want my writing to rehabilitate the Black person, her beauty, her smile, her walk, her genius ... his too. I also want to explore the reality of Canadian society ... which I must free to include me. I use words like 'black' and 'white,' etc., in situations that both question and highlight the historical connection. So I constantly talk of blackness and night as warm and safe and enclosing. I want to describe Black people with words that are *real* ... word/object/connotation become one.

JANICE: Do you see parallels between your project of renaming and the work of lesbian writers? Daphne Marlatt's 'hidden ground' is a forgotten space on the periphery which is rehabilitated in order to displace the 'perversity' of lesbianism.

CLAIRE: Exactly, yes, the same thing. Except, with us, we have an even more – or perhaps it is the same problem – we have a history as well to recover. In my new book, 'Drawing Down a Daughter,' the poem is a stream-of-consciousness writing of the entire day before a woman gives birth to her child. It ends with the first real contraction she has. She needs to make the world safe for her child; the poem prepares a safe space. The mother points out that a truly 'civilized' people don't ... can't consider human life fair exchange for political and economic power.

JANICE: Joy Kogawa's reading of racial oppression recognizes the colonizer in the consciousness of the colonized. How would you interpret this reciprocity?

CLAIRE: Yes, of course, but I think that the one who is colonized, her recognition and consciousness of the oppressor has to be based on truth – on her intimate knowledge of the absolute savagery which absolute power over human beings can conjure. The oppressed know that misunderstanding the effect and the extent of power can lead to unrelieved grief, suffering, and death. Physical survival demands that she understand the other. And understand him/her as an individual. At the same time, in order to survive as a human being, she must understand the source of this power. This source is always technological, but is allied with a quality of character, a willingness to view the other with an absolute ruthless ferocity. It seems to me that there must be a stage of reluctant admiration for the technology, and the uses to which it is put. However, racial oppression is of its essence indiscriminate. It is the lack of discrimination which forces the oppressed, whatever her education and life experience, into a recognition that the source of the technology and its final purpose is a denial of life, of the importance of life. And this frees the woman of any desire to be like the other. At the same time she has this tremendous intimate knowledge of the other, because if you despise people there is no need to dissimulate in their presence. At whatever horrendous costs, it is a gain.

Unfortunately, the oppressor must think of the colonized as less than human and pay no more attention than one pays to stones, or donkeys. At the same time that self-respect demands that they see the other as less than human, the nagging knowledge of humanity demands ruthlessness, because, so the nightmare goes, one day they will turn on you. One day they must turn on you. Worse, one cannot allow oneself the luxury of really knowing *any one* of them as individual. To maintain the myth, they have to be a faceless mass. Since you are 'good,' they must be 'evil.' Hence the pseudo-scientific, the religious rational, the 'swamped by evil' attitudes of racist societies, where all forms of 'knowledge' must support the power structure. Hence the people who can say with a straight face *you are different*, and think it a compliment! In the end, both knowledge of the other, and of themselves, is denied them. The only knowledge the oppressor gains, if he is lucky, is the intimate knowing of his own capacity for evil, for self-delusion. In the end, the oppressor loses everything, except, of course, his capital, and his very narrow endangered world. And if he has any self-awareness, he knows it. He cannot even afford to examine *all* his life! The unexamined life, as we know, is worth nothing.

The sad thing is this continues to have repercussions. People don't want to be responsible for the evil of their ancestors, but they want to continue to enjoy its benefits. They delude themselves with more 'subtle' forms of racism, sexism, classism. They continue the search for justification. Or more commonly, they simply accept things as they are and don't think! These attitudes in themselves are a measure of their fear and pain.

JANICE: Carolyn Cooper of the University of the West Indies wrote an essay on the Sistrene Theatre Collective, which begins with the discourse of literary theory and then halfway through shifts into Creole, a shift she describes as a departure from the authority of English as the exclusive voice of scholarship in the West Indies. She works to bridge the gap between the 'scholarly language' of textual analysis and the language of oral stories. A White male colleague of mine who describes himself as a 'curmudgeon' said that if he were in the audience when Cooper was delivering the paper, he would leave the room because he wouldn't be able to understand the dialect.

CLAIRE: That is racism, because I don't think the problem is that he would not be able to understand; it is that he does not want to see 'standard' English challenged, and particularly not from that height. He would thoroughly enjoy West Indian languages if the person speaking was a maid, not a person, especially a woman, with his own qualifications. Note that he does not describe himself as he is – or his effort at silencing her ... his hubris is made lovable: he is a 'curmudgeon.' In another world circa 1940 we would recognize him. That's partly his own insecurity, of course. I have looked really closely at the question of dialect; most people writing Trinidadian dialect translate the sound of the language. Every now and again they change the grammar, but it's minor changes. It's like 'he book' instead of 'his book.' But the really important words, the verbs and the nouns, stay the same. It is 'd-e' instead of 't-h-e' and that sort of stuff that gets changed; 's-o-m-t-h-i-n' instead of 's-o-m-e-t-h-i-n-g,' 'd-e-y' instead of 't-h-e-y.' But language is more than pronouns, and pronunciation, more than inversions and lost auxiliaries. If in English 'L-e-i-c-e-s-t-e-r' can be pronounced 'Lester,' I fail to see why 't-h-e-y' cannot be pronounced 'dey.' It is a matter of power. Now, on the other hand, dialect can be used very effectively to make important political points. When I'm talking to kids in school, they tell me, 'We don't have an accent,' because an 'accent' has come to mean something stupid, funny, not good, so White Canadians can't have an accent. The people who come from the West Indies have an accent. Asians have accents. Poles have accents. Politically, it is important to make the point that everybody has an accent, and a dialect. This is the way one wrenches languages into the shape of one's world. New world: new dialect. If you choose to write in Jamaican dialect, either you are writing to all your Jamaican friends of this generation, but the next generation in Canada is not going to understand; or you are writing to Jamaica, where everybody knows that particular dialect form and its connotations. But it seems to me you lose half your ability to say what you want to say when people reading you do not get connotation. And most people don't really get it. I use the tone and rhythms of West Indian speech, its elisions, its vocabulary. But I have just written a 'lit-politics' essay in dialect ... to annoy ... to amuse ... and to make a point. If one lives in the Northern Hemisphere, it is essentially a political gesture, though not an empty one.

JANICE: This also helps to create your rhythmic patterns and the musicality of your form.

CLAIRE: Exactly, a tone, a space, an attitude. But I don't see the point in changing the way the language was written because of pronunciation.

JANICE: In the midst of the long winter of the prairie, one of your poems introduces an exotically organic, luscious vocabulary of flowers and 'jalousies.'

CLAIRE: People don't hear these words any more. African, early modern English, French, they are part of our history ... And I love the land. It is so lush; language is organic to land.

JANICE: You use double narratives in your work and juxtapose prose poems with short-line verse. In some, you split the narrative horizontally and juxtapose different texts. In one of my favourite poems you juxtapose a highly literary verse account of a woman with the oral testimony of Guatemalan revolutionary Rigoberta Menchú. What effects are you writing towards?

CLAIRE: This is what I think I'm doing, though I shall probably discover five years from now that I'm doing something different: when I come to write about something that is so terrible – one thing that strikes me about Canada is how innocent everybody is ... First, everybody who knows anything about Latin America knows that the U.S. sends people down to Latin America to teach people how to torture people. It's called 'counter-insurgency training.' Now, the very idea that the 'good guys' would do that is just not something that anybody wants to believe. Imagine in the last decade of the twentieth century the luxury of believing in 'the good guys'! ... We Canadians have been denied our own history warts and all in favour of a dreadful social sanitation. We object to the illustration of the horror and beauty of the human race. It isn't polite! Still right here in Alberta, even in this day and age, three-quarters of the Lubicon people have TB. We like our dirty work done for us, as long as it's decently hidden. Now, I want to tell this society, 'Look at what the world is like,' and 'If we go along with this, we are responsible.' The simple linear idea ... I mean, everything is happening at the same time ... all these different voices in my poetry are a very small way of commenting on physical reality. Also, in such a poem, there is a quality of impertinence ... one steals a life ... puts a high-fashion gloss on it ... I was blessed to discover the narrative – so that the woman could speak in her own voice ... fact and emotion given form ... the quality of language should reflect the landscape. There's a need to say this is a factual thing, life is not simple, and is rarely a matter of choice ... especially for. the powerless. In one of the poems I have the story on one side, and on the other side I have a long series of historical assertions, in which all the facts are accurate, of similar incidents that have happened elsewhere in the world. The idea is to keep saying, 'This is what we are. If we are not going to behave like this, then we have to make an extra effort, because *this is what we are.*' We have to prevent people from saying, 'Oh, that's those Latin Americans,' or 'That's those Africans,' or 'That's those ...' which is a favourite attitude here, a remarkable attitude when you think of the history of the West, of Europe, of Canada; but that's how it is. Equally important to me is the idea that this poem is an artefact. I can do anything with form ... anything ... to make meaning visible.

JANICE: When I spoke with you in 1986, I didn't identify myself as a White feminist critic because I didn't quite know how to address the issue. How does one make out the specificity of my experience as interviewer and critic?

CLAIRE: The place from which you come and where you stand now. You're a White Canadian; you can't help being Euro-centric. It is as always a matter of degree. But, inherent in Euro-centric criticism is the idea that there is a norm, and that everybody else is reaching for it. This always puts the critic up there looking down on the peasants. There is no acceptance of variation, of difference ... It is interesting to read the criticism of somebody who is reaching out to try and understand the work, who recognizes where she is coming from and that she is in a particular place. If you say something that is clearly racist, you know that next time I write an essay, I may very well pull it out and discuss it. But that's part of the dialogue, and part of a way of opening the question. It's necessary to identify oneself ... say where one is coming from. To be a woman is to be a feminist ... I'm inclined to think that one has to go beyond that ... sometimes critics say that my writing is full of rage, but the only poem I've written that's full of rage is 'Jaywalking,' and in the last verse I turn it back on myself, because in the final analysis, the responsibility for my reactions, whatever the circumstances, is mine ... I would like to think that my work has/is born of a certain clarity, that it is emotional ... but a controlled emotion ... I'm wary of the automatic assumption ... Black writers are enraged ... Right! So I'm enraged!

JANICE: But in your most recent poetry collection, the women experience a 'cold rage' / which changes something.' Does the resolution of the anger/coolness dichotomy you've expressed suggest a new voice for you?

CLAIRE: OK ... I have a problem with the word 'rage' as used by White women ... because historically there has been an assertion that Blacks are too 'irrational' ... that this 'irrationality' is part of their 'childishness.' This is why they need the 'great White father.' Of course, part of Black irrationality is their impertinent assumption that they are capable of running their own affairs, describing their own situations. And their righteous anger at the various canards used to deprive them of this right. It seems to me that much of this remains in the society ... this pernicious assumption makes it easy to dismiss the work of Black writers, the ideas of Black writers, and therefore the criticism of Blacks, their desire to move the society towards a more humane and civil place, a truer place. That is why in my own work the rage is cold. It is not a matter of emoting! It is a matter of putting passion to work. I believe, passionately, that women as a group have much the same problem ... Now to answer the question specifically. Yes, there is a new voice – I'm not sure it's a new voice – it may just be a new form, most certainly a new attitude. While most of my work is written 'out of Canada' as much as 'in Canada,' it isn't really about what it is to live in this 'stolen land all its graceful seductions.' Well, *Conception* showed it was time to get down to the nitty-gritty. It took all that time, twenty years, for me to realize that this was home. As far as an immigrant can have a home. So now it's time to write truthfully and accurately about Canada. You know in spite of ... perhaps because of ... everything I have learnt in the past twenty-six years ... what I have learnt of the human condition ... I would do it all, exactly the same, all over again for fear I'd miss something.

JANICE: In our earlier interview, Claire, you spoke of your hesitancy to write about sexuality in your poetry. But your 'Conception of Winter' poem is about a vital sexuality which challenges the culture which privileges you as a heterosexual. The women in your poem 'resolve to invent passion beyond the tired conventions of western romance.'

CLAIRE: The thing I've noted about sexuality in Canada is how much social/personal hypocrisy there is. Look at the various problems with the AIDS advertisements. I merely wrote about the actual in *Conception*, in the sense that much of the poem is based on real people who took real trips with me. But real passion has to do with being open to risk and to generosity. And it has to do with action ... taking and holding a new space, part of the wholeness of the autonomous woman. I have begun writing about situations in which expressed sexuality is natural. To pretend it didn't exist would be to make the situation false. So the poetry has taken over the cultural reserve. I know that some idiot is sooner or later going to bring up the vicious Western myth of the 'sensual animality' of the Black woman ... either we are asexual or we're strutting it ... in either case we're not really women at all ... but that's your myth: your responsibility. Mine is to ensure that the work is 'true.' You say the society 'privileges me'! How? Every day I must face the racism of the streets, the culture, the bedrock myths, the language I speak. People see an African woman. A large African woman. Clearly Aunt Jemima! Who cares if she's a writer? A teacher? A taxpayer? Ain't it great I'm not into paranoia?

JANICE: Can you describe what it is to write 'without a net'?

CLAIRE: We write outside of Native culture (the descendants of Africans, enslaved, transported, de-acculturated, are always and everywhere in exile) in a society in which our point of view is not merely perceived as in/valid, but we ourselves, our very *presence*, is also perceived as physically in/valid. Moreover, we are educated, churched, socialized to believe in our own 'wrongness.' To write, we have to challenge even the forms we write in. The language we use, every thought has to be tested for its truth. It takes a long apprenticeship before we conquer the hydra within; even so, should we be lucky enough to find *ourselves*, we must always be on guard. I go over my work line by line to be sure I am not adding to the measure of lies. I can't take any of the received wisdom for granted. At the same time we have to be certain that we are not letting ourselves be distorted by the political realities of our situation. It seems to me that there is a danger that the writer may become a mouthpiece for a particular point of view, for what is 'politically correct,' which is nearly always as simplistic as any other 'quick fix'; you do that, you caricature yourself ... a danger to your own craft ... your own 'truth.' Because in the end the most important problem we face is the problem of being human. The normal cultural safety nets, the subconscious ones, are missing as well once we leave our Islands, so one always has to be looking out for one's self. I mean to whom *exactly* am I saying all this? I don't know! I do know the effort that has to be put into such interviews if the questions are not to be traps ... one gets so bored and so tired of laying the groundwork first. I suppose I'm an optimist at heart ...

Calgary 1989

Smaro Kamboureli

Fragments from a novel in progress, 'Various Blues' (tentative title)

Her icon.

A string of pearls, sapphire and ruby rings, diamond crosses and pendants, gold bracelets – her hidden image a necklace around her neck.

Hail Mary, full of grace – a greeting studded with diamonds. She must be there, you don't greet someone you can't see unless she is as absent as the Lord who is with her.

The icon rests under the glass of a gold-gilded frame. Locked in because of its double preciousness. It is guarded from the fervor of worshippers by the still wings of two golden angels suspended one on either side of a cross at the top of the frame.

Danger in love is always immanent. Yiota, sailing toward Tinos, knows this. Once again, she will walk up the steep broad avenue leading to the white cathedral to look at Our Lady of Annunciation. She wants to remember the sixteen-year-old girl genuflecting (at request) in front of the icon that some say has the look of St Luke's brush.

The icon of another girl, a teenager even younger than Yiota was then, whose image adorned as it is cannot be seen. For all Yiota knows, Mary might not be there at all.

Our Lady of Intercession, of Pity, Mary the Pelagiotissa, the Hodegetria, the Perivlepousa. Her gothic image blackened. Mary with parrot and puppy. Mary in strawberry bed, with strawberry book on her lap (is it a gardening book, the book about the perfect lawn, a diary, the journal of her creation?). Earth Unsown. Eastern Gate. Fleece of Heavenly Rain. Mary with cherries. And with a bunch of grapes, scrawny baby, and shut book (on her lap, her arms being full), Gipsy-Mary. The burning bush in her mind as she rocks her baby boy in his cradle.

Yiota has seen all of them.

Always, she thinks, inside her there is the outside.

Sightseeing, she called it – this looking for a believable shape, a lived life. She played hookey from school so that she could visit yet another church, another chapel.

She had been seduced unawares.

The grander the churches the smaller she became. Her neck strained as she peered into their designed darkness – the better to hide. She leaned against their cold pillars polished by the leaning backs of devout and tired Christians, their marble softened by the melody of hymns. She often clasped her notebook against her chest, telling herself she was cold. Sometimes, when afraid to look, a peek sufficed.

She was faced back by clones of Mary.

Ivory, marble, cloisonné enameled, pebbled virgins.

Iconic bodies, looking at her with their wooden gazes.

Imagination incarnate and the real woman brushed aside into the foreignness of the real, onto the grain of apple, cherry and pine wood.

Behind the fact of Mary's absence. This invisibility the only proof of Our Lady's existence. All Yiota wanted was to enter that absence. She longed for a wisp of her perfume, the brush of her heather-purple tunic – right here on her arm. That figment of flesh, that tender body denied not so lovingly. Mary's liquid tongue on Yiota's bare shoulder.

Smaro Kamboureli and Lola Lemire Tostevin

'where the imaginary takes over'

JANICE: Nicole Brossard wrote: 'To write: *I am woman* is heavy with consequences.' What are the consequences of writing as a woman for you?

SMARO: As a woman, I can't afford to erase sexual difference in my writing because that would eliminate who I am. It's important to be reminded that gender and consciousness go together. My signature as a writer permeates my writing, and this signature includes, of course, my gender. But this doesn't necessarily imply that my writing is always *about* sexual difference. It's important, I think, that some women writers have moved away from those stories and images that deal exclusively with, say, housekeeping and motherhood and, indirectly, perpetuate the female roles that patriarchal tradition had codified as the only alternatives for women. These stories have to be retold from our point of view. To do this, I think we must, like Nicole Brossard, find a space for ourselves in language, appropriate it, let language speak us in our own terms. The consequences of this act are important, not only for women, but for men as well.

LOLA: Woman writing instead of woman being written is in itself a consequential and political act. However, having to take a political stand in one's writing means that you are always writing in opposition, in relation to someone else. This was and is still important for some women to extricate themselves from cultural and social constraints, but for others, it's important to move beyond that. What I want to achieve in my writing is a point where it is taken for granted that I'm a woman as defined by myself. That is how I want to live and that is how I want to write.

SMARO: This writing of woman becomes another version of the authorial signature in writing, where the writer signs her or his name in various ways by playing around with autobiographical elements. But I think that, somehow, the symmetry we find between a male writer and his signature assumes different configurations. I like the plurality that implies.

JANICE: Let's consider the specificity of the female signature. Isn't it ironic that at this moment, when more women have access to writing, when they are writing 'as women' and exploring female subjectivity, critics like Michel Foucault and Roland Barthes are pronouncing the author dead?

LOLA: When someone pointed out to me recently the importance of ridding oneself of the 'I' in writing, I said, 'Great, I'll lose it as soon as I find it.' One of the poems in *Double Standards*, 'Les Trois Ailes de mon nom,' is a deconstructive wordplay on my name, where the self is suspended and the primacy of language is emphasized. However, the question of how and what is written can't be separated from the one who writes. Ultimately, the exploration of language leads back to the self, or preferably to different selves.

SMARO: More and more people these days talk about 'writers,' not about 'authors.' This is so because of our increasing understanding of the primacy of language, of how discourse operates. For Foucault and Barthes, the author is dead in the same way that God is dead. That's why, as I said before, signature becomes so important – and I have in mind here both Foucault's and Derrida's writings about signature. Although there are many differences between their positions, one of the things I like about their work is that they both see contradiction as the key to all the systems of closure we've inherited from our tradition. Contradiction becomes the main thrust of discourse and of culture. This indicates a movement away from the humanistic position that foregrounds the self as ego towards a polyphonic presence of the self, where we have many versions of the 'I,' many stories to tell, which all contradict each other. The self is aleatory; it keeps changing. We can only perceive it through its contradictions. It's like that Greek monster: you kill it, but it grows another head. Although my book is written in the first person, it's called *in the second person* because of a dialogue between the self and its many others. The others speak too in the first person, but they do so in the lower-case 'i.' So the composite or polyphonic self that emerges out of these different others is the self that exists within the spaces created between contradictions. Someone asked me to define how these different selves in my book are reconciled. They are not. I didn't want to define my so-called 'ethnic' identity; I wanted instead to explore the plurality of my immigrant experience. Nor is this concern with the self a narcissistic one. Since I try to get rid of the ego, there is no precise figure in the mirror, on the page, to gaze at.

JANICE: I'd like to readdress the question of politics. As a feminist, I'm committed to imagining, and working towards, the transformation of our often deadly culture. We assume that it isn't literature but people who change things. In our writing, we attempt to reappropriate language, and at the very least disrupt the canonical status quo. As a 'symptomatic reader,' I want to know the relation between our writing and social change.

LOLA: That takes us back to your first question, about the consequences of writing as a woman. You say that as a feminist you are committed to imagining ... Well, as a feminist, I am also committed to imagining, but as a writer, and not as a politician. I try to move towards a space of the imaginary that offers something that is perhaps more subtle than the political. I agree with Julia Kristeva when she says we have to add something more subtle to militant feminism. I also agree with her that it is wrong to think that we understand a human being by classifying her in a particular class, or at a particular pole, which is what the political does. She dismisses certain aspects of the political, such as not giving the individual her value, but if you read her *Revolution in Poetic Language, Powers of Horror, Histoires d'Amour*, these are very revolutionary books. Hélène Cixous, for example, who also claims that she is a writer and not a politician, continues to emphasize both in theory and practice the need to exceed masculinist ideology. These are important relations between writing and social change.

SMARO: Let me say first that feminism doesn't have to do only with women. Quite the contrary: it has to do with all aspects of culture.

In other words, it is a political movement that seeks, among other things, to undo the political rhetoric of our tradition, which is a rhetoric of polarities, as Lola said. So feminist writing as an activity is – has to be – iconoclastic. I agree with what Alice Jardine says in the beginning of *Gynesis,* that we should move away from our obsession with identity to a concern with difference, from wholeness to incompleteness, from representation to presentation. This kind of movement is, for me, a political gesture that deflects the status quo, be it literary or social.

JANICE: In *Double Standards,* Lola, the speaker is located in a particular space I find reminiscent of your own autobiographical roots in a bilingual northern Ontario town.

LOLA: The past impinges on the present, there is no doubt about that. But the autobiographical references – which are inaccurate by the way – they've been interpreted designedly – are the beginning of the book. They don't move back, seeking to retrieve. On the contrary, from the very cold climate of northern Ontario, the book moves to a warmer place, that of language. The last piece, 're,' is a reading of the present, the moment of writing.

JANICE: Does language then become a utopia?

SMARO: No. But I like the way Lola puts it: it's as though you're changing geography. Geography becomes geo-graphy: the writing, the graph of place. The place becomes writing. I think what you're doing, Lola, is very interesting, especially given the context of Canadian literature, where there is such an obsession with place both in fiction and poetry. You're writing language as place. What I'm doing in *in the second person* is dealing with the self as 'the place of language.'

LOLA: The place becomes language and not a utopia because it keeps generating new language. One word generates another word, another thought. It is never static in a utopian sense.

JANICE: This sense of language as generative reminds me of your 'Do not be deceived by appearances' poem. Through a poetics of negation, 'I am not a woman' repeated over and over again gives way to the sudden appearance of the woman in the text.

LOLA: We were talking of subject and woman at the beginning. Trying to find the 'I' in order to lose it. 'Do not be deceived by appearances' is that kind of process, where you negate the woman in favour of the poem, the sequence, the words, until finally within the words, there is woman defining herself.

JANICE: Smaro, your *in the second person* os organized as a series of journal entries. The journal form always appears paradoxical. On the one hand, we imagine it reveals the self, in acute 'subjective' terms. But once written for public circulation, the writing becomes 'objectified,' a textual space where the subject can be scrutinized. Journal texts are also filled with the doubling contradictions of both history and the fictive. Daphne Marlatt talked about her *What Matters* as 'an enactment of journal writing in terms of a narrative.' How is personal history enacted in your writing?

SMARO: Through reading and rereading, and writing and rewriting the journals I kept. *In the second person* is a journal exactly because it is a recording of my reading of those journals. Those three journals I refer to in the book present three different versions of my history, and I tried to capture just this, my many histories. So history is there, but it's activated when you relocate it in the present tense, and I like the energy that's generated through the transposition of the past into the present. And when the familiar self and its seemingly familiar others emerge out of the past and surface in the present, that's when fiction starts emerging as well. Fiction, not in the sense of being a pack of lies, but a fiction that creates what Lola calls 'a space of the imaginary.'

LOLA: Where you interpret designedly.

SMARO: Exactly. I had to give a design to that rereading of my journals and to the writing, the book, that came out of it in order to make the private journals public. This is not the sense of concealing the 'real,' but in the sense of giving it an aesthetic design. So I made up a lot of entries to create a narrative that would make my immigrant experience more accessible.

JANICE: Like the scream in the kitchen.

SMARO: No, that one is real, actually.

JANICE: Then the double scream: the one that sounds and the one that doesn't.

SMARO: There are a lot of screams in the book, or, I use the word quite often, screaming. I think of screaming as a different version of language, a different kind of utterance, or articulation of my linguistic condition, of being on the edge of two languages. The scream as voice, as sound, the language of the inarticulate.

LOLA: It's very articulate, actually. It expresses those emotions that can't be expressed in words.

JANICE: Lola, your poem about violence against women provokes the reader to questions about experience and writing. Why is the title 'Not a Poem'?

LOLA: 'Not a Poem' receives so much attention and that wasn't my intention. I don't like to talk about it; it speaks for itself. My daughter and I discussed my publishing it and she very graciously gave me permission. I named it 'Not a Poem' because traditionally poetry has been associated with all the tricks of language, such as metaphor and simile. When you try to write about something that has affected you as much as the event in the poem affected me, then you realize that there are no metaphors, or similes, or poetic functions that will transfer what you are registering emotionally. Yet there's a need to say something. The metaphor 'there is a garden in her face' comes from the Song of Songs and was used by Elizabethan poets such as Campion to convey the serenity and beauty of the Virgin, or a virgin. I wanted to reverse that and use it to convey the different kind of garden present in our young women's faces after they've been attacked.

JANICE: Would you talk about what it is to write in Canada as opposed to what it would be to write as a woman in another cultural community? Though you are divided differently, both of you write through a divided cultural tradition, and challenge the notion of a uni-vocal hegemony.

LOLA: I came to writing quite late because I felt divided by my two languages. Then I realized I could make it work to my advantage. It's another aspect of this multiplicity we were talking about. I don't feel I'm writing in another culture; two languages is my culture. Writing as a woman, as a French Canadian who writes mostly in English, has provided me with more material because of the recent emphasis on multiplicity. I feel I've struck a vein. And there are other writers who understand the importance of this plurality. Of course, this sense of difference has its problems as well. On our cross-Canada reading tour, Smaro and I were accused of being too cerebral. I think that is unjust since I feel Smaro has definitely reached a balance between emotions and intellect in her book, and I hope I have too. But as women, we're not supposed to have a mind. Having to write in a Canadian context about things that are not traditionally written about in a Canadian context makes some people suspicious. For me, writing means taking risks. Fitting within a Canadian context is not something I worry about.

SMARO: But that's an artificial thing. Since you are a Canadian writer writing in Canada, you do belong here. What you are referring to is the canon decided by a certain number of people and a certain kind of politics.

LOLA: I don't worry about the canon.

JANICE: What about you, Smaro? Your difference has to do with immigration.

SMARO: Yes, coming from another culture and language. It would have been very difficult for me to start publishing in Greece. Even some of the big presses there operate without contracts. Besides, if you're not part of the literary establishment in Greece, you don't get to meet the writers. We don't have public readings or grants for writers – at least that was the case when I was still there, and I don't think things have changed. I only know one Greek woman writer, and I got in touch with her after I came to Canada. It's partly through my interaction with the Canadian writers I know that I felt encouraged to write directly in English. But, on the other hand, there is one thing I don't like here: the inferiority complex Canadians have about their literature – now I'm talking as a Greek, I guess. Canadian literature is great by any standards. There's another thing that also disturbs me, and this has to do with reviewing. There is a certain kind of anti-intellectualism, a fear of ideas. Many reviews, particularly the ones done by journalists, are totally off. If a reviewer doesn't understand something about a book, then it's the writer's fault for not reducing his or her vision to a so-called common level. This kind of reviewer often underestimates the reader's desire to discover new things, to read new forms. This is something you would never find in Greece.

Italo Calvino's *Mr. Palomar*, for instance, was serialized in a Greek magazine that would be equivalent to, say, *Saturday Night* or the *Canadian Forum*.

JANICE: You both talk about the opportunities for writers in Canada. What about the very particular problems for women? I was just reading through the Women and Words Conference proceedings, *In the Feminine*. The epigraphs of the book, a litany of statistics, point out the inequitable material conditions and institutional support for women writers: 'Forty-two per cent of Canadian freelance writers are women ... Eighty per cent of the people in Canada who buy books are women ... fewer than twenty per cent of the jurors [of the Governor General's Awards] have been women and twenty per cent of awards have gone to women ... In Canadian newspapers ... women writers get only twenty per cent of review space.

LOLA: I wouldn't say that women writers have finally made it in Canada, but there is a willingness to publish, to tolerate, women writers that has only happened in the last few years. Of course, it's still a problem. Women will have to keep writing, and their standards will have to be very high.

SMARO: Well, my feeling is – but maybe I'm wrong – that women writers have no real problem getting published. The problems appear when we talk about reviewing.

LOLA: Women reviewers will have to review women's books. I'm asked all the time to review books, but I can't do more than I'm doing. I do feel, however, that if a woman has a good book in Canada at this time, it will be published. Women may even have a slight edge right now. I wouldn't want to be a man writing in Canada at this point in our history. Of course, I wouldn't want to be a man, period.

JANICE: You both pay tribute to various women writers in your work. One of the conventional ways of describing the male line of influence has become Harold Bloom's paradigm: the 'anxiety of influence,' the Oedipal struggle, killing off the literary father. How would you describe your relation to other women writers?

LOLA: In *Double Standards* I use words, lines, from other women writers. I turn them into my poems to see how much of these women still live in me. H.D., Anne Hébert, Mina Loy. Something in these women's writing touched me. Their work lingers on. It's not so much an influence, or competition with our predecessors, but a link that continues to flow between mother figures and their daughters.

SMARO: I don't feel that I have to kill my literary mothers or fathers.

LOLA: No, I don't either.

SMARO: I find Bloom's theory very interesting, but I don't agree with him. It's kind of contrived. It's too Freudian, too male. I'm influenced by both men and women writers, and I certainly welcome this influence – after all, you can't write in a vacuum. I read both men and women, both literature and theory, although I've been reading more feminist theories as I become aware of them. And I've got a lot of support from both male and female writers. My criticism deals with both male and female writers. No, I don't have any 'anxieties' about this.

JANICE: I've saved the notion of the erotic pleasure of the text for the end of our interview. What is the place of eroticism in your writing, Lola? Your *Gyno-Text* is an embodied anagrammatic puzzle where you take language apart and eroticize it in a very concrete way.

LOLA: I think of eroticism in language in a Barthesian sense. It exceeds social function in its wordplay, in its texture. I think he said that the pleasure of a text is in the moment when the body is allowed to pursue its own ideas. I'm interested in layering different kinds of language. The verbal lay, French and English, narrative fiction and poetic underlying narrative ... When there is interaction, penetration of one genre by another, or, as in *Gyno-Text*, when you break up language for the sound of it, you get a textured erotic text.

JANICE: In *Double Standards* you begin with the line 'for a long time I couldn't decide whether to be a story or a poem   the story always losing its way as it scribbles towards some equilibrium.' Throughout that first poem, there is a movement towards the sonorous, to an almost onomatopoeic language. Is that part of the erotic process?

LOLA: Yes. The 'I' in *Double Standards* is the book speaking. But the many aspects of the book intersecting make it erotic. I think of the last piece, 're,' as a site of bliss, of bodily rhythms, fluidity.

SMARO: And then that love poem where 'your legs close on me / like a book.'

LOLA: It's the book speaking. I believe very profoundly in the moment of writing, when the narrative line, the poetic line, take on a life of their own. Many times I've written something and not remembered having written it just a few hours later. That's how strong the moment of writing becomes. It takes on a life of its own, generates language, energy.

SMARO: Do you think that loss of memory has to do with entering the space of the imaginary?

LOLA: Yes. Somehow you move to another space, a margin, where anecdotes get lost. Where the imaginary takes over and generates new possibilities.

Toronto, March 1986

Joy Kogawa

Excerpts from *Obasan*

There is a silence that cannot speak.

There is a silence that will not speak.

Beneath the grass the speaking dreams and beneath the dreams is a sensate sea. The speech that frees comes forth from that amniotic deep. To attend its voice, I can hear it say, is to embrace its absence. But I fail the task. The word is stone.

I admit it.

I hate the stillness. I hate the stone. I hate the sealed vault with its cold icon. I hate the staring into the night. The questions thinning into space. The sky swallowing the echoes.

Unless the stone bursts with telling, unless the seed flowers with speech, there is in my life no living word. The sound I hear is only sound. White sound. Words, when they fall, are pock marks on the earth. They are hail-stones seeking an underground stream.

If I could follow the stream down and down to the hidden voice, would I come at last to the freeing word? I ask the night sky but the silence is steadfast. There is no reply.

Where do any of us come from in this cold country? Oh Canada, whether it is admitted or not, we come from you we come from you. From the same soil, the slugs and slime and bogs and twigs and roots. We come from the country that plucks its people out like weeds and flings them into the roadside. We grow in ditches and sloughs, untended and spindly. We erupt in the valleys and mountainsides, in small towns and back alleys, sprouting upside-down on the prairies, our hair wild as spiders' legs, our feet rooted nowhere. We grow where we are not seen, we flourish where we are not heard, the thick under growth of an unlikely planting. Where do we come from Obasan? We come from cemeteries full of skeletons with wild roses in their grinning teeth. We come from our untold tales that wait for their telling. We come from Canada, this land that is like every land, filled with the wise, the fearful, the compassionate, the corrupt.

Obasan, however, does not come from this clamorous climate. She does not dance to the multi-cultural piper's tune or respond to the racist's slur. She remains in a silent territory, defined by her serving hands. She serves us now, pouring tea into Mr. Barker's cup. She is unable to see and stops half-way before the cup is full.

From *Obasan* (Toronto: Penguin 1983)

Joy Kogawa

'In writing I keep breathing, I keep living ...'

JANICE: A polycultural politics is central to this Commonwealth literature conference [in Aachen, Germany]. How do you respond to this?

JOY: What I found exciting *here* was a tension between the aestheticists and the politicists and how that tension is being lived out in people's lives. I sense around me an effort to answer the problem of how to prevent the uglification of one's soul.

JANICE: Could you talk more about your sense of the 'uglification of the soul'?

JOY: There is an uglification of the soul that happens with one-dimensionality, and this is one of the dangers of political endeavour. One can be so overcome by the desperation of a political struggle that the despair becomes the reality, and that alone. In the midst of the struggle, in many instances, you realize you are going to lose and *are* losing, but you keep on struggling anyway. I didn't understand Wilson Harris's address. But I thought maybe he was saying that the way not to get uglified is to embrace our lostness and our failure – which is our heritage and our present political reality – and to see ourselves as indispensable parts of a complex therapeutic community of people. To be open to encountering one another rather than to be focused on an incestuous Oedipal destruction that leads to guilt and remorse or to the mentality of conquest. I think one can be so involved in striving for therapeutic community that the necessary political endeavour can be nullified or diluted. That's a possible danger, and maybe it's even uglier than getting swallowed up in the despair. This morning I was wondering: if we're not going to win, what do we struggle for? What are the rewards? In my struggle I have been discovering a sense of rightness, and that's a reward. With a sense of rightness, you just go on. The sky is bluer, if nothing else, just because your soul does not feel destroyed. I've also been thinking on this trip that one sometimes has to see the victimizer as genuinely victim. I met a beautiful South African couple whose one-dimensional view of their own terror was that they could be killed by Zulus. So I felt that to engage in dialogue with the victimizer demanded first an acknowledgment of their own very genuine sense of victimization.

JANICE: This discussion of the victimized reminds me of your human rights talk, 'Is There a Just Cause?'

JOY: I wrote that a long time ago now, but, yes, I do think we are all broken. There are pure victims in that infants are born and die, and they are not victimizers. But when a Hong Kong war vet tortured by the Japanese says, 'You're responsible,' it's an inadequate response simply to scream and say, 'No, no, I'm a Canadian.' I do have a connection to my Japaneseness. Better to say, 'Yes, what happened to you was so much worse than anything that happened to me, really, truly, it was.' As a person who has those genes, whose ancestors came from that country, I can't just dismiss him, walk away, be angry. My heart has to be, get, touched. In terms of the women's movement, I feel passionately the responsibility of White middle-class women to understand and identify with women in oppressed groups, because there is a tremendous hope in the women's movement. When I was in Israel last year at a women writers' conference, Jewish women from around the world got together and went as a group to support the Palestinian women. The power of that act, the power of women's solidarity beyond cultural differences, was wonderful; there was tremendous hope. But I've found that women who struggle from within oppressed cultures do not generally – and this is a very general statement – have time for the women's movement, naturally because they have a prior, more urgent, pressing, survival concern. A lot of women in Israel were saying, 'No, we can't be involved in the women's movement. We have to be involved in the survival of our country.' One first has to understand that statement by women of oppressed societies and then reach out and say, 'We're here, not to divide you from your men, but to support you in your struggle as an oppressed group.' Because I have been dealing so much with Japanese-Canadian politics recently, I've been wishing that I could reach out to the considerable resources of women's groups to assist the Japanese-Canadian group. But NAC [National Action Coalition] refused to support the NAJC [National Association of Japanese Canadians] because they said it's a male-dominated organization. That was their unseeingness of a political reality. Women have got to see that we risk becoming Margaret Thatcher if we don't identify with oppression, period, not just with women. If we don't, there's a failure in the political vision.

JANICE: When I first crossed the Belgian border into Germany, I experienced the dread of remembering Nazi Germany. One of the German opening speakers to this conference spoke to my dread when he reminded us that members of that anachronistically titled Commonwealth had to remember the Germans learned racist techniques and propaganda from Victorian England. Any account of the Japanese-Canadian internment camps in Canada echoes this uprooting of populations and the dehumanized treatment of people.

JOY: Political endeavour worries me in that people can become so bound up in the definition of what belongs and in winning that we lose sight of the humanity of the 'other.' In my new novel Aunt Emily struggles with the labour of birthing community and with politics and justice; I'm still struggling with many questions.

JANICE: The point of contestation in your own work is very interesting because Obasan opened up such an important moment in history to an audience who might not read the non-fiction accounts. I've taught Obasan to university undergraduates who have no cultural memory of this period. The tensions between Obasan and Aunt Emily help them to see different cultural and historical influences on a young woman's life as well as different attitudes towards political change. The novel is an important political work in that over time it disseminates a new story through our culture. But you also participate very actively in the lived struggle for Japanese-Canadian redress. How do you balance the writing and political activism?

JOY: Bharati Mukherjee said that if you are a minority writer and you're in Canada, you either have to get politically involved, because it's so overwhelming, or you have to write. She left Canada. I have been trying and trying and trying to write this novel, but the phone rings all the time and I can't say no. If you love people and they're hurting, you just don't. You wake up at night thinking how crazy it is that they're hurting so much, and you have to talk to this person, talk to that person, rally here and rally there. You get involved and don't have time to write. So I find that I can't write. If I want to be a writer, I'm going to have to get out in some way. I can't turn my heart off, and even when I leave I can't stop worrying. It's not as if they're being herded into camps any more, but the people who were herded into camps are the same hurting people, and that pulls me. I can't stand it, I get so mad. I've been worrying that so much emotion has got to be blinding at another level. I should be able to draw on some power to feel better, to feel differently. The writing would help me to do that. I was in the middle of writing, and I didn't really want to leave to travel here. It was terrible: wrenching myself is like being shot with some tranquillizer which I don't want. I've become so political, and in many ways very one-dimensional, that I'm afraid of destroying the poetry, the richness, of realities other than political realities. There are thousands of realities, but the political reality is so overwhelming in the world, I get drawn to it now. My involvement in this small political reality has opened an avenue to see the other analogous realities; it's like looking into a prism. It's been valuable to me as a writer to simply get involved and get my hands dirty and discover that I had to do that in order to get clean, or cleaner. When that door to the unconscious is dangerously narrowed, and the head gets bigger and bigger and more full of fact, it's like you're walking around in a starker and starker world. If the door to the unconscious is kept open all the time, the other stuff rushes out. I've been afraid that the door has been getting narrower and consciousness has been cutting out my poetry. I don't know what this novel's going to sound like. I may decide not to let it into the light of day because it'll seem so banal, the answers will seem like pills, not rich, real food.

JANICE: Is it more important to provide answers, or to provoke people to seriously consider issues which are meaningful to you?

JOY: What's important is to be fully engaged. It's a matter of being absorbed in the discovering.

JANICE: Bharati Mukherjee's introduction to her short-story collection *Darkness* is a very angry account of her experience in Canada. She presents the United States as a place where racism is articulated differently, where it is easier for visible minorities to live free of discrimination. Do you agree?

JOY: As a person who's never lived in the United States, I wouldn't know how to make that contrast, but I accept that that's her experience. One has to acknowledge that another person's expressed reality is her reality, and that's hers. I've always felt like a Canadian nationalist, a person who wants Canada to be strong, but I've been one of those people saying with chagrin, 'Look at how much better the United States was in the way it treated Japanese Americans.' In my brief journeys through Californian Japanese-American communities I've seen a lot more political consciousness among the people. They seem to exist even more strongly as identifiably separate groups there than we do here. This seems to be a contradiction. We're the people who have the mosaic and they're the melting pot, and yet I experienced it the other way around completely; in the Canada I grew up in we were supposed to become English. I found many Asian Americans thinking of themselves as a political unit, especially in the artistic community – the Chinese, Japanese, Filipinos. There was a feeling that they needed to be together in their big White country. In Canada the multicultural program gives a grant to this or that group, and that's the pie. We fight each other to make sure we get our grant, and our voices are kept distinct and separate from each other, controllable, smaller, and less united. That seems very destructive. Bharati felt that an official malevolent racism existed in Canada consciously from on high. I don't know how conscious all that is; maybe it works to maintain the power of a few elite Whites. Obviously, there is no one White group in Canada, but certainly there are powerful Anglo-Saxons. It's a complex question, and certainly different from the United States. There are times when I'd like to leave Canada and go to Hawaii. But I would identify with other people's struggles there, so there is no place to go, really. But I was interested that Bharati said what she needed to say, and she was a powerful person to say it.

JANICE: As a Japanese-Canadian writer, what is your relationship to the White Canadian writing community?

JOY: First, as a Japanese Canadian, I grew up needing to be the only

Jap in town, which was what we were taught we had to be and why we're all spread around and don't know each other. So I'm familiar with a sense of isolation. Jackie Kay said she would look in the mirror and be surprised that it was she whom she saw there. I used to feel like that a lot. I experienced myself as White almost all my life, until very recently. I just felt like a White member of the writing community for the longest time, and didn't have the guts or the consciousness to stand up and say, 'Well, I'm not.' At the Writers' Union conference a couple of years ago in Vancouver, I had been so politicized by the Japanese-Canadian endeavour that I felt I had to ask the Writers' Union to support Japanese-Canadian redress. I didn't have the nerve to stand up and say it myself, so somebody else said it for me, but even that was a big step. There was some debate, and we knew that if we let it go on too long it was going to be defeated. The chair, Rudy Wiebe, let it go through quickly, which was great. At that point I keenly felt my isolation as part of this tiny minority, a minority among minorities. I looked around to see the other minority people in this big White group. I wanted them there, but they weren't. On one level I experienced a great deal of discomfort, but on another level I felt a calling, 'That's what I'm here for. I might as well do it if I'm going to be true to what's happened to my life thus far.' Robin Mathews once talked about being burdened by an identity. I sometimes feel he put himself in a corner by presenting an identity with which he was then burdened. I too feel burdened by an identity because it was foisted on me, but on the other hand I chose it inasmuch as I started to talk about it, and by that act got doubly burdened by it. So there's no escaping my identity, which I cannot tear off at night any more, although I would like to escape it. If it were just a mask, I could take it off. But that's part of the human condition; we are limited by our mortality and by the realities of our condition, whatever it is.

JANICE: During one of the sessions yesterday Claire Harris and Sharon Pollock criticized Robin Mathew's presentation, in which he didn't consider race and gender in his account of colonization. Sharon dramatically announced, 'My country is not just Canada, my country is women!' What is your self-identification?

JOY: There is an identification as woman, as a Japanese Canadian, the identification with trees, with creatureliness. The search, if there is one, is from moment to moment through all those different identifications for something that is either at the base or that is a single focal point. For some reason human beings seem to be intent on finding single points, like searching for but never finding the ultimate building block of matter. In my search for a primary identification, I come to what I would call a spiritual point, a sense of unity like a spiritual explosion of joy, which I don't experience often. I experience despair as much as other people, inasmuch as I lose sight of those moments of joy which are very powerful antidotes to despair. The discipline that I would most seek for myself is a more accessible awareness of that spiritual resource below the surface of consciousness. It's like a stream that goes by as you sit on the bank. Fish come down that stream, and one is nourished. One can be constantly nourished by whatever goes through this life. From time to time, there is an amazing experience of allness, of complete belongingness. What makes it recognizable to me is the emotion of very great joy that attends it. The only feeble thing that seems appropriate to say at such moments is 'thank you.' That moment's identification is the one I wish would inform all my other identities, especially when the others become as heavy and painful as hair shirts you want to get rid of. If you have to put the shirt back on again, you can struggle and *survive* because of this other, for want of a better word, 'spiritual' identification.

JANICE: What kind of writerly decisions did you make in constructing the fiction *Obasan* between opening and closing texts: the introductory text is poetic, while the concluding document is historical?

JOY: I was so unconscious when I was writing. I just felt Emily's consciousness, which is Muriel Kitagawa's consciousness, and I felt myself having to work with that. And with Obasan. It didn't feel like it was part of me but a part of *them*, and they were demanding the right to exist and I was saying, 'Yes, Emily, yes, Obasan, you can exist. What is it you've got to say?' I wasn't aware of really making decisions; it was their doing. And in what I'm writing now, Emily has really invaded me. That's what worries me because I've often felt that Emily is one-dimensional, a person who is present, political, immediate, a person who feels now. Obasan's voice goes beyond from yesterday and tomorrow and from the stone: she *is* the stone, and the stone can speak if you listen to it hard enough. You listen by watching. Her hands make enormous speech if you have the capacity to hear. When I wrote *Obasan*, I was wrestling with their two voices. I still honour the greater power of that which is coming forth and not yet conscious. The practice of poetry for me is the sweeping out of the debris between the conscious and the unconscious. It's engaging the discipline of dreams. *That* was my primary commitment which most moved me when I was sitting down with a pen. What worries me is the smaller-mindedness of conscious political activity which informs Emily and which informs me now. It worries me because I think my work will be far less as art, but I'm doing it anyway because I seem not to be able to stop. This new book is in some ways similar to the basic structure of *Obasan*. This one begins in 1983 and then goes back to the fifties, proceeds up to 1983 in the middle, and then beyond to an unknown present. I'm in about 1985 now, and it's getting increasingly truncated because of my impatience and dissatisfaction with it. I want to engage Emily with the *obasan* even though she has died within this book, or engage Emily with herself and her own despair. If I can do this, the book will be OK. But what I despair is that I'm so tired I'll just give up on this book, but there are about twenty-five chapters more or less done. And all that is happening right now seems so obvious to me. There's less richness in it, and the imagery is not there because it's all political talk.

JANICE: Does your poetry give you some respite from the long rigours of novel writing?

JOY: Not much. I never carry my books of poetry around. When I feel a poem coming on, I might scribble a line or two, whereas in the past I would wrestle with it until it shaped itself. I don't do that any more. I've just lost the confidence to do that, and I don't know why.

JANICE: How does your 'discipline of dreams' inform your poetry?

JOY: In 1964 I was in a crisis of ideals in my life and thought I needed to know more and desperately escape from unattainable ideals I believed so powerfully in. The problems of evil seemed to me to be so enormous, so impossible. I felt there would be answers in the dream world. I woke up night after night with a pen beside me, and it was just like a volcano: the dreams, the images were so suggestive; they were *more* than suggestive, they were almost directive and instructive. I was so amazed by them. Sometimes there was a kind of unconscious writing. I'd wake up in the morning and there'd be this poem, which made no sense at all when I was writing it and yet was so obvious to me in the light of day. I kept that up for years, and the discipline of it was in simply insisting on remembering and then playing with it, not giving up on it, and trying to find out what the meaning of it might be. Part of the discipline of dreams was simply paying attention to them.

JANICE: If your poetry is a way of apprehending life through your own psyche, does *Obasan* work differently? Did you have a sense of who your readers might be?

JOY: When I was writing *Obasan*, especially the first draft, it was an extension of writing the poems, and so there was no audience in mind particularly. There was just the compulsion to do the act as an act of discovery and that was purer, somehow. Now I'm more conscious of publication, and that bothers me.

JANICE: How much of your writing is autobiographical?

JOY: A lot. In the future I would like to get away from that. I'm trying to make the current novel less autobiographical and more imaginary. In writing prose, you take a little thing here and a little thing there and make composites. What you are true to is the feeling and not the situation. Not the facts as such, but the facts of one's feelings.

JANICE: In fiction we can construct alternative worlds. How does *Obasan* translate or transform the trauma of your displacement as a child during the internment of Japanese Canadians?

JOY: It's all connected. Of course it relates to the way my family was traumatized and how my mother's and father's realities broke down for them. It is certainly interwoven with the history of racism, but it goes beyond that. My mother used to be such an elegant woman. Debbie [Gorham] told me she thought that I had made these two female characters, Naomi's idealized mother of childhood plus the *obasan*, because I wasn't able to cope with the reality of what happened to my real mother. She had been a very bourgeois beautiful, elegant woman with a lovely house, lovely clothes and furs, and china and furniture and music lessons. She was a musician. She had all of that, and suddenly she was out in the prairies in this dusty place and an important part of her gave up. She didn't seem to care any more what she wore, and I used to feel embarrassed to have people come around. She was always clean, but so poor. Her clothes had patches, and she could never buy anything. That was one reality. She was also very, very tough inside. But increasingly she retreated from the semblances of things that children need. It's difficult for me to talk about this.

* * *

JANICE: Daphne Marlatt writes that *real* women – that is, small *r* – *real* women ... Isn't it terrible how I have to re-appropriate 'real' away from right-wing R.E.A.L. women? ...

JOY: ... the terrorism of language abuse ...

JANICE: ... Daphne said that her work is autobiographical because for her most accounts of women's lives are fictional, artifice. She wants to write something that has to do with *her* being in the world.

JOY: I would like to write something that is real, too, and I was trying to do that in my poetry. The problem I have with what I'm writing right now is it feels less real. You're helping me with that question. The problem with Emily is my experience of myself with Emily feels somehow less real. The political reality, real as it is, is somehow an imposition of order on something that is much more complex, and if I am going to be true to what is real within me, I will attend far more intently to that complexity; that is, tap the spiritual thing that I was talking about. But I don't feel that I *really* talked about it with you because the language was abstract. I couldn't say it in a way to convince you or myself. So what I would like to do is to go back into the spiritual feelings, to look more fully and say, 'This feels more real.' It's not to say that Emily's not real; she is very real. But you know the uglification we were talking about earlier – *that* is so great a danger, and *that's* what feels less real to me. Probably I'm having a hard time with this novel because that other dimension is lacking and not being properly pulled forth. That's a problem I have: I can *never* get to that point where it really feels real; it *never* gets there. It's just not ever accurate, and one can go crazy wanting desperately to get to that point of clarity. Though in the political struggle there is a feeling of becoming increasingly clear about certain things, and that feels great and clear the way a star in the distance feels clear. You can see it, but it isn't clear in the way warmth that completely surrounds you feels clear. What I want is my body, and that is the big problem that Naomi has. She is so divorced from her body, such a repressed prude, and I don't think she's ever going to come out. I have such trouble with her. And Emily doesn't have her body either. There is a lostness I despair about because I don't know how I'm ever going to have my body.

JANICE: Feminism has raised the question of the female body in a non-objectified way. Wouldn't feminism have helped Naomi with her own disengagement from her body?

JOY: Yes, if there is a genuinely political feminist voice in the novel, that should engage her, but she is still so removed as she has developed to this point. I keep wanting her to come forth, to come forth, to come forth, but she hasn't done it. There are people who go through life and this doesn't happen to them, and it could be that she never will. There is no conspicuous feminism in this current book but maybe there needs to be. There is a character, a priest called Father Cedric, and what he is doing we can only guess at. He and Naomi go off into the woods and she imagines what goes on, but we don't know what's real.

JANICE: What kind of space does her naïvety allow you as a writer?

JOY: I have no idea. I feel terribly frustrated with her and with myself too. Why she has developed this way only she knows. I guess I'll have to ask her: 'Why are you like this? I don't like you.' So she'll say, 'OK, we'll split.' It reminds me of a dream I had in which there were three characters, a terrible prude and a prostitute's daughter and the writer. The prude was going to kill the prostitute's daughter, and the writer intervened and said, 'No, no, if you kill her, you kill all three of us. We have to co-exist. We can't live together, but every once in a while we've got to get together.' If Naomi represents that terrible prude who is struggling, and we have Emily, we still don't have the prostitute's daughter in the novel, unless she enters at this late point in the novel after twenty-five chapters. But there's not going to be any sense of the woman's wholeness if she arrives so late. I was picking on Naomi and wanting her to do something which she obviously can't. She can't have an affair and she can't feel her body.

She has experienced rage, and that has been so debilitating that it's resulted in a further calcification. But rage is a beginning and maybe she'll proceed beyond this. But maybe she won't and just have to be one of these horrible characters, I don't know. You see, I think that I truly am one of these really repressed people, too. Deep down it is so severe and the scarring is so great that maybe I'm not going to come out. I don't know. Maybe that's part of the struggle.

JANICE: Is writing then not only a process of self-exploration but also of change?

JOY: I think it's all those. It is more like a compulsion without really knowing what results from it, except if I don't do it, it feels like I'll collapse. In writing I keep breathing, I keep living, and it feels so good when I've got that right word out.

Aachen, Germany, June 1988

Lee Maracle

Excerpt from 'Maggie'

Mama worked. In the early morning hours she rose, set crab traps with our little skiff, and after breakfast she pounded them up and sometime in the afternoon she took the crabs somewhere to be sold. She came home near to our bedtime. Maggie told me she remembered the very day mama went to work for cash money. Maggie knew why too. Mama's marriage was a mess. Sometime after our dad left, she acquired a lover who didn't care much for her dependants. Maggie told me he was just a plain brute. I remember doubting her, thinking maybe it was us. All four of us where there, unwanted by our own dad, when he can. I could never see the point of wanting more from this stranger than what our own dad was prepared to give, but Maggie wouldn't hear it: 'He is sick.'

It was 1956. The year we got a television. Mama tried to finish work by six to watch the news. Maggie popped the corn and made tea and got the rest of us settled in to watch the show. The new black and white console stood out in stark contrast to the bare walls of our old house with its overly simplistic furnishing. An old couch and chair, an oil heater which never seemed to have any oil in it, and a brand new television. All of us lined up on the couch quietly staring at the news, none of figuring these things really happened.

When mama was late, Maggie mocked the newscaster, filling up the broadcast with words of her own. 'Anti-colonial Black movements in Africa threaten' came from the newsman, followed by Maggie's 'to "kick ass," with white folks today.' We laughed nervously. No one in our community dared used the word 'white' when talking about the others. No one told us it was forbidden, but we had never heard white people referred to by anything except 'them people', and always they were mentioned in hushed tones. Maggie's cheek and brass scared us. She knew something was amiss and somehow figured 'kicking ass' could fix it.

After the news, Mama closed her eyes and asked Maggie to read. Mama had four books: a Bible, an unabridged dictionary and two novels, *Germinal* and *Les Miserables*. Maggie threw her heart and soul into her voice when she read, dramatizing her own passionate dream of poor people 'kicking butt' with 'them people.' Mama never suspected a thing.

In the early morning light I would sometimes wake up and catch Maggie writing in her diary, painting with words whatever pictures of the world she wanted. Travelling to places she had not been, and imagining herself doing things she would never be allowed to do.

Sat. Dec. 10, 1956
'Joey, Joey, Joey,' an exasperated mother picked up bits and pieces of an electric train, shut off the power source and muttered softly the name of her errant son.

Joey was long gone. His little league cap plunked jauntily atop his fiery red hair, a glove in one hand, a bat over his shoulder and a softball in his ass-hip pocket. He had sauntered off to the cow field for a game with the boys.

On the little league team Joey was the back-catcher, but on the cow field he was agreeable to whatever position his mates wanted him to play. Today, he was first at bat. Tony was the pitcher and he threw Joey a dandy – WHAP! A line drive heading straight for sleepy Dave.

'Shee-it ... chrisst ... jeezuus,' and a half-dozen bewildered boys circled Sleepy Dave, who lay peacefully motionless on the field about where the short stop ought to have been standing.

'Will ya look at the lump on his head?'

Yeah' ... 'What a beauty,' and other such mumbling carried on while Gary ran for hid dad. The story ends here, because adults are not allowed in the diary.

She finished reading me her story. I asked her how come mothers were allowed in the story.

'Mothers are girls, silly, they never have to grow up.' Maggie shaped me. Maybe it was what happened a little while later which made her words stick so well in my mind. What she said was true. Even the ladies from our own community called themselves girls – little girls, growing girls, old girls, but all girls nonetheless. It took twenty-four years, amid much brouhaha and some pies in the faces of a few politicians whose names I dis-remember, for me to say *women* and not girls, but it happened. It was kind of hard for me. I was among the first young females to gain adult status, and it took me a long time to figure out what being an adult entailed. Maggie must have known:

Tues, Dec. 13, 1956
'Ann, put that down. Annie for gawdsake.' A firm wrist jerked the hammer from Annie's hand and the mouth who owned the hand spat out some nonsense about 'gurlz, 'n' hammerz, 'n' shugger 'n' spice' and other such clap-trap Ann tried not to think about.

'Why don't you play with your Barbie doll or something, for chrissakes.'

'Cuz Barbie don't drive truck and I don't like pointy tits.'

The woman cursing Ann gasped, turned white and red by turns, and finally sent Ann to her room: 'Until your father comes home.' In her room Ann lay back and laughed about the look on Mary's face when she had found her pounding nails into the garage floor. Even more precious was her mother's look when Ann disclosed her awareness of truck driving and tits.

From *Soujourner's Truth* (Vancouver: Press Gang 1990)

Lee Maracle

'an infinite number of pathways to the centre of the circle'

JANICE: Your public readings are dramatic in that your stories are teaching stories.

LEE: In the tradition of the Big House speakers and storytellers there is a way of presenting story. In the Big House there are powerful people who know the history, the families, the relationships between everyone. And they're also the people who are asked to articulate whatever it is that people want to decide or discuss. They have a cadence and a drama when they speak, which matches up with our songs and story dances. Inadvertently, I suppose, I'm influenced by that. My poetry comes from, first of all, a desire to write and, when I was little, to confront the differences in how people interact. Old people are one way; people in the next generation are another way. And the people in my mother's generation were, I think, very confused. They're the students of residential school, the students of abuse. These were not the kind of residential schools that supposedly forced us to learn English. They were basically industrial schools, where males learned to farm and females learned to cook and clean. When they came out, my great-grandmother used to call them crippled two-tongues. They couldn't speak either language as adults. When you're an adult, it's time to marry, procreate, work, provide for your family, not the time to learn to speak a language. They never did overcome this. There were a few exceptions. My dad was one, but we didn't live in the same house. I went to public elementary school. Our folks wanted us to learn to write, to learn how to live with these people. In the course of that public schooling, I learned about story – Dickens and Fitzgerald and Chekhov and all these people. Zola. I love Zola. I read them at a very young age. From the time I was ten until about thirteen, I read furiously. I suppose from my own background and the way we speak English and the things we look at and see and the structure of Indigenous story comes a kind of poetry that's not poetry in the European sense and not story in the European sense either. I think Marlene Philip has termed it – oratory.

JANICE: Your poem 'Perseverance' is set in Toronto, where you figure yourself as a dandelion on Bay Street 'Perpetually rebellin' / against spike heels and blue-serge suits.' In the poem there is pain as well as a fierce fighting desire for survival. You write, ' I really hope I keep the elite awake at night.' How enabling is fight-back rage?

LEE: First of all, it's *out*raged. At one time it was *en*raged, and I think that's destructive. Wow, that poem comes from a number of places. It comes from a five-hundred-year history of silence, a largely self-imposed silence because no one was listening. Our folks believe we will know when people are prepared to hear. That poem is actually fairly old and comes from an experience in Toronto when I was sixteen or seventeen. It had been eating away at me for years, but I didn't write it until I was about thirty-eight. Two people, I guess, contributed. One was Patrick Andrade, a Black man from the West Indies who had just left Toronto. In a letter to me he said he felt like 'his skin had been scraped off him.' And I thought, 'That's it'; that's what I needed to hear. So there's Black rage, which is why I ended with a Black desire. In the poem there's also one of my relatives who always wondered why people don't think dandelions are beautiful because they are medicine, they're a clothing dye, and they're so much like a sunburst. And they survive anywhere on almost *nothing*. I thought of myself in that way. I hadn't asked this world for anything. And neither had my ancestors. We got nothing. We got less than nothing. But still we had a kind of grit about the future – the forwardness. So it's not totally rage. There is a contradistinction between the destructive kind of economic development that created the urban centres, urban madness if you will, and the kind of development that we imagine could be. There is an element of hope in the forwardness and the huge desire that Native women have to rectify, not just life for ourselves, but the colonized land and the impoverished people capitalism naturally creates. There's great beauty of perseverance under terrible conditions. There's not so much pain in it as you might imagine. At least not for me. I love that piece.

JANICE: As a White woman, there are certain experiences I can in part share with you about my own history which have to do with discriminatory structures, sexual abuse, whatever, but on the other hand, institutions and structures of authority are set up to confirm my racial privilege. What do you imagine my role as a White literary critic should be in relation to your work?

LEE: It's easier for me to see things in metaphor. From our perspective we think of life as climbing mountains. Some people don't climb very many. Some people don't even make it to the top of their first mountain. Doesn't matter. But every time you confront something that's an obstacle, it's a mountain. For me racism was a huge mountain. We come at it from two difference sides, White and Coloured. It's only when we've scaled and reached the summit that we have much to talk about. I can tell you how racism is for me and how it is to undo it, how it is to keep going up that mountain and keep falling back and keep going up because I know at the top, no matter how hard it is to climb, you can see the world. You can see the magnificence of being a small creature in the world. At some point, someone's going to get up there with you. At some point I'll get to the top too. I think I'm probably closer.

JANICE: I'm sure you are.

LEE: That doesn't matter, I'll wait there. I'll enjoy the wait, I think. I can't answer that question for you, you see, because I'm not undoing the dilemma you've been caught in, and being deprived of me is a serious thing. It's a serious thing for you to pursue and undo.

JANICE: So in some ways it's up to me and other women like me to try to work out in ourselves a space which is self-critically enabling and doesn't appropriate. In fact, you dedicate I Am Woman to two White women who supported your writing.

LEE: Always remember – I think it's a significant lesson – 'everything you do and every word you speak, either empowers or disempowers.' And you have to always double think. I know I have to make these decisions every time I'm in a white audience because sometimes a momentary disempowerment in the end is long-term empowerment. I'm extremely open with what I think. I decided on a January day in 1988 it's time to take on all this stuff out there in the public world and so I do. I started in Montreal in June of 1988 asking White women in the feminist movement to 'move over' – actually *telling* them to move over. In their own interest they must move over because half of them is missing and I'm that half. Not me personally, but Native women. There's no other way, there just isn't any other way. I think some of these American White women have learned that in their relationships with Black women. They still have to learn it in their relationships with Native women, either English-speaking or Spanish-speaking, they're all Native women to me. I think it's a devotion to be critical of White feminism. I think it's a kind of love and devotion we have inside us, and it's not seen as that. It's seen as pain and rage. And it's not! Otherwise I wouldn't bother talking to you if I didn't *feel* you were prepared to listen.

JANICE: One of the problems I sense in these discussions is that one of the only models for difference of opinion is oppositional confrontation. Some of the critical engagements that have happened over the last while between White feminists and Women of Colour seem *so* painful for everyone that I wonder what kind of conversation we could have that would work through our differences without the aggression. Or is the aggression implicit in it? I agree with you, it's generated not just by one group of women necessarily.

LEE: This is a complex one. Canadians definitely have a parasitic culture. It's also a male culture. It's a utilitarian culture. It's a culture based on pain where courtesy is a class question. A sense of courtesy in Canada is developed by upper-class people who have no respect for the lower classes in their own communities. It's based on nuance, inference, and hiding that typifies a sense of politeness. One doesn't say *this* because you might hurt the person's feelings. I want to say something about this because it moves and motivates me. When you get cut, at first, you hardly feel it. Next day when that flesh, and those veins, and that skin start to mend, you experience the pain of having been cut. Social pain and social healing is not any different. For you to become a racist was painless. For you to un-become and become something new is going to be excruciating. Just like me to become self-racist is painless. The shame part was easy to learn, easy to internalize. The un-becoming is very, very difficult and very painful. But it's healing and there's no other way to heal. There's no other way to knit things back together except to go through it. People say, trust hurts, but the hurt of it is the healing. It's not the infliction of a wound. The infliction of a wound is silence, and women in this country are silenced by the culture that is parasitic and upper-class White male. I really want to get specific here because there are some White men who just shovel dirt and don't know anything about how this all came to be. There are conventions around what you say and what you don't say which are really killing people. They're killing Native people in huge numbers because there's no way for us to express ourselves and how we feel, and the reality is that deep in our hearts we do want to be at one with other Canadians. Despite all the racism, despite all the neglect, despite all the abuse, we still dream, deep inside us, of unity. Even when we don't like you, we still dream of it.

JANICE: *I Am Woman* was published by your husband's Write-On Press. Was that a decision that had to do with the way publishing organizes itself in Canada?

LEE: First of all, I come from a culture in which asking for something is almost a crime! I come from a situation where I didn't want to be up on the stage and talking, but at the time I wrote it someone asked me to send in a manuscript. A Woman of Colour press in New York rejected it. One of the comments which was made was that it was too beautiful for a political non-fiction book. But that's my political discursive style. It's written as oratory because I don't really know how else to put politics plainly so my folks can understand it. It's a collection of things in my life which shaped me; it's a summation of my life from different angles. It's an attempt to give a picture of colonialism as a whole, not in abstract theoretical terms, but as it affects us in our real lives – how Native women relate to White folks, and our own folks, our children. It's all about the worst that has happened to us.

JANICE: So you were addressing an audience where politics wasn't just a theory.

LEE: Well, it's theoretical, sure, but not the way that Europeans theorize. It's a real dilemma for most scholars – all scholars, whether they come from Africa, India, America, are Black, White, or whatever. Everything is taught and expressed in a White, upper-class male style. Anything else is weird, or impossible to market as politics or ... So she asked me to send it to her again, and I said no, I think I'll do it myself. It was probably a dumb think to say! But I told my husband to do it and he did.

JANICE: You have a whole range of readers – the Native community, feminists, specialists in Native studies. Do you have a sense of an audience you write towards? You said you want to locate your writing in a particular way.

LEE: Native people have a great command of oral language. First of all, they want the raw, bare truth, and secondly, they want it put with energy and as beautifully as possible. It is the raw, bare truth. A lot of people say my book is very angry. But most of my folks say it's a very inspiring, empowering book because there's an energy there that never lets up. There's a thread that says to them every sentiment they've ever had about the world they live in is a good one. Every doubt they've ever had is a wonderful doubt. It makes us sharp. It makes us brilliant. It makes us very powerful just to see – just to see.

JANICE: So the Native reader finds experience affirmed, while the White reader is confronted by the pain of your experience. You write: 'I really hope I keep the elite awake at night.'

LEE: Mm-hm. Yeah. They just have to look at something they've never looked at before and didn't want to see.

JANICE: M. Nourbese Philip sent her manuscript of poetry out to twenty-two publishers before she finally published it. Many Native writers have talked about problems of access. What do you see is the solution to discrimination in Canadian publishing?

LEE: Access to capital. The development of our own presses and our own publishing houses.

JANICE: Like Pemmican and Theytus.

LEE: A non-discriminatory kind of access. Usually what happens is only the people with a certain politic gain access to money, which acts as a kind of censorship. I've experienced it in my own life. Status of Women wanted me to do an article. But a political organization said Native women don't want to write and be identified with other

Women of Colour and squelched the project until a survey was done. This happens to us. Writers do not represent anybody. What they represent is a personal direction, a new humanity and a new sense of the world. That's something this world always is going to need. Chekhov did not represent the Russian people, but his work contributed to the dismantling of serfdom in his country. Zola did not represent the Basque people in France. Dickens did not represent his class when he began a process of undoing the child exploitation which existed in England. And *I* don't represent anybody either. But ten years from now, people are going to be different because I'm a writer, just like Chrystos, Jeannette Armstrong, Maria Campbell, etc. Every single Native person who writes is pointing to a road over there. I don't necessarily agree with every writer who ever wrote something. But it needs to be said and thought about. It needs to be approached from every angle we can. There's not enough of us out there. There are *tens of thousands* of Canadian writers; there should be *thousands* of us. There are *thousands* of Canadian presses; there should be *hundreds* of ours.

JANICE: My grandmother was a rural Manitoba schoolteacher, and when I visited her house as a child, the first poetry I read was Pauline Johnson's. Her popularity meant that she represented the tradition of Indigenous writing by women. I connected with her as a young White girl who wanted to write. What is your relation to Johnson's writing?

LEE: I loved her when I was nine; I still do. Betty Keller, a White women, wrote a good book about her. She talked to a lot of older Native people who know quite a bit about Pauline's family history. She was raised by an English mother. Her father was Native. So her writing skill arises out of an English tradition, but throughout her life she struggled to capture her heart as a Native woman.

JANICE: Not only did she hobnob with royalty, but she travelled across the continent fourteen times and brought her poetry to many small communities along the way.

LEE: I have tremendous respect because she did it at a time shortly after they'd hung Louis! It stuns me to think that there was a man in her audience who had actually done some of the killing, who would listen to this poetry and be moved by it. She moved a lot of Canadians, and I like the fact that her hundreds of readings may have prevented an awful lot of conflict.

JANICE: Discussions about Native writers have been hindered by the fact that they are often framed from an outsider's point of view where you locate a single writer as representative and lose sight of a diversity of writing and positions.

LEE: I've got a story coming out. It's called 'Polka Partners, Uptown Indians, and White Folks.' 'Polka Partners' is a kind of urban metaphor, Métis for courting. Uptown Indians and White Folks have a lot in common. There is this tendency to look upon us as a monolith. When we break that monolith, White people are terrorized by it. Someone said that the reason people don't like Chrystos is because of homophobia. We have no way of knowing that. But this woman was so sure because 'homophobia exists in our community.' So does internalized racism! So does sexism! So does alcoholism. Perhaps it's that she's not an alcoholic that people are prejudiced. There are a whole number of reasons why people could be upset with Chrystos. Perhaps it's because she wants a different world, and there are conservatives in our community. I think conservatism is a whole bunch of things – it's sexism, racism, homophobia, and all the rest of it. Perhaps there's professional jealousy. That exists. We have all of these contradictions, and we can't go on speculating that it's only one and be so categorically sure of any single one. All of the contradictions this woman sees exists everywhere in the same degree. That's part of the racist legacy we're left with. I want to say something on the good side, though you may not agree with it. The women's movement, much more than the rest of the country, is willing to look inside at their own motivation and really consider what the impact of their actions or words is. I'm not saying all women are that way and certainly not every feminist. Maybe it's a legacy of patriarchy, I don't know. But there is a sense women have that maybe we don't know everything, maybe we ought to get in there and look at everything. We've changed enough diapers to know dirt is not that bad; cleaning it up is not so horrible. So I think we're a lot better equipped to look and clean up. Homophobia to me is organized rape. And I think that it exists in our community. Residential school is filled with sexual abuse. Two things happen when kids are sexually abused: one, they internalize it and develop a victim consciousness; and two, they become perpetrators. Generally, males become the perpetrators, females become the victims. The children were taken from their homes, sometimes hundreds of miles away, and had no upbringing by their own people.

JANICE: There are Native myths in which homosexuality is revered and Native histories which talk about homosexual shamans.

LEE: In White culture homophobia is a kind of rape because we're forcing everyone to submit to what *you* decide. But I think of homosexuals as people with a dualism, two-spirit people. It makes them good healers because they understand both male and female sexuality. We don't have a he/she in our languages, so we don't have the homo-, hetero-, and all that other kind of sexuality; it's just human sexuality. And choice. Nobody can tell you how to express our sexuality. Sometimes men and women form a marriage in which their sexuality is actually expressed homosexually between them. All kinds of things happen in the bedroom nobody knows! The whole question of your sexuality is very very personal and private and determined by the spirit inside you. If you have two spirits, you're considered more powerful, because you have twice as much as everybody else.

JANICE: You teach part-time at the En'owkin Native writing school in Penticton. How do you see your role as a teacher?

LEE: When you're teaching, you're not actually doing anything except encouraging learning, and when you've written as long as I have you learn some short cuts. We need many more Native writers in this country very quickly because publishers are starting to see they've got to publish us, and they're going to start looking for manuscripts. Six Native writers are not going to do it for this country. There's got to be hundreds of us from all different cultures. The En'owkin school is made up of people from different cultures. We try to hot-house the students' own skills to build what's in their own selves. It's the way Native people teach and learn. My parents, my mother anyway, encouraged me to realize myself rather than battering me with useless instructions about don't touch this, and sit at the table, and be still, and don't talk to much. I was given choices at a very early age, either reading or working. I always chose reading. To *recreate* that skill in someone else from his or her own perspective is marvellous, like watching a flower going from seed to flower in a human being.

JANICE: You're working on a novel now. How does this project differ from your earlier work?

LEE: A novel is a whole piece. It's not a long short story; it's a whole chunk of somebody's life, how people interact, how they come to being. Mine is about the kids who were sold to Americans in the fifties, and what happened to them. I wanted to articulate in it what we call tribal memory. We believe every one of us is born with the memory of the essence of who we are. In the novel, a child, who is completely divorced from her heritage and grows up in L.A., is abused and then rescued by an unconscious tribal memory which finds its expression in her relationship to a place in the hills around Topanga Canyon. Here she rescues herself in traditional fashion, but she doesn't know this till much later. She's a frightened child. In the end, the three women, the natural mother, the adoptive mother, and the child, come to a kind of understanding among each other, and you get the sense at the end of the novel a new direction is in store for all of them.

JANICE: How do you come upon a form to write a novel such as this?

LEE: Probably accidentally. A young guy asked me indirectly; he just said that that story had to be written. He knew I was writing on women and hinted in good Indian style that I should take on this responsibility. And so I did. I started to do a bit of research about the case of a young man who was sexually abused, and then became an abuser. His life came to light in his trial, and the scandal of being sold to an American family also came to light. I couldn't bring myself to use his story. First of all, I don't know what it is to be male and sexually abused, and my imagination would tend to be angry about him becoming an abuser. I decided to use a woman character. I decided to put her through things and find a way for her to rescue herself in the course of her life. Secondly, the man, whose case became quite well known in the papers all over the place, was from the Midwest, and I don't have a sense of the landscape and the weather. So I used a young girl on the West Coast.

JANICE: If your relationship to other Native writers is cross-cultural in that you have different tribal histories, languages, and customs, is your reading of each other's writing a process of translation?

LEE: Before White people came, a lot of trade routes led to the development of cross-cultural kinds of thinking. And certainly some of our very, very old stories relate to a relationship with other people on this continent. We didn't have the massive communication that now exists, and we certainly didn't have a common language, so it was a limited cultural exchange which took place. In the last thirty years there has been a pan-Indianist movement at least in the cultural sphere. We writers no longer feel isolated from each other the way we used to. I met Paula Gunn Allen and fell in love with her *Woman Who Owned the Shadows.* Jeannette [Armstrong] and I haven't met Lenore Keeshig-Tobias, but I'm sure I'm gonna love her when I do. I just edited *Songs of Rita Joe,* a Micmac woman's poetry book, and I met the artist Joan Cardinal-Schubert and have seen the work of Jane Ash-Poitras. They are all influential in bringing about what is common to us. We come from our own specific place, but we have a commonality and a common dream.

JANICE: What's the effect of reading someone like Paula Gunn Allen?

LEE: She makes me laugh because she is inside all of us. Some things she writes about are tragic, but at the same time we're laughing because her manner of expression is exactly the way we think. In *The Woman Who Owned the Shadows* every now and then this tornado of words and thought happens. I think it's how we actually think, at least it's how I think. There I am – [mini tornado sound] – and I love that tornado, it's very disquieting, but you know the end of the tornado is this wonderful peace, and calm, and knowledge. For most of our people knowledge is sacred. Here she is actually writing a novel which is after all just a novel, but every now and then, there is a wonderful tornado of thought, perception, sense, and then clarity. It goes back to being a regular European-style story, then *sheooo* it happens again. I just love it. She's becoming an influence, at least an affirmation in my life.

JANICE: *The Woman Who Owned the Shadows* isn't separated into conventional chapters. Episodes are interrupted by poetic lines. For

me, this way of breaking up the narrative initiates a reading meditation in the middle of unfolding events.

LEE: I think of it differently. I always think of by-plays. In any situation there's something else underneath it all which happens at a
level we don't quite understand. Some people call it the spiritual level;
some people, the centrifuge. I don't know how to define it myself.
There's always something else going on sparking the imagination. I
love that part of life. People are so complex. I don't know if that was
Paula's intent, but it doesn't matter what her intent was anyway, does
it?

JANICE: How is your spirituality connected with your writing?

LEE: Writing is like ceremony for me. I have to be in a certain place
to start talking to those dead trees, the paper that was essentially
murdered so I could put little black ink etchings on them, draw little
word pictures. It's a relationship I have to trees, to the oil from the
ground that makes up the typewriter ribbon. It's a relationship to the
people in my life who need to have their lives articulated and to
myself when I need to go forward out into the world. It's a huge
ceremony for me.

JANICE: Within Canada, who are the writers with whom you feel a
kinship?

LEE: I don't read very much. I read and listen to a lot of Jeannette
Armstrong's work and Dionne Brand. I read Joy Kogawa's *Obasan*
and Roy Kiyooka's poems. But I don't think I draw inspiration so
much from other people's writing. A lot of Native writers will be
writing from a different place, about the same thing, and come to the
same place. We call it the medicine wheel and there are an infinite
number of pathways to the centre of the circle. Chrystos is another
writer I like a lot, though she's not Canadian. I don't look to any
other writer for something to write about; I don't think they're de-
serving of that kind of attention. *I'm* not either. The people who
deserve to be written about are those who will never sit down and
write. They won't sit in the closet at two in the morning and cudgel
themselves with a dictionary and a blank piece of paper. Those are
the people who need to be talked to and spoken about. Sometimes
it's animals ...

JANICE: I think my spirit guide is a dog, Mars.
LEE: Just like wolf, right. Mine's supposed to be a wolf. Someone's gonna send me a werewolf story ...

Edmonton, April 1990

Daphne Marlatt

There is a door

There is a door other than that which opens to the known world

      drawn in the steamed up windows of the house a house (windows and mouth, lopsided plume) that bares opaque aspects of the soul (no kidding) the way words exit her place of abode, steamed up, where is she anyhow? keeping house as if keeping herself meant hugging a shadowy wall she is playing house without the means with all the right words (keeping it nice) and somehow still feels left outside

he has a full house, three of a kind and a pair no repairing to where she hears he is scaling walls, floodlit

the depression of solitaire: for fear of claws in the legal because (she is tied up inside it all) believing what they said, that she would die if she went through that door ...

where women meet where the words face up, are heard – i know what you mean – in these small houses walls are falling

while his back meeting rain on the street slickers into the Buccaneer, relief, the reign of conversation here behind glass fogged up and closed in it's in-house news exchanged with change or beer the currency of who makes it here

playing to a small house, house of the ascendant, house of commons, stars parading through their phrases, stars or tiny lights –

that there's only so much power, not enough to go round, to light up windows on the outside of town / the known

the indifferent news –

we are giving up on, moving out of solitaire into a clearer sense of what relates us, this solar river this windy oikos simultaneous her *sisterfire* at the mouth at the mouth borne inside each of us saying what women see is flooding out the old inside / outside of our minds.

From *Salvage* (Red Deer, Alberta: Red Deer College Press 1991)

Daphne Marlatt

'When we change language ...'

JANICE: I want to begin by asking you about your current work. Your project 'Salvage' is a rereading or revisioning of earlier writing in the light of your developing feminist consciousness. Is this a critical consciousness that recalls the feminism implicit in your early writing, or is it a consciousness which looks back and recognizes gaps?

DAPHNE: It's more looking back and recognizing, not so much gaps, but places where I was blocked and I couldn't see my way out because I didn't have the theory that would have helped me do that. So now with the benefit of some of that theory and having done a lot more writing of a different kind, I can go back and read my way through those earlier texts for the hidden dynamic that's operating. For instance, a piece which Penn Kemp published in the women's issue of *IS* (14 [1973]) in the early seventies, 'Steveston. Support. Fish,' has become 'Litter. wreckage. salvage,' and I discovered it took a veer from Steveston to skid row in the original because it's really about how difficult it is for women to be on the street and how they don't occupy the street in the way men do because it's a public space that's basically male. I realized that the buried image for this was agoraphobia, quite literally 'fear of the marketplace.' We've had this long tradition of women on the street being seen as available somehow – they get whistled at, stared at, yelled at by men, because women on the street have been seen as being there for men, to service men, they're on the sexual market in some way.

JANICE: You talk about the rapport between your writing as a feminist and your reading of feminist theory. What feminist theories have influenced you?

DAPHNE: There's so much, it's hard to say. I became very interested in the kind of theory that Nicole Brossard was writing, which I first encountered in the issue of *Ellipse* (23–4 [1979]) that was devoted to *La Nouvelle Barre du jour* and *Open Letter*, and I loved the piece – it wasn't even the full piece, it was just excerpts from 'E muet mutant,' the silent feminine *e*. I began to get very interested in the possibility of writing carrying the feminine, so that led me to French feminist theory, and I started reading Cixous and Irigaray and Kristeva – Duras before that, but not so much for theory. The thing that drew me to what Nicole was doing was her writing always as a woman in the process of *writing*. I'd been reading Anglo-American theory before that, I mean in the seventies, women like Greer and Friedan, some of Juliet Mitchell, Elizabeth Gould Davis, and that spoke to me too, in the same way that when I read Simone de Beauvoir's *The Second Sex* in the sixties I just felt devastated, because there was so much that she was naming that I recognized. Always that's the excitement in reading feminist theory – having names and articulations put to what you've been aware of, but you haven't been able to articulate in any clear way. But it was an even greater excitement reading Nicole because she was talking about an approach to writing as a woman. It was the same kind of excitement reading Mary Daly's work with language. So then I got into reading Chodorow's *The Reproduction of Mothering* – I seem to have approached Freudian theory first through the Americans, through Chodorow and, more recently, Dinnerstein. And as I've been circling around the subject of mother for a long time in my own writing, I find the writing these women are doing, talking about what Freud didn't manage to talk about, that pre-Oedipal stage and its extreme influence on us, I find how that links up with Kristeva's sense of the semiotic in language very illuminating.

JANICE: Traces of this fascination appear in your *Ana Historic*. The rapport Annie has with her mother is very powerful and complex. As a woman reader, I recognize the compelling ambivalence of, on the other hand, being nurtured *by* and identifying *with* the mother, and, on the other hand, feeling overwhelmed and repulsed by her.

DAPHNE: That's right, a lot of the feminists who have worked out of Freud's theory talk about this, about how difficult that bond is between the mother and the daughter, because the mother herself is ambivalent towards her daughter; she wants to be nurturing, she wants her daughter to have everything she didn't have, but at the same time she's raising her daughter to accept the limitations of being a woman in a patriarchal society, and so she's always setting limits to her nurturing.

JANICE: How much does the writing free you from ambivalence? I'm thinking of feminist theories of individuation as well as of my own experience as writer and critic. Acknowledging my own ambivalent relationship with my mother and working through to a deeper understanding of her helped empower me to write.

DAPHNE: Oh, I think that's the key: it *is* empowering, and it's such a mishmash of very primal emotion that, well, working with it probably occupies a lifetime. I'm not finished working with it. I had a very close bond with my mother, I realize now looking back to when I was little, and I can actually see in my relationship to her such an appreciation of her femininity that it almost supports Freud's notion (although I dislike this notion because he couldn't recognize a female libido as female; it always has to be modelled on the male libido) of the little girl as the 'little man' courting the mother. I can recognize that behaviour when I look back. But then we went through such a difficult time together during my adolescence when she had such a bad time. We ricocheted away from each other, and she denied me and I denied her, and we never really got back to any kind of *rapprochement* before she died; so writing about her is my way of doing that, of getting to a place where I can feel some of that affection and empathy and understanding. It's a really different bond from the little girl's bond, because my understanding comes from empathizing with her experience as a mother, having had my own experience as a mother. And recognizing in myself the difficulties I had as an immigrant, and seeing how those were magnified for her. I can only realize what we had in common by also expressing where I felt she betrayed me as a mother, because she was in such deep psychological trouble herself that she couldn't go on mothering.

JANICE: You write about memory as overlap. Louky Bersianik writes about 'rites of memory, *memoir*, that is a *portmanteau* word, sometimes mother, mine? and sometimes me, condensed word.' Is there a memory-mine-me-mother in your work?

DAPHNE: I was amazed when I read that passage in Louky, because it reminded me so much of what I was working with in the memory poem ' "abandoned," ' in 'The Month of Hungry Ghosts,' the experience of being back there in Penang so many years later and remembering, and yet not consciously remembering, having a memory that was in the body somehow, but wasn't consciously accessible until I got there. I couldn't have said how to get from A to B, but at a certain point, rounding that corner, I got an immediate flash of what I would see when I got around that corner, and I could not have foretold it until I was in that actual movement around that particular spot. And memory seems to operate like this, like a murmur in the flesh one suddenly hears years later. There is in memory a very deep subliminal connection with the mother because what we first of all remember is this huge body which is our first landscape and which we first of all remember bodily. We can't consciously remember it, but it's there in our unconscious, it's there in all the repressed babble, the language that just ripples and flows – and it isn't concerned with making sense. It's concerned with the feel: the 'feel' of words has something to do with the feel of that body, of the contours of early memory. The wholeness of memory, these early memories that suddenly flash upon you, probably has something to do with the earliest sense of a whole body image, and later, much later, a whole landscape. Anyhow, it's only later that we separate ourselves and everything into subject and object.

JANICE: There's a moment early on in *Ana Historic* when the mother says something like, 'I am not your mother,' and the daughter cries.

DAPHNE: She says, 'Your mother's gone.' Yes, I think that's a very primal experience to have the mother turn into this person who denies that she is the mother figure, that she is the one who is always there, always nurturing, always patient, that figure the child counts on as some kind of basis for existence. It's a very early lesson in language, because she is saying what the child feels has to be impossible, and yet, because she is saying it, language makes it real and her absence is suddenly there as a frightening possibility.

JANICE: Toni Cade Bambara talks about how she's trying to break language open and get to the bone. She's trying to find out not only how a word gains its meaning, but how it gains its power.

DAPHNE: I wouldn't call that 'the bone.'

JANICE: No. What would you call it?

DAPHNE: Well, in *How Hug a Stone* the bone is like the seed, the germ of the word, using that neolithic concept of the bones being planted back into the earth in order to bring forth new life. I saw that bone in the Anglo-Saxon root of the word and wanted to revivify it by putting it in a contemporary context. But in terms of how the word gains power through usage, through time – that's really a history of political usage. Mary Daly did a primary job of renewing certain words for women and showing how they had been turned from their original usage, which didn't involve a negative value, as the oppression of women increased.

JANICE: Thinking about this question of language and power: I was teaching Adrienne Rich's lesbian love poems, and my students were embarrassed about naming the female body and female desire. The power embedded in the classroom made it impossible for them to identify what they have been socialized to ignore, and they simply could not find words.

DAPHNE: Woman's body is never present in its own desire, so if you start writing about it, you have to combat a kind of fear that you feel because you know you're breaking a taboo. Di Brandt has talked about this, and it's something that I recognize very strongly in her work where, in order to make it present, she has to write so-called 'scandalous and heathen' things; scandalous and heathen from a conventional Christian point of view. The only way you can bring the significance of our sexual being into the language is by making it so present that you can't get around it, you can't deny it, you can't euphemize it.

JANICE: It's interesting to me how in some lesbian writing the body is absent, as in Phyllis Webb's *Naked Poems*, where the female body's being is its absence; the furniture is rearranged around a poetics of loss and longing.

DAPHNE: That's true, and the lover's body is also evoked through absence so poignantly by her blouse, those little details. It's like drawing everything around it, and the thing itself becomes simply the white face of the page, its contour outlined by everything around it.

JANICE: There's something different in your lesbian love poems than that absent presence. Your lesbian body is excessively present.

DAPHNE: Yes. Okay – why? It has to do with my attitude to language, I think. I feel language is incredibly sensual. The more musically we move in language, the more sensual it is, I suppose, because, as Kristeva would say, it's the closest that we get to that early sensual experience of fusion with the mother's body. And lesbian eroticism involves this incredible fusion, this merging of boundaries, because our bodies are so similar in their way of touching, of sensing each other, so I'm always wanting my language to somehow bring that into itself, that opulence of two incredibly sensual bodies moving together. I want that movement there in the way the words move.

JANICE: I don't know what I'm going to say after that except to recall a different sensuality: Toni Cade Bambara's 'touch talking.'

DAPHNE: That's it. That's a lovely metaphor for it. There's a kind of push and pull in Touch to My Tongue which has to do with touching even though the book was written against the lover's absence. Most of the poems were written on my way to, and while I was in, Winnipeg – and later in Vancouver when Betsy was ill. They're written with longing, and I suppose longing always does have an aim. Desire as moving towards, and specifically moving towards that arrival point of being together. [The poem] 'down the season's avenue' is the epitome of that, driving down a street here imagining her there. There's always this longing to go where she is, but also there is this conjuring of the actual lovemaking, as a presence that is triumphant because it combats the absence the yearning is trying to do away with, trying to elide, trying to collapse into the moment when I'm together with her and all there is is our being together.

JANICE: I'm wondering, too, if this writing of lesbian desire isn't simply a representation of a transgression of a heterosexist culture.

DAPHNE: It's not 'simply a representation of transgression' because that overlooks desire which is ongoing in this movement towards the other woman's body – it fails to be erased finally when that movement is concluded, it's never concluded, that's the point with desire, especially women's desire. I had that problem structurally with Ana

Historic. Once I had located Annie as a very sexual woman, the writing kept moving towards her actually making love with Zoe, and yet that could only come at the very end of the book, because she had to go through all these shifts of identity and coming to consciousness of what the latent desire really was. Yet I didn't want that final scene to be the end of the story, because it's never the end, it's always the beginning of new stories, so how could I honour that? The only way I could honour that was by moving back into the writing and the reading, using the metaphor of the continual turning of the page as the working of desire. There is always the next page, the next page, even if it's not yet written, it's imminent there. I suppose this has to do with where I put myself against Christianity, which has taught us to defer bliss to life after death. Yet language itself, especially writing, is another kind of deferral. In the humanist tradition it was thought to be a vehicle pointing to what was real beyond the writing. And we've now come to think of it very differently as a signifying process present to itself *within* the writing. To speak of what has been excluded from the world of literature, which is women's desire, and to make that present in a language of presence is a challenge.

JANICE: *Ana Historic* interrogates notions of history as a story of dominance, mastery. In Mrs Richards's journal there's slippage between fiction and historical document. In the novel you write: 'What is a fact, (f)act? the (f) stop of act, a still photo in the ongoing cinerama.' What is the relation between language and women's history?

DAPHNE: If history is a construction and language is also a construction – in fact, it actually constructs the reality we live and act in – then we can change it. We're not stuck in some authoritative version of the real, and for women that's extremely important, because until recently we always were – the patriarchal version was always *the* version, and now we know that's not true. We can throw out that powerful little article. When we change language, we change the building blocks by which we construct our reality or even our past 'reality,' history.

JANICE: I'm interested in Annie as the hysteric Anna O, the German feminist Bertha Pappenhiem treated between 1880 and 1882 by Josef Breuer, who called the psychoanalytic cure 'the talking cure.' Juliet Mitchell writes about women's novels as hysterical, as women's simultaneous acceptance and refusal of patriarchal capitalism. When I first read the excerpts of your novel published in *Writing*, I was in the middle of my own analysis with a feminist psychoanalyst and reading feminist revisions of Freud's work. I was excited by your 'hysterical' narrator, your dreaming voice which opens an interpellation to the reader – 'Who's there?' As a reader, I'm called by Annie. I'm the intruder into your writing asking myself, how did I get here? how do I enter this text? who am I? As a woman reader, I can feel threads of my being pulled through the narrative.

DAPHNE: This brings up the notion of audience: who do you write for, and how does that actually shape the writing. I began to feel that as a very important element of what I identify as feminist writing, and I don't want to say it's the only element or that all feminist writing has to have this, but, as a reader, when I feel that pull, when I feel that I'm being directly spoken to and drawn into what I'm reading, I'm answerable in some way, I create some kind of response to this writing that speaks to my own experience as a woman. When that happens, I am so compelled, I underline these books, I make notes in them, they make me think of my own writing, they give me ideas. I want to open similar spaces for this kind of conversation with readers of my own writing. It makes for a different sense of writing. I first began to feel it maybe in *How Hug a Stone*, because I knew I was working in the mother area, the mother's so strong, and we all have this in common, we all have these ambivalent relationships with our mothers. It has increased with *Touch* and now with *Ana*, and the experiences of reading to that audience last night [29 Nov. 1988, at Common Woman Books] was a delightful experience for me, because in that laughter I could hear so much recognition, and it wasn't the men's laughter I was listening to, it was the women's: it's almost a painful kind of laughter, and it's releasing when you can laugh like that and it's named collectively, then the pain of it begins to dissipate.

JANICE: Not everybody touches you with unconflicted identification. Yesterday we heard Claire Harris read 'Where the Sky Is a Pitiful Tent.' Afterwards Claire talked about her dialogue with Guatemalan revolutionary Rigoberta Menchú's oral testimony and the complex thoughts she had about repeating another woman's story – how, as a Canadian Black woman with Caribbean roots, she related to a Latin

American Indian woman's words in terms of both her difference and her identification.

DAPHNE: Right, and whether she's exploiting it.

JANICE: Whether she's exploiting the other woman's experience and appropriating her world of daily political oppression.

DAPHNE: Perhaps anyone who has felt any oppression at all can use that anger to help her understanding of much worse oppression. You know that you may not have felt anywhere close to the intensity of oppression in Guatemala, but you know as a lesbian what it feels like to live in a patriarchy, and Claire knows as a Woman of Colour what it feels like to be erased by racism. So you're never entirely an outsider. You can certainly question how you're using that material because we have so much privilege, and here my 'we' is a very doubtful we, because as a White woman I have even more privilege than a Woman of Colour living in Canada, but both of us, as women living in Canada, where freedom of speech and the freedom to act are more extensive than in Guatemala, we have this privilege, and yet we also have some consciousness and we know we can build from our own experiences of oppression, we can imagine ourselves into a little bit of that life, and it's very important to do that imagining. Exploitation happens when you as the writer remain on the outside of the experience, but if you can move even a few steps towards the inside – and I don't mean take over, appropriate, someone else's experience, I mean evoke the grief and rage and pain it brings to you as a witness, a person involved, and make that real to others – Claire's poem did that for us.

JANICE: I'm having flashes about the reader and the therapeutic power of writing. Writing as homeopathic, as an inoculation and healing process, a recognition in difference and identity, and as catharsis.

DAPHNE: And that is political.

JANICE: Ah, is that one of the connections between feminist writing and feminist political action?

DAPHNE: I don't think you can have action without consciousness first. Consciousness precedes action, because if you don't act with consciousness you act irresponsibly and you may end up supporting exactly the thing that you're trying to undermine. So you have to have consciousness, and consciousness is constituted by language, so you have to look at the language first of all. It's a very complicated interaction. Changing consciousness by itself isn't enough; you can change the consciousness of individuals, but if they don't get together and act collectively, nothing in the social world changes. So the two have to happen together.

JANICE: You've written poems which are explorations of your own experience in a colonial culture, Malaysia; as a young child, you lived in a very privileged class position. 'In the Month of Hungry Ghosts' explores that experience of trying to find a structure of language to 'carry this being here.' What conflicts do you feel as a writer about an experience which appears intrinsically contradictory?

DAPHNE: I haven't finished exploring this yet; in fact, in some ways I feel as if I've only just begun, and I don't think very clearly. It's difficult to write of my childhood experience or my parents' experience without sounding like an apologist for colonialism, which is definitely not what I want to do. But the issues of racism and classism are so subtly bound into that experience, even though, as a child, I wasn't aware of them − or maybe especially as. The patriarchal oppression of women and colonialism are two different faces of the same coin, and I can see that in my mother, who knew nothing about feminism but was in some ways an instinctive feminist, even in that colonial situation − and despite the really deep habits of classism she also had. I don't think the conflicts of thinking women in a colonial situation have been adequately explored. My mother could identify with the women who were her servants to the extent, on one occasion, of standing up to the Catholic priest who was visiting one of her servants to rail against her, a Tamil woman who was a Catholic and, according to the priest, living in sin because she wasn't married to the man she was living with although she was about to have a child by him. My mother was furious and threw him out of the house and was herself aware, not only of supporting this woman's desire and this woman's lived reality, but also aware of the social system under which Tamil men often left their legal wives in India and came to Malaysia to work, sending money back home to support their families. This might begin as a temporary situation but didn't end up being one because there was no work for them in India and so gradually they made a life for themselves in Malaysia and had another family.

There were also the kinds of conflicts my mother felt being a woman and being limited in the ways a woman is limited in that society to the domestic realm. The resentments that she felt about having a life that had no meaning, that wasn't valued as productive – that was all there. But there was also this, that although my father might be dining out with wealthy Chinese business colleagues, my mother was at home where she was in close touch with the domestic necessities of the Chinese or Tamil women who were working for her and also living with us. For instance, we had a gardener who would get drunk and systematically beat up his wife, and my mother was always trying to figure out how she could intervene in this, respecting the fact that it was, after all, their marriage, and their relationship, and yet trying to stop the beatings. In some senses the colonial women were brought in closer touch with the realities of the lives of colonized people than the colonial men were, and I think they felt the conflicts more deeply and saw the effects of colonialism on a day to day level more clearly than the men did. On the other hand, I don't know what our servants really felt about my mother – I mean, on the surface, there was a feeling of loyalty and this feeling that she was a good 'Mem,' but what did they really think underneath that? I think she used to worry about that too. She wasn't really committed to that system as a way of life and in fact gave it up quite readily, and I think this was because as a woman she had a political awareness my father didn't have – or maybe I should say a disinterest, a political disinterest in upholding the Empire, and I mean 'political' in the broadest sense of power relations.

JANICE: One of the things that comes up when you talk about this colonial setting is the material world. The contradiction you're trying to locate in your mother in this colonial setting is between gender and class. The material conditions of class and race are central to your early work, including *Steveston*. Later gender as an issue becomes predominant. Can we talk about this shift?

DAPHNE: Yes. I suppose what feminism forced me into was an examination of the creation of my female psyche – it was a very inward thing. It forced me to look at childhood, it forced me to take Freud seriously. It forced me to look at the origins of consciousness and how deeply in conflict we are at that level. So in that sense it's a retreat from an analysis of class and race, which are large problems that feminists have to address, and, in fact, the feminist movement has seen that that is number one on the feminist agenda right now. I guess I don't want to be forced into an over-generalized position, one that would say that women's psyches have all been formed in the same way, because clearly they haven't – the historical and class and racial conditions all have a different part to play in shaping us. But maybe this shift has something to do with coming to terms with the actual material of my existence as a writer: language. I had to come to terms with the oldest layer of my language, the language I inherited from my mother, which was generated within certain national class and period mores. Victorian stifling of female sexuality is something that comes under severe attack in *Ana*. I had to come to terms with this before I could do anything else, and I don't really know where I'll go from here.

Edmonton, April 1988

Daphne Marlatt and Betsy Warland

'in companionship with another voice'

JANICE: Daphne, *Double Negative* echoes your previous writing 'The Story, She Said,' which documents a different train ride and a collective process of composition.

DAPHNE: There's a real difference, though, because 'The Story, She Said' occurred amongst eight writers on a train from Vancouver up to Prince George for this Writers' Festival we were doing there. There were three women and five men, and the collaboration became quite competitive, with a strong aspect of game-playing as it went on. We all started off writing, but it lasted for several days, and by the time we were taking the train back, there were only three or four of us, and I was the only woman still writing. I felt frustrated because we weren't so much collaborating as upstaging each other with verbal wit, so whatever narrative there was kept being pulled in different directions. Of course, what other people write always provides a context for how your entry is going to be read, which can be illuminating and fun, but in this case there was alot of contextual conflict. That's why when I got back, I wanted to write my own version of what was going on. But with Betsy, collaborating is much more *collaborative*. For one thing, we were not so much competing with each other as trying to open out the experience of being women together on this train. We both had this project of writing our lesbian bodies into the phallic symbolic of the train. This allowed not only for more sharing, but for a lot more eroticism and joy in the writing. The experience of that writing is more sensory and physical than the experience of the other writing, which is much more head-trippy and resistant on my part.

JANICE: Betsy, how did you work together and maintain two distinct voices within the collaboration?

BETSY: Well, we were on the train for three days, and the two rules that guided us were that we were to alternate entries and read one another's previous entries. The second rule was to refer to the names of the places we were passing through; you had to at least mention one in each poetry entry which makes up the first part of the book. We seemed to make two entries each day, so there were four altogether each day for the three days. It just happened that way. The middle of the book is the interview section, where we talk about wanting to break the frame of the lyric poem, go off track, so we could be free to explore all our sub-textual thoughts that we had set aside because they weren't located within the narrative context of the poem. In the third prose poetry section we take excerpts and phrases from one another's poetry and spark a whole derailing of thought. The interview and prose poetry sections were done in Canada. It was a lot of fun to break the frame ourselves, and to do that twice: to find out what happened when we wrote beyond our own endings.

JANICE: In the notion of collaborative writing I'm concerned with what happens to the autonomous female subject. How do you maintain strength in the particularity of the voice, as well as elaborate a sharing? In collaborative work, do you fear losing the distinctiveness of voice?

BETSY: Yes, I think there is always this fear with anybody who's collaborating, and that's why lots of people don't do it. But, in fact, I don't find that's the case in collaborating with Daphne, and I would like to do more with others as well. I find it actually sharpens my voice, because you're writing both in companionship with another voice, but also to some extent in resistance to it. This continually pushes me beyond my habits in writing and thought. When I'm writing, I never know really where I'm going, and that sense of mystery is doubled in collaboration. Some readers don't distinguish whose voice is whose and some do. Basically I feel it doesn't matter. It probably isn't that important for those who don't distinguish the voices, while for others, who know our voices more intimately, the distinction is important. Part of what this is about is the patriarchal concept of ownership of the written work – which we're calling into question with our collaborative, unmarked texts. What about you?

DAPHNE: Well, a joint project pushes the elaboration of thought. That's where the playfulness comes in, because one of us can be using a word that we play with in a certain way, and the other will see other possibilities and deconstruct it differently. We each bring different ways of reading to the writing, shaped by our differences in background and approach to language. Playing back and forth between these differences actually furthers a collaborative process of thought.

BETSY: In addition to using each other's phrases, there are a number of quotes which float through the text, so there are several voices actually in collaboration with us. This is very much how life is, really.

DAPHNE: I don't know if you can say that they're in collaboration with us, though. We choose them, right? They don't get to choose us.

BETSY: Yes, but we collaborate with what gets said.

JANICE: There have been several recent commentaries by women writers which critique writing which uses postmodernist theory towards feminist ends. Could you comment on this criticism?

DAPHNE: Well, it's a hard thing to talk about, because the ideal is that here we all are feminist writers together in this great project of creating the female subject. But it doesn't work that way, because we all have our differences where we get threatened most. Some other women writers, who either see themselves as feminists or could be called by others feminist because of the themes in their writing, feel they're not living up to or not writing like a number of us who more consciously combine postmodernism and feminism. As soon as you have this kind of feeling, then you have a sense that there's 'moral prescription' going on – or if not moral, at least prescription. That's difficult, because those of us who are writing this way don't feel we are being prescriptive. We're trying to create a space that hasn't existed before. There isn't a conspiracy going on, as we've been told. We each basically are doing our own work, and write quite differently. But because we're breaking new ground, others who are fracturing the language less, or not as radically attacking the patriarchal symbolic embedded in it, feel their writing is devalued in comparison. I feel upset about this because I think there's space for a lot of different kinds of women's writing and we each rewrite the patriarchal real in our own way.

BETSY: I agree that we are breaking new ground, Daphne, but in another respect it's not entirely new ground: we do have the writing of various women writers who started to shape tradition that we're elaborating on. I'm thinking of H.D., Djuna Barnes, Stein, Mina Loy, and Woolf; there's a whole collection of writers who have been quite crucial to our work. I feel angry at the accusation of prescription when, in fact, the women writers who make this charge are also working within traditions, usually the capital T tradition, which is certainly prescriptive and often quite oppressive for women. In an inverview recently it was said that Nicole Brossard is the only 'original' and the rest of us are 'cookie cutters.' I remember living in the United States about twenty years ago when we could have one Black writer, James Baldwin, and that was it – the rest was inferior literature. This is tokenism. It's part of a strategy which silences people who have been marginalized. One is enough – thank you! It's very dangerous. Yes, there are certain writers who seem to be originals, but we don't know until we look back how this all shakes down, and even then it's questionable. It's all relative in terms of your point of view and your values. I would like an honouring of a whole flowering of dialects among women writers and a recognition that we are each developing a dialect, none of which is superior to another. We are all attempting in our particular ways to open up language and writing, to break the constraints we have all suffered from, creatively, psychologically, and socially.

JANICE: With a critical eye informed by such radical relativism, how do you respond to questions of literary value? Traditional academics are always asked how particular writers measure up to the received literary canon.

DAPHNE: That's where it gets really political, because the embedded value system is of the dominant majority, which is the White colonizing majority. We can't apply those standards to all literature without colonizing the differences and saying that the cultures of Native writing or Black writing or lesbian writing have to be replicas of the dominant White male bourgeois culture.

BETSY: If that's the critieria, we can't exist. It's that simple. So we have to come up with other ways of evaluating writing. Part of what I look for is what drives the writing; is it generated out of a felt necessity. Do we need this text? Does it enlarge us? Take us beyond ourselves and our givens – either formally or in terms of content, which usually happen together fo me. Does the writer bring some new slant in their awareness of the communities (literary and social) within which she or he collaborates or resists? We are so inundated with print, to the point of meaninglessness, so as a reader it's essential that I feel this necessity of text. Even if the writing disturbs me.

Edmonton, December 1988

Erin Mouré

Song of a Murmur*

Having been satisfied with the weight of
silver,
having measured with a small spoon the portion
of manganese in the internal heart,
having done this,
having done these things, & more,
having seen to the softest tears of the vagina,
the sickness of the seed which our children have become
because

it is so small living inside of this seed
inside of this air
inside of this latitude of the air
where the air is,

inside of this seed.

———

Having been satisfied with the measurement of the bank
accounting of the rich, who do not recognize us
in these forbidden sweaters,
in these sweaters we have been forbidden,
our mouths above their knitted necks & shoulders speaking

like graffiti on old bridges
this 'like' making sure of the intelligible insistence
of the similar, the architecture of analogy that functions
in the head as thought
that we think 'thought'
in thinking

———

because at first, when I was young, I suffered so
from the cranial dichotomy
I wanted mirth & toast, & accepted to remember
thoroughly
everything
in the permitted strength of original comparison

& no other way
& not to listen to the crying of the seed
where so many of us are living

———

it is cramped space & at night we are kept awake

by the internal heart we have remembered
the deafening splinter in the soil
that will grow into a tree
before we are free of it
By which its cardial insufficiency, oh
reader

———

does your mitral valve flutter?
if so, are you ready to obey it?
three straws for the manganese of your shoulder?
your bank account?
are you satisfied with the weight of it?

if so, are you ready to drop your drawers, sir?

To DM, SH, and others it may concern: *This is a complex poem whose socio-political implications deserve deciphering.*

---

*What the murmur is singing is that the capitalist system, based as it is on individualism and individual greed, separating human beings, stinks.**

Note to people who have difficulty laughing at themselves: the above note explains nothing and is a JOKE. You may well ask: WHAT socio-political implications? It is clear that the poem doesn't have any. Ideology and art don't mix.*

In some schools, jokes are not allowed in poems. And the poet must be very polite, politer than this one, who ends her poem as if to say: get fucked or get your ass kicked. What business is it of hers to adopt this superior tone, appropriate for a seasoned politician, not for a respected artist?*

****However, please remember it is the murmur who is singing this. The poet is only an observer, a private individual, and the murmur is an act of the imagination.

From *Sheepish Beauty, Civilian Love* (Montreal: Véhicule 1992)

Erin Mouré

'my existence whenever
I start to think'

[clatter]

JANICE: OK Erin, so it's Sunday, December the ...

ERIN: Seventh.

JANICE: Seventh, 11:36, and you're making pancakes. 'Domestic Fuel.' [Clatter; banging.] In your letter 'To Speak of These Things' [*Tessera*, 1986], you discuss a movement away from a notion of an 'I,' in quotation marks, and 'the dream of the individual.'

ERIN: Well. I started to get tired. For a long time I fell for it too! There are so many poems that are like − 'I got up, I went outside, I chopped down a tree' or 'I sat down, my friends came over, we had coffee, I feel anguished today.' A poetry of personal anguish that's supposed to somehow transcend the individual ego, but in the end it doesn't and just perpetrates this notion of the 'individual.' What's wrong with perpetrating the notion of the individual? We're all individuals, you say. True, but our correspondences and reflections together are at the base or there are no individuals. The dream of the individual really buys into patriarchal capitalism, as consumption, and so we should get rid of it. [Laughter.] Because it prevents people from speaking out. If everybody's just an individual then people don't take, can't take, responsibility for themselves in a political sense. They start to think − 'I feel this way but I'm the only one who feels this way.' Plus they start worshipping other *individuals* − or only noticing individuals − like even progressive people see something wrong with Reagan but they don't see anything wrong with the American way

of life, the way everything is directed towards individual purchase
and consumption. Life is much more symbiotic than that even in
physics, like in my 'free trade' poem called 'The Producers.' What
separates me from the atoms on this table?

JANICE: A naïve feminist story goes: 'women have been silent.' This
has been criticized by lots of feminists, including Himani Bannerjee,
who talks about how Women of Colour have not been silent at all.
But in 'a culture of the deaf' their voices aren't heard. What do you
have to say about this particularity of voice?

ERIN: The problem is, if we're all only 'individuals' here, some of
us are more 'individual' than others you know, like Ronald Reagan
and Mila ...

JANICE: Mila!

ERIN: Mila!

UNISON: Mila! [Laughter.]

ERIN: [Serious:] Privilege reigns. So that actually this notion of the
individual can suppress difference in the end. We're all interdependent *because* we're different from each other; we need each other.
Women come from different communities, different classes; we have
to valorize each other by making space to listen to others. Not by
making 'individual' noise! Himani Bannerjee is right that listening
is key.

JANICE: What about the lyric voice?

ERIN: I don't want to have the 'one voice' you know. I don't want
to be the big poet speaking 'literature,' getting the sympathy and
nodding heads of readers. You know it's a bad role model.

JANICE: Then how do we recognize Erin the poet?

ERIN: And how are you enjoying the pancakes – they're good eh?

JANICE: Mmm – they're delicious with orange –

ERIN: And maple syrup.

JANICE: Mmm – mandarin oranges –

ERIN: Mm-hm. Um Erin the poet. I don't like Erin the poet very
much. We've always ended up with this language objectifying things
that aren't things ... like Erin the poet really doesn't exist – there's
Erin the woman, Erin the human being, but I'm not like oh, 'you're
Erin the VIA Rail employee.' I mean you write things and people read

them. But then they take them away into themselves [pulling chair, as if to demonstrate], into their lives. [Scraping.] Did you have two last time or one?

JANICE: Two.

ERIN: OK this one here. Whoops! – oh – I don't want to write so that people get something out of my work and next year it's recuperated so that Ronald Reagan can use it in his campaign speech. But poetry *can* start off a kinetic motion inside of readers that makes them think more about themselves. But it's not gonna change the world.

JANICE: What is the relationship between poetry and social change then?

ERIN: I don't think it's possible to talk about poetry in those terms. When poetry starts to have a public relationship with social change, then somebody gets co-opted into one more way of maintaining the patriarchal order. Poetry should bug people. Then *they* can change.

JANICE: In some of your writing you contrast poetry with political newspeak.

ERIN: Poetry exists within the same discourse as newspeak, alas. There's a lot of things written that I don't even bother to call poetry; it's just what I call 'the ego masquerading as the soul.' Real poetry makes you develop a kind of self-critical relationship with language. You can't just use words without thinking of all the cultural and class forces that are in a language. And even the structure of the language divides objects and processes, makes distinctions in thought possible that aren't *there*, really. You end up objectifying things like space and time. I mean time is a noun. Objectified! Phase is a name. But is it an object? Touch is a name. But touch is an *action*, I mean, it exists in time then stops existing. *Naming* all these 'durations' or 'movements' that aren't *objects* at all brings thought to a point where it's co-opted by the public order again. Using language unthinkingly, then, maintains its hierarchial power. Its power to close off and isolate *relationships* as *things*. Separate. Individual, again! [Dishes clattering.] Language organizes things and, like a camera, leaves out so much. As soon as you speak a sentence, you've left out every other possible sentence. The organization of structures, whether it's a social structure, a political structure, or whatever, should evolve according to need, which is why friendship is so interesting because the structure evolves simply according to need. There's never more structure than is needed. Two people don't meet and say well who's gonna be president of the board of directors. That's jumping from one end of the spectrum to the other, but that's what you end up with when you create these social and political organizations because language simplifies too much. But we're afraid. We don't wanna exist on the edge of confusion where our boundaries might not be distinguishable from the boundaries of this table ...

JANICE: Well how do you ...

ERIN: They're only distinguishable because we objectify space and time. Otherwise you could interview this table. It would be fun. You would like it! You could interview this pancake.

JANICE: A morbid prospect.

ERIN: In my job I tell people over and over you *have* to exist on the edge of confusion, in order to find what we *need*, instead of deciding what we need in advance and then trying to fit in all our expectations. [Banging.]

JANICE: How do you feel about –

ERIN: Embarrassed.

JANICE: ... your poetry intersecting with a community of women readers involved in the women's movement, activists and ...

ERIN: My readers? Oh I like them all! Poetry is sound, and I can't just listen to the sound of my own ego; that's like the sound of one hand clapping. I absorb things from my environment, from what other people say; I mean I can't think all on my own. I don't get any further in my thinking if I just do it all by myself, and that's what's important about women readers, their responses. If you can get out of this hierarchical notion of the poet who is now going to tell you all something ... The poem is part of the organic process of the whole community that congeals or is visible or evolves or comes together as a group of sounds, a process that moves on. What appears on the page is just a record of those sounds. My poetry's been getting messier and messier because in a poetic like this there's lots of room for mistakes. This is what's starting to get me away from the notion of the poem that starts at the top of the page and ends at the bottom with a punch-line.

JANICE: In 'The Jewel' perspective is shattered. There is no resolution that isn't in the act of reading itself.

ERIN: Mmhm. I'm not recording everything for posterity or catching things that don't belong to me. 'The Jewel' is interesting as a poem because it's part of a diversity of voices, a diversity of expression, a community of writing. What makes this poem interesting is what other people are doing or not doing, not 'me the poet.' A very weird looking thing, this pancake.

JANICE: What did you put in here – is it – it's not nuts?

ERIN: Sesame seeds. It's healthy.

JANICE: I'm trying to get at this notion of accessibility –

ERIN: Oh you are – well why didn't you just say so?!? Let me tell you about accessibility – [scraping] want some more?

JANICE: Um yeah – but that's my limit.

ERIN: OK. They're looking weird but they're OK. My poetry is very –

JANICE: Is your poetry becoming more 'inaccessible,' the more multi-faceted it becomes?

ERIN: Accessible is just a way of reading; we're all taught to read, so that we can read the newspaper, you know, and become 'consumers,' also known as 'citizens.'

JANICE: Barthes calls that reading 'the already read.'

ERIN: The argument for accessibility in poetry goes like this: nobody buys poetry; it's hard to market because nobody understands it. Why don't they understand it? They don't understand it because it's not accessible. Some poets jump into this discourse and they say, well then we'll just have to make poetry accessible. But you can't start off with this marketing question – 'Why don't people buy poetry?' – follow a certain line of logical thinking, and afterwards go out and write accessible poetry. That's how they figured out how to write Harlequin romances, but why should poetry be like that? The words are so powerful; they catch forces, things, processes, feelings as sounds. In fact, I think poetry has an influence even on people who don't read it. Books influence people who don't read them!

JANICE: [Surprised:] How do they do that?

ERIN: Just by existing. They just take up this much air. [Indicates.] They have an influence. They bug people who don't read them! I don't see why we should tap into the way that people read the newspaper. That's how people get trapped inside this house of language that is actually diminishing them, their differences, which are also their connections. If we are just accessible, then a lot of questions, important questions about structures, don't come up. I was talking with this friend of mine, Lou Nelson, who is taking this course in feminist ethics, and she's trying to argue through the whole course that you can't have a class in feminist ethics because you're just tapping into the same thinking set-up of other ethics. I guess you can have a class called 'feminists-talk-about-ethics' or a class called 'feminist-approaches-to-ethics,' but if you have 'feminist ethics,' then you're attaching the way feminists do things into this whole dynamic that is, really, opposed to feminism. If you put all arguments on the same road map, it is going to alter your perception of the terrain.

JANICE: Mmhm. It's going to structure it.

ERIN: Yeah. Even if you're saying, oh, no, we're not going into this with a ready-made structure, folks, it's still going to structure. I was a major in philosophy at university before I dropped out, so I had to take an ethics course, the structure of which I couldn't stand. Are you trying to get me onto another topic?

JANICE: OK no.

ERIN: No are you trying to?

JANICE: No, well there is no topic. I'm just trying to catch up with some of the things I was thinking about while you were talking. You talk about the sound value of poetry, and Nicole Brossard talks about the problematic status of a lot of Anglo-Canadian women's writing which is as she says 'story-story-story.' Last night we saw a film by Kay Armatage, *Storytelling*, where you could see the stories embodied in these storytellers' bodies, their gestures, pauses, and histories. The narratives broke each other apart. Armatage did her doctoral thesis on Gertrude Stein, who said ...

UNISON: 'A narrative is any one thing following any other.'

JANICE: As a poet how do you deal with 'story' –

ERIN: Well I think the narrative is any one thing following ...

JANICE: ... any other.

ERIN: I like confusion myself. I think we should have more confusion. Anybody who says a story has this kind of progression, that kind of progression, this kind of progression, is putting a structure onto the story before the story happens that maybe the story doesn't need; it's going backwards. That kind of process of story is the same process as having a board of directors for your thinking before you've even figured out if your organization needs a board of directors. It's like creating this massive structure and then waiting to dismiss things that don't fit in with it. I see it in my dealings with people at work and how we can work together to serve the passengers on a train, and I have spent a lot of time on trains off by myself trying to supervise these people inside this train, this narrow 'world.' Because social structures are left behind to some extent on the train, I was able to think about some of these things. The storytelling impulse is older practically than human beings, something like forty thousand years old. Story is a way of connecting new information to old, altering our perception of experience, and even of memory. A dogmatic, static approach to poetry can distort even memory! We've been telling stories to each other forever. Yet story can be a very organic process because people can say, yes, I belong to this part of it, I recognize that, and then they can integrate the whole of what's being said into the whole of their experience. I notice when I teach adults to supervise that when you teach leadership styles everyone wants to tell stories about the railway. 'I remember when this happened and this and this happened.' The new information gives them the impulse to tell the story, which means to the instructor that they're working through in a verbal and auditory way what you've just told them about leadership styles. They're integrating it somehow into their body by making these sounds. Now I'm off on another little track: that sound. Here's a story: I went to physiotherapy for my back and the physiotherapist told me how I should be making sounds when I'm doing breathing exercises because sounds have an effect on how well your organs work; organs actually absorb different sounds and different sounds help different organs, like the noise of the letter a helps the lungs.

JANICE: What do you think about Brossard's comment about most Anglo-Canadian poetry as 'story-story-story'? It's something other than that.

ERIN: She's talking about anecdote in a particular way. I think she's saying the same thing as I am when I talk about the ego masquerading as the soul, like 'I got up, I went outside, I chopped down a tree, I went to the store,' – you know. Also in English poetry there seems to be a separation between ideas and actions, as if ideas weren't actions or thinking isn't acting. Maybe it has to do with the sound of French. In English we're always so dispassionate when we talk about ideas. In French you can really get emotionally involved in ideas. I too have written 'story-story-story.' I still have the impulse to write like that occasionally.

JANICE: What do you do with that impulse?

ERIN: I mostly stop it because it goes nowhere. I look at what I've written and I ask what's the real poem? I'll sometimes end up with a word or a line and I say that's it, that's where I touched on something. That's where the nerve is. If I pull at that, I'll find where the poem is. It's like my ex's landlord went out in his yard one day and there was a piece of metal sticking out of the lawn. So he pulled at it, you know, he pulled at it and it got longer and longer and it was kinda half coiled; it got about this long and he still couldn't pull it out of the ground. So he went and got his deep-sea fishing rod that he used to fish hundreds of pounds of sharks or some goddamn thing, and he went out there and he was trying to fish this metal out of the ground and he pulled and pulled and he couldn't do it; so he went and rented a tractor and he hooked it up to the metal and put the cable around a tree and pulled and what came out was a whole mattress, its springs under the lawn. His house was built in an area that used to be a dump and this mattress had worked its way upward through the landfill. All the cloth part of it had gone; there was just the metal, and then one day a little spring of it came out of his lawn and he thought, 'I can't have that there where it will wreck my lawn-mower.' That's the process of writing poetry. When I write something that turns into the lawn, I say, 'Well, where's the mattress spring?' And then I discard the lawn and just save the mattress spring to pull on later. And then I end up with something different in the poem. Homer would roll in his grave if he heard me talking about this mattress. But then things all actually have to do with each other, organically in the brain. Memory plays in sets of neurons that are in a sheet form, and can be triggered by what happens over here, in the sheet beside it. If one area in the brain is really overstimulated, the sheets of memory can be altered, even if they're only 'close by.'

JANICE: You talk about memory in your *Tessera* essay. Is memory palimpsestic? Your writing is a bit like recuperating what's been rubbed away through writing and over-writing.

ERIN: In showing the parts where something's rubbed away, you can see part of what's underneath in conjunction with what's on top. And you can see the part that's rubbed smooth. To have the under-layer and what's on top, at the same time! You can accept the surface or you can try and pull the underneath of it if you want, but ...

JANICE: What's specific about women remembering? Earlier you told me about your mother's linoleum wearing away where she stood in front of the sink. The linoleum became a written text where her body's work was inscribed. I was swept away by the nostalgia of this bitter-sweet story until you laughed and told me how your mother went out and got a job and came back and put new linoleum down.

ERIN: Women and remembering. Since there are structures of thought, we forget certain things because they're not acknowledged in the structure as important. But really we haven't forgotten them; they're still there, encoded. If you don't remember them, they do sort of get rubbed away, so you have to call them back. But then what are you going to do with it? You're just gonna end up with material; you'll end up with a thing, turn the story into a thing, and it'll become a story-story-story. As women, we're sometimes in danger of that. We'll recall our own stories as if only a certain view of the personal is political. People sometimes think of language as just a 'thing' to use. They forget in recalling stories that they're encoded in language and ways of speaking and that *those* have to be examined as well. Memories are there, though some of them seem to have been rubbed away. They are accessible to us and we should do something about them, but we have to examine the language at the same time. And also examine our own class and race and how they colour our perceptions and anxieties. Certain ways of thinking are open to me because of who I am and where I come from. There are a lot of things that I still have trouble understanding because of the way I was brought up.

JANICE: How were you brought up?

ERIN: Well, some people can always tell who's a WASP and who isn't, and I can't, except I know some people I thought were just people from Ontario. It's this uptightness or something that WASPs are supposed to have that I can't tell. My mother told me when I was growing up that there were English- and French-speaking people in Canada. So I thought everybody was English and French! I didn't know what French was, but my Dad said they said 'avec jambon' and other things, which we didn't say. We lived on the south side of the Bow River and spoke English, so I thought that French-speaking people must live and speak French on the north side of the Bow River. That was my image of Calgary. If people had Ukrainian names, I didn't realize that they had different names, that they weren't 'English.' Growing up in the West, there was never this history of the WASPs or Loyalists. Though we had Louis Riel and Bishop Grandin. What really bugs me about Loyalists was some of the early Loyalists were the Nova Scotian Blacks, who still live in poor housing and still have lousy access to jobs and are still treated like shit by the mainstream structures. In Ontario a big tourist celebration about Loyalists doesn't say anything about *these Loyalists*. Bugs me. [Whistling sounds.] We have to go.

JANICE: OK wait. OK I just have – I wanna ask something about –

ERIN: We're gonna run out. Ask fast!

JANICE: I wanna ask you something about desire in writing; in narrative there's memory, and then there's desire – an in your poems, ah, 'Like the Rain' and 'Gale Force,' in particular, poems that give words to lesbian desire. I love the line where you talk about how you dream of women's 'tough reusable wings.' These aren't texts of lesbian victimization, but of strength, of versatile wings, of toughness. Even in the sections of your writing where you are clearly writing love poems, there's a sense of mutuality without loss of identity or merging. You spoke earlier about your dis-ease with the 'individual,' but in some other lesbian writing, there's a sense of merging and absolute symbiosis. You avoid this. How?

ERIN: Oh, you mean sometimes everybody turns into amoebas and trot off into the sunset.

JANICE: Yeah, amoebic dissonance.

ERIN: Oh, just amoebic. Amoebas aren't dissonant! I don't think of things as merging or loss. I think of it as heightened, as opening up all your pores so that you can see out of all different parts of your body instead of just having ... some parts 'sexual' and some not. It's heightened sensitivity from and in all of the body. We're interdependent bodies, too, and if we're interdependent, that implies 'more than one thing' or you don't have any need for 'inter.' That's how individuals come into the picture, for me. You give expression to each other in this space wherein you're both speaking. And speaking not just being words, but we speak differently out of different areas of the body. I think that all our cells can see. That they can all speak, too.

[later]

JANICE: OK Erin, now it's dinnertime, and instead of pancakes it's eggplant parmesan.
ERIN: And I'm grating cheese.
JANICE: And you're grating the cheese. We just went to see the launching of Dorothy Hénault's film *Fireworks*, otherwise known as *Les Terribles Vivants*, after Louky Bersianik. A more literal translation might be 'the furies.' Your next book of poems, *Furious*, is still in manuscript form. But how much of *Furious* is informed by the furies and how does rage engage your work?
ERIN: I actually never intended the title to be taken as 'rage.' Still, *Furious* has a rapport with rage. I think there is a lot of rage in my work, because people tell me that. But it's an undercurrent, something that I'm not consciously working on. I mean I am mad, I'm mad. [Very softly:] Pissed off.
JANICE: Why?
ERIN: I'm consciously working through my anger, but I'm not using it as a device at all. But 'furious' as a title is meant like Snoopy when he's writing a poem on top of his doghouse and he says, 'The author was sitting at his table writing furiously.' That's the kind of furious that is like ... furiously doing something furiously.
JANICE: Passionately.
ERIN: Intensely. Impulsively. When you said it would be a good

translation for *Les Terribles Vivants*, I thought, you're right, it's '*terrible*'; it's a terrible compliment to say that. What I mean by 'furious' is to be terribly terrifyingly alive. *Furious* is radically different from my other poetry because I'm working, progressing, and changing. The title actually comes from a word in 'Hooked,' which is a more traditional poem than a lot of the others, a love poem. It talks about how two women in love are publicly displayed even if you're in your own home, where you can't kiss because the neighbour might see. You're always visible like you're in an aquarium. You can't walk outside and give each other a big hug. There's one line in it, 'the wounds you bear because of my furious glances.' But I mean those glances to be terribly alive in my work, not angry.

JANICE: But why shouldn't you be enraged and angry about your vulnerability to others' homophobia?

ERIN: Why do you think I'm mad? To never have one's difference acknowledged! Except in terms of the structures of heterosexual desire ... not to mention having one's partner excluded from benefit plans and so on!

JANICE: Is your writing addressed to women readers?

ERIN: How does one address to cats?

JANICE: *Rapport d'addresse. Rapport de mouse.* Do you address yourself to particular readers?

ERIN: This afternoon, Nicole [Brossard] said there's a reader looking over your shoulder and a reader out there you're going towards. I don't feel that in my writing. I feel sort of a sense of a reader, a reader who is part of myself too. Who am I addressing? I'm talking to women, and if I'm talking to men that's I think when my furious, my terrible aliveness, becomes rage. Because I have this strong sense that there are lots of problems right now with heterosexual love. Men don't acknowledge their love for each other in the same way that women do. A lot of heterosexual love is men using women as an intermediary to get at their love for each other. What's displayed in pornography, for example, is men's love for each other through this object which is woman. I perceive my audience as mostly women. When men like it or want to read it or comment on it, that's OK with me, but I don't perceive them as my audience anymore because I'm tired. They're my audience at VIA Rail. I have to deal with them all day there, and that's fine but when I come home and write, excuse me, I'm tired of it. [Sizzling frying sounds.]

JANICE: Does your particular rapport with women readers orient you in terms of the subject matter of your work?

ERIN: The books are just as accessible to men as to women. I don't shut them out. I think my subject matter is sort of everywhere at once, 'cause I talk about political things. It's when I think about men's role that I'm not talking to them any more. There's only one way to talk to them and that's if you're pretty much like them or acceptable to them. I went through the trap of being acceptable to all these men. I was held up as a woman writer who's progressive but is swell about men. I started to realize that I was letting myself be used. I don't know how you can ever describe this in a written interview but there's something there. I suddenly realized that I was being used, so that they didn't have to question themselves.

JANICE: Did this discovery come about during your participation in the symposium 'Split Shift,' which focused on the topic of work? In your statement of poetics and the talk you gave there, you were very explicit in saying, 'After all, the work we do is not the reality of our lives, but one part of us that we live as integrated, intermingled, with our own desires. What of our erotic selves, our mortal souls, our search for spirit in the muscle light of others, ourselves and others.' You're trying to recuperate an integrative category 'work' ...

ERIN: ... as it is perceived by them; it's often disfunctional. I think 'work poetry,' as they say, has a lot of validity to people in terms of the sociology of work. That kind of poetry *is* important for people to become aware of themselves and their relationship to their jobs and their work. If it's accessible like the newspaper's accessible, it's probably OK to some extent. But, curiously, when I've read poems to people who work at VIA Rail, they may recognize themselves in the work poems but the poems they're really moved by or that they relate to and can integrate into their lives *aren't those poems*. Part of the problem is the class thing, of saying 'what we have to do for these workers is make writing accessible like the newspaper.' It's really speaking from the position of the privileged, and talking down to people, in effect. It's patronizing.

JANICE: So to categorize writing in terms of work would be a very different process for a feminist because you would have to take into account –

ERIN: Existence.

JANICE: Yeah, all kinds of work – like reproductive work and domestic work ...

ERIN: And more than work! We aren't *separate* from the work we do! And if anything is work, then why isn't *theory*, 'cause theory is work too. But if only surface 'job' work is validated as real work, then we get: 'I got up, I went outside, I chopped down a fucking tree!' 'I came inside, I took off my boots.' And like, a lot of work poetry is that, the story-story-story anectodal mode. There are fewer women work poets because women I don't think see their experience in those terms. In Vancouver Phil Hall and I had that struggle sometimes, over a series called 'Work to Write.' [Scraping.] We'd organize poetry readings every year and invite two men and two women. [Sizzling.] At first some other members of the group wanted to look for women who wrote of 'work' in a particular way. But finally the women we invited, like Libby Scheier and Bronwen Wallace, talked about reproductive work and various kinds of work in *their* way.

JANICE: What does theory have to do with work?

ERIN: Theory has to do with the act of thinking. [Chopping.] It's a way of acting and a way of doing, a process; it's not a thing that exists out there which you academics own. A lot of people think it is. I get mad. I'm an ex-smoker, you know. The worst people to be down on smoking, as everybody knows, are ex-smokers 'cause only an ex-smoker can know how stupid it is to smoke. I'm an ex-person-who-thought-theory-was-all-academic. I used to go through this touchy-feely relation to my poetry, which was about *me feeling things*.

JANICE: What made you change your feelings about theory?

ERIN: It was through meeting feminist writers, and particularly Gail [Scott], whose experience in the Left had made her think about things in a rigorous way, and valorize that thinking. 'Theory' wasn't over there with oh ... Robert Kroetsch at the University of Manitoba; it was here and now, happening.

JANICE: How has theory informed your work poems?

ERIN: 'The Jewel' was a work poem! If I didn't have to work, I never would have written it. Thing is, once we start to really write work poems, a real work poem, then 'work' becomes no longer useful as a category.

JANICE: Why is 'Jewel' a work poem?

ERIN: 'Cause it talks about a woman's rapport with her body, and her attempt to be different in that office environment, to distinguish anything of her 'self' in that environment. It's about coming to terms with who you are in terms of your own memory and in terms of sexuality itself, which is always present but has to be 'suppressed' at work. To me sexuality isn't a person in a kimono lounging on the bed. Sexuality permeates existence and it permeates my existence in that office. I have to come to terms with it. In 'The Jewel' I lie there, I fold up my pajamas, I put them away gently to go to the office. But I have to come to terms with my memory and its relationship to the present tense. Memory is what makes the past present in *the present*. It's important to have memory, but I have to displace that memory from my head into this office, and I have to displace this sexual-remembering-person-that-I-am into this office. The poem ends with the facts that permeate my existence whenever I start to think – 'it's bloody time to go work.' The last little section of 'The Jewel' is 'I have to go to the office, I have to get dressed.' It's this whole paranoid thing I go through. 'I have to look nice.' 'I have to do this.' I have to wear nice pants because these pants here, for example, are not acceptable in an office; they're too casual. So I iron the shit out of the clothes I own and starch them, and they kind of fade out for a while, so [pause]. This is my life.

JANICE: Right.

ERIN: This is why I drink. [Sound of clinking glasses.] As my friend Lou says, 'Welcome to reality.'

Montreal, December 1986

M. Nourbese Philip

Discourse on the Logic of Language

English
is my mother tongue.
A mother tongue is not
not a foreign lan lan lang
language
l/anguish
    anguish
– a foreign anguish.

English is
my father tongue.
A father tongue is
a foreign language,
therefore English is
a foreign language
not a mother tongue.

What is my mother
tongue
my mammy tongue
my mummy tongue
my momsy tongue
my modder tongue
my ma tongue?

I have no mother
tongue
no mother to tongue
no tongue to mother
to mother
tongue
me

I must therefore be tongue
dumb
dumb-tongue
dub-tongued
damn dumb
tongue

Edict 1

Every owner of slaves
shall, wherever possible,
ensure that his slaves
belong to as many ethno-
linguistic groups as
possible. If they can-
not speak to each other,
they cannot then foment
rebellion and revolution.

Those parts of the brain chiefly responsible for speech are named after two learned nineteenth century doctors, the eponymous Doctors Wernicke and Broca respectively.

Dr. Broca believed the size of the brain determined intelligence; he devoted much of his time to 'proving' that white males of the Caucasian race had larger brains than, and were therefore superior to, women, Blacks and other peoples of colour.

Understanding and recognition of the spoken word takes place in Wernicke's area – the left temporal lobe, situated next to the auditory cortex; from there relevant information passes to Broca's area – situated in the left frontal cortex – which then forms the response and passes it on to the motor cortex. The motor cortex controls the muscles of speech.

THE MOTHER THEN PUT HER FINGERS INTO HER CHILD'S MOUTH – GENTLY FORCING IT OPEN; SHE TOUCHES HER TONGUE TO THE CHILD'S TONGUE, AND HOLDING THE TINY MOUTH OPEN, SHE BLOWS INTO IT – HARD. SHE WAS BLOWING WORDS – HER WORDS, HER MOTHER'S WORDS, THOSE OF HER MOTHER'S MOTHER, AND ALL THEIR MOTHERS BEFORE – INTO HER DAUGHTER'S MOUTH.

but I have
a dumb tongue
tongue dumb
father tongue
and english is
my mother tongue
is
my father tongue
is a foreign lan lan lang
language
l/anguish
  anguish
a foreign anguish
is english –
another tongue
my mother
    mammy
    mummy
    moder
    mater
    macer
    moder
tongue
mothertongue

tongue mother
tongue me
mothertongue me
mother me
touch me
with the tongue of your
lan lan lang
language
l/anguish
  anguish
english
is a foreign anguish

A tapering, blunt-tipped, muscular, soft and fleshy organ describes
(a) the penis.
(b) the tongue.
(c) neither of the above.
(d) both of the above.

In man the tongue is
(a) the principal organ of taste.
(b) the principal organ of articulate speech.
(c) the principal organ of oppression and exploitation.
(d) all of the above.

The tongue
(a) is an interwoven bundle of striated muscle running in three planes.
(b) is fixed to the jawbone.
(c) has an outer covering of a mucous membrane covered with papillae.
(d) contains ten thousand taste buds, none of which is sensitive to the taste of foreign words.

Air is forced out of the lungs up the throat to the larynx where it causes the vocal cords to vibrate and create sound. The metamorphosis from sound to intelligible word requires.
(a) the lip, tongue and jaw all working together.
(b) a mother tongue.
(c) the overseer's whip.
(d) all of the above or none.

From *She Tries Her Tongue; Her Silence Softly Breaks* (Charlottetown: Ragweed / Gynergy Books 1989)

M. Nourbese Philip

'writing a memory of losing that place'

JANICE: You've recently published two books. One is a novel, *Harriet's Daughter*, written in a form accessible to teenagers. Your new collection of poetry, *She Tries Her Tongue; Her Silence Softly Breaks*, is innovative in form and addresses different readers. You're developing a very wide readership through these different genres of writing. bpNichol had a way of talking about writers on a non-hierarchical continuum from language researchers to popularizers. Your own writing seems to replicate this continuum from language research to more popular writing strategies.

NOURBESE: I have two books of poetry prior to *She Tries Her Tongue ...*, *Thorns* and *Salmon Courage*. It's important to understand that *She Tries Her Tongue ...* came out of a particular period. I decided to stop practising law, and that becomes very relevant because I felt I needed large unbroken chunks of time within which to work. Out of this period came this work and another companion manuscript called 'Looking for Livingstone: An Odyssey of Silence' [published in 1992 by Mercury Press]. It started out as the last poem in *She Tries Her Tongue ...* but grew so long it became a book in its own right. It deals with the idea and concept of silence which presented itself after I delved so deeply into language in *She Tries Her Tongue...* One of the reasons I got into writing fiction was that I felt that I couldn't earn a living writing poetry. I wanted to spend my time writing, and I thought – and I still believe – that we no longer live in an age of poetry. I think poetry requires a certain kind of attention that very few people today have or are prepared to cultivate. Still, being very committed to poetry, I thought that if I got into writing fiction I stood a better chance of earning a living to pay for my habit, which is writing poetry. On the surface that's one of the reasons. I say 'on the surface' because the issues in the poetry also surface in my fiction, in a completely different way, of course. For instance, in *Harriet's Daughter* I have the young girl, who's the main protagonist, telling a friend who's just come up from the Caribbean that she wants to be bilingual. She wants to learn Tobago talk, and what I realized only very recently was that the entire book is, in fact, a metalanguage. One of the things that I have argued is that writers coming from the Caribbean inhabit a spectrum of language – Caribbean English. It's neither dialect nor standard English. *Harriet's Daughter* is evidence of how one inhabits this spectrum. It's not something I was conscious of when I was doing it, but various characters in the book speak in various registers and styles ranging from the very stiff, staid kind of English that I learned when I grew up back there to 'dialect,' what I now call demotic language. I began writing fiction also because I was very concerned at the time I began *Harriet's Daughter* that there weren't enough good books for young Black people. My son was a teenager at that point, and I thought, well, why don't I try and write something! So my motivation to write fiction ranges from the political, like providing more and better literature for coming generations of Black people, to what we can say is maybe a more crass reason, trying to earn a living at writing. I suspect more than those reasons are at work in terms of fiction because I'm presently working on another fictional work, and I have a sense that much of my engagement with fiction is a very personal exploration and process of learning.

JANICE: In the context of patriarchal language women adopt a kind of double-speak. Is this parallel to what you are talking about as the Caribbean spectrum of language?

NOURBESE: That's an interesting question, and I don't think I have an answer to it in terms of the Caribbean *yet*. And I say 'yet' because what I was particularly engaged with in *She Tries Her Tongue* ... was subverting in a very conscious way all the traditions of poetry. Poetry came to us in the Caribbean as another form of colonization and oppression. So, for instance, in the poem 'Discourse on the Logic of Language' I set out to subvert the poem itself. Usually a poem is centred on the page with the margins at both sides clearly demarcated. Also there is the prescription of certain traditions like Eliot's objective correlative: you remove the poem from its morass of history, so to speak, clean it of its personal clutter, and anyone anywhere ought to be able to identify with and understand it. I deliberately set out to put the poem, that particular poem, back in its historical context, which is what poetry is not supposed to do. The centre-piece of this poem is an unbroken refrain on the ambivalence of English being both a mother and father tongue; I surrounded that with a short story of a mother blowing words into the mouth of her newborn daughter – this I ran along the left-hand margin of the page; on the right margin I placed historical edicts about African slaves being prohibited from speaking their mother tongues and having their tongues removed for breach of this edict. On the pages facing the poem – it runs for two pages – I have a physiological description of how speech takes place and a series of multiple-choice questions. I haven't forgotten your question; I'm coming back to it. What I was mainly concerned with in 'Discourse ...' was the colonizing experience – how what we call a mother tongue, in this instance English, was, when you traced its lineage, really a father tongue, in that it was the White male colonizer bringing us language. In that sense there are parallels with the feminist project of delineating a 'patriarchal' language. But in terms of the language in which I believe very strongly – the Caribbean demotic – in which the people in the street have loved, lived, hated, and spend their life, a language which the aspiring middle classes shunned, I really can't say that that language is less patriarchal. It is certainly less White – Euro-centric, if you will – since so many of its tonal, linguistic, and rhythmic resources are African.

JANICE: In *Harriet's Daughter* the protagonist talks about Harriet Tubman. And your new book of poems 'And over Every Land and Sea,' begins with the mythological daughter Persephone, a story of a regenerative feminine history. You dedicate your recent poetry book 'For all the mothers.' Can you talk about this mother/daughter genealogy and the particular connections you make in your writing?

NOURBESE: Part of my hesitation in answering is because that is a pretty loaded area for me. It's loaded on several levels. The first poem where Ceres and Persephone play their part, 'Questions, Questions,' was conceived when I went back to Tobago for the first time after many many years. Given the fact that I was born there and only spent my first eight years in Tobago, it plays a very important part in my writing life. I think that is where my writing comes from, and what set the poem going was some memory of losing that place. There's also, I believe, some personal stuff within my own experience around the emotional loss of my mother, which I believe many women experience. I think those two experiences came together in that poem. On a still larger level – beyond the personal – is the leitmotif of seeking and returning to the mother as in the motherland, Africa, that continually plays a part in almost all writing by New World Africans. In *Le Pays Natal* Haitian Québécois writer Max Dorsinville advances the argument that this archetype of a search for and return to the lost mother is found in the work of many writers of African heritage living outside Africa or even those from Africa. Loss and return play an important part in their writings, and sometimes as in the case of writers like Aimé Césaire and Maryse Condé, there's actually a physical return. There are three levels on which that archetypal configuration plays itself out: for what I call 'Afrosporic' peoples, there's the greater loss of Africa; then in a more personal sense, the lost place that for some unknown reason I was and am very close to; and in a much more immediate way, the loss of familial relationships caused by emigration, which you see cropping up in both the fiction and poetry.

JANICE: When you talk about this multi-levelled relation to archetypal structures, it's clear that your writing experience and myth-making would be enriched by a reading informed by diasporic writing. Margaret Atwood's first book of poems, *Double Persephone*, and Daphne Marlatt's rewriting of the Persephone myth in *Touch to My Tongue* ... create different Persephone figures. How do you see your writing in the context of traditional Canadian literary studies and Caribbean studies?

NOURBESE: That's an important question. People talk about *She Tries Her Tongue* ... as postmodernist. It certainly on the surface has that kind of sensibility, but I never set out to write a postmodernist work, and while I was conversant with it, I certainly wasn't immersed in it. I'm not saying that my work can't be read or analysed in terms of something like postmodernism, but if one only sees it in that way, one loses a lot of the fundamentals which give rise to it. For instance, one loses sight of the Caribbean and the New World, which for me represent massive interruptions in time for different people – for the aboriginal peoples, whose time was permanently interrupted, for the Africans and Asians who were brought there, and even for the Europeans who came. I never seem able to write anything through from start to finish without interrupting it somehow by some other discourse. Some other voice is continually interrupting. That's the historical and social matrix from which my writing is partly coming. It's in touch with or resonating with that historical material. Also, growing up in the Caribbean, you grow up knowing that you're going to leave home. For one thing, the societies are too small to absorb all their trained people, so you have to leave. On a psychic level you are continually looking elsewhere; nothing that is immediately around you is ever looked at with a sense that 'this is valid, this is where it's at,' so to speak. These circumstances can and did lead to a lot of negativity. In a more positive light, the interruptions that I mentioned earlier can be seen as part of the African musical tradition, particularly that of jazz, where you might have the main riff going and the musician interrupts and goes off on another musical path. It wouldn't surprise me if that tradition is there in the work. So, I live in Canada. And what am I doing writing this kind of stuff [laughter]? I was thinking the other morning that I had never written a poem about winter. It's very interesting! It's true. The closest I've come to it is a poem called 'E. Pulcherrina' from my first book, *Thorns*. It's about the poinsettia being forced to bloom, overseas, and while winter is implied, it's never mentioned. But I've never written a poem about winter and how cold or hard I find it. I think it's because my imaginative life doesn't take place here. I suppose *Harriet's Daughter* is maybe the closest I have come to placing myself here in an imaginative sense. But it *is* a novel of return because Zulma, one of the girls on whom the novel focuses, wants to go back. The critical problem in terms of the Canadian literary scene is what do writers like myself do – writers who come to a new land with imaginative and psychic resources formed already? How do you begin to mediate between where you've come from and what's going on here. And is the scene here relevant to us? Canada is unique when compared to the States or England. Both of these places have strong traditions of Black writing and Black literature. Canada doesn't, although it is being formed now by people like Maxine Tynes, Claire Harris, myself, Dionne [Brand], George Elliott Clarke, Lillian Allen, and others. It will be interesting to see what comes out of this work. As a Black writer, it has been very painful to survive here – where there was nothing that you could either resist or go along with as a tradition. There is a danger of falling into the void and just giving up. But if you come through that, the work becomes stronger for that reason. If I had gone to the States or England, I don't think I would have written *She Tries Her Tongue* ... In both those countries the tradition of Black writing is so strong that I would have had to come to terms with it somehow in my writing. In a sense I could be more daring here in Canada. The critic Leslie Saunders, who attended the First International Caribbean Women Writers Conference last year [1988], said she felt that Canadian writers were the strongest writers there. I think what I'm saying explains in part what she means, because we have had to wrest our writing out of what has been in most respects a very unfriendly environment. Maybe this is where the metaphorical Canadian landscape comes in – the nothingness, the void, where you go to the frontier and seemingly there's nothing beyond it. It's going to be very sad if the Canadian literary scene doesn't begin to realize what an incredible contribution and potential there is, not only in Black writers, but in all those writers who are coming from different cultures who, I'm sure, are confronting this problem in their own way. Canada in a sense allowed me the space to produce something.

JANICE: Claire Harris and Dionne Brand are from Trinidad. Your origin and your utopian space is Tobago. Does this different milieu inspire a different writing?

NOURBESE: Tobago is very rural, very quiet. The residues of African culture are a lot stronger in Tobago. Trinidad, on the other hand, is a very modern place; there is also a 50/50 split between Africans and Indians in Trinidad. The sensibility is very different; they're a very fast, quicksilver kind of people. I smile when I say that because there's something very appealing about them. Tobagonians tend to be much more serious, phlegmatic, if you will. If they give you their word,

that counts for something. Both my mother and father are from Tobago. In the Canadian context different kinds of writing come from
women from the different islands. Jamaicans, like Lillian Allen and
Afua Cooper, seem to emphasize the oral tradition in their work,
whereas Dionne, myself, and Claire appear to be more page-bound
[laughter]. I think the critics will have to figure that one out.

JANICE: You've written a lot about the politics of voice in Canadian
writing. bell hooks has talked about the problem of returning to some
bipolar system of Black/White writing. She asks ironically about what
happens if a Black middle-class writer wants to write about a poor
Black person. Are they authorized to do so?

NOURBESE: I don't believe that you can issue an edict that no one
ought to write about, x, y, or z. For starters, it's quite unenforceable.
So there's a problem.

JANICE: I hear your legal mind speaking ...

NOURBESE: Why make a law if you can't enforce it! Having said
that, I recognize that African peoples certainly suffered through what
we now call appropriation by the modernist artists like Picasso and
Brancusi. Many of these artists were influenced by Africa and the
African aesthetic particularly in the plastic arts. And then to add insult
to appropriation, these artists then said they weren't influenced at
all! It also happened with our music in the U.S.A. In Canada some
Native artists are trying to resist that appropriation by saying, 'we
don't want you Whites writing *about* us. Keep your hands, your words,
and your word processors off our stories.' I certainly respect that point
of view and think it makes a certain degree of political sense. This
culture is so attuned to issues of censorship that such an attitude has
political value in bringing people up sharply so that at least they start
engaging with the question of whether or not this is censorship. Appropriation happens wherever you have inequities and inequalities
between cultures, and the more powerful culture poaches on the other.
What I hope is that eventually we have some sort of cross-fertilization,
because you can't have two cultures living side by side that do not
cross-fertilize. But appropriation will only cease and possibly become
cross-fertilization when there is greater equality between the cultural
practices of First Nation peoples and those of the dominant culture.
I do think, however, that we have to go beyond prohibition into more

positive areas such as increased access for artists from those groups who have been traditionally marginalized and whose cultures have been appropriated. If you tell White writers or any writer not to write about this particular group or culture and they do stop writing about it, how does that guarantee that writers from the other culture are going to get heard unless you also make inroads into publishing and distribution organizations? Publishers have tremendous impact on writers. We might not like to believe this, but we all know that before you send your work out you ought to make sure you know what the magazine or publisher is looking for. If publishers begin to take a responsible approach and are serious about looking at work by people from cultures they have traditionally overlooked, as well as being more discerning and critical about work by White writers *about* other cultures, the message is going to get through to *all* writers. I don't think that a White writer, for argument's sake, is going to spend six months to a year working on something about a culture they're totally foreign to, knowing that at the end of the road, the manuscript might be severely critiqued because they're not from that culture. I'm not saying that that is right, but the message has to begin to come from all levels that writers and publishers have responsibilities which both groups have to begin to examine. Publishers who are getting federal monies need to be made more accountable for whom they're publishing. Contrary to what many people believe, publishing in this country is not market-driven. We all know that it's heavily subsidized. I would like to see publishers, if they're not willing to make the changes voluntarily, having to report on how many manuscripts by African or First Nation authors they have read. I'm not saying that they have to have a quota which requires them to publish a certain number of books by such authors because you mightn't get good enough manuscripts in a particular year. But publishers have to begin reading such manuscripts seriously, which means they have to get readers who are sensitive to such material. That's where I personally would be willing to put energy – in improving access, because I think that once you have more writers coming from such groups and cultures the problem will solve itself. I might also add here, Janice, for those who will object strenuously to this tinkering with 'Literature,' that we have a notorious example of official tinkering here in Canada.

I am talking of CanLit, which, as we all know, came about as a consequence of government fiat. The result – many, many years later – are writers who are renowned both domestically and internationally. James Baldwin said that when Black writers came to voice that would in fact solve the issue of colour. The interviewer didn't seem to understand what he meant, but he went on to explain what I am saying about Native writers, African, and Asian writers. The profound political problem that we have now will begin to settle itself when these writers are published. I believe that if you have a good writer writing from within a specific culture and a writer from outside that culture, all things being equal, the writer formed inside the culture is going to be able to give you much more nuanced work – a richer work, which I believe publishers will be able to market. I should also add that you may, also, have appropriation *within* cultures, between say the rich Asian and the peasant Asian, or between the upper-class and the working-class Black person. All writers, not necessarily moving across a racial boundary, but into areas where there is systemic inequality, have to ask themselves very seriously *why* they are doing it. In *Books in Canada* Brian Fawcett in his defence of the 'right' of the writer to write about anything deplored the possibility that we might have more middle-class White writers writing about themselves. That says a lot. If the reason White middle-class writers are moving into other cultures is because they think their particular culture is boring or of no interest to White middle-class readers, that is, to my mind, the worst reason for a writer to want to engage with another culture, because then they go looking for exoticism, and usually they find it. That to me is very dangerous. That's where I see the responsibility of the writer lies for all of us – to examine our motives and to be as honest as possible – not dissembling boredom with one's culture under the guise of so-called liberal freedoms.

JANICE: Brian Fawcett's comment comes at a time when many White women are publishing very powerful stories which are threatening and frightening. I'm thinking here of incest narratives and accounts of male violence. Gender issues don't seem to have informed Fawcett's comments.

NOURBESE: Exactly.

JANICE: There is a rich context of stories and internalized oppression which needs to be told about White culture.

NOURBESE: While willing to fight for freedoms, people often remain blinkered to the fact that those very freedoms are based on somebody else's oppression, so the freedom to write *about* anything and everything in this context is quite often based on silencing other people. It seems to me we should be trying to move towards all of us getting heard, not just that you get heard and that's based on my silence and vice versa. Jeannette Armstrong was recently on a CBC panel with me, and I was very struck when she said that she was not going to tell people that they couldn't write about this or that, but that she was talking about writers having integrity and beginning to take responsibility for knowing when they were moving into a culture, particularly one that has been suppressed.

JANICE: At the same time, I have a difficult time following your argument about appropriation between classes. In a class society many of those at the bottom haven't the means or the time to write and represent themselves. Your title poem hinges on a semicolon and points to how women's silence isn't broken until she is able to test or try her tongue. Virginia Woolf's classic demand that women have 'a room of one's own' and a living wage underscores how material conditions disable many writers. A number of Canadian writers are middle class; I hate to think they would always necessarily write about themselves, though many of them do. We can work to change and imagine a more equitable society. In the interim, should we simply read about moneyed classes? Perhaps I'm simply circling back on the same problem of access.

NOURBESE: Aren't you suggesting by your question, Janice, that because we have to wait for a more equitable society to hear more voices from the working class, that this somehow justifies a middle-class writer writing *about* them? Isn't this rationalization similar to the one made by Fawcett which I mentioned – his concern was about the production of more books about White middle-class, middle-aged angst. It seems to me the challenge for writers is to try and make what they're writing about interesting and engaging even if it's White middle-class angst. The implication behind your question could serve to rationalize doing nothing about increasing the number of voices from the working class, for instance. For instance, the Writers' Union could certainly become more actively involved in trying to solicit such voices – why hasn't it, for instance, sponsored writing workshops in working-class neighbourhoods? I know of no such projects. Am I suggesting that a middle-class writer ought not to write about the working class? No, what I'm saying is that the writer ought to examine why he or she wants to write about that class – she might very well decide after reflection that she *has* to write that particular story. But she ought not to justify her writing about that class by the fact that we're waiting for more equitable times to arrive – that I believe is a specious argument. And this concern of mine has nothing to do with believing that the imagination is or is not free. To set up the argument that way is ill-advised – we have to understand first how the imagination is socially constructed. Furthermore, if we talk of the 'right' of the writer to write, about anything, we have to understand the social underpinning of that right and we must then try to identify what the accompanying obligation is. But all of this I've already argued elsewhere. Before leaving this topic, however, I want to make one final observation. The novel I'm presently working on is partially set in the Caribbean, which is where I was born. I can say with some authority that I know the society I come from and to a lesser degree the other island societies. Yet, I find it surprisingly difficult to render these societies truly – maybe I carry the burden of being a writer too heavily, but my obligation demands nothing less than the most authentic image I can present. How much more difficult must it be to render truly and honestly a society, a people, a group to which I am a stranger. What is the source of the arrogance that assumes one can discharge this obligation as lightly and easily as some appear to suggest?

JANICE: Recently, I heard an interesting exchange between Rudy Wiebe and W.P. Kinsella. Rudy Wiebe was critical of Kinsella's appropriation of the Hobbema reserve, just south of Edmonton, and pointed out that while Kinsella was writing fiction, he was using the names of actual Native people who live on the reserve. W.P. Kinsella responded with entrepreneurial opportunism, saying, I'm doing something important because people want to read my work, and my responsibility is to my readers, not to the integrity of those I'm representing or misrepresenting. I was struck by the class politics, where Wiebe was trying to make a space for the disenfranchised Native poor to find a space to write, while Kinsella was talking about his pocket-book! He became more repellant when he talked about his writerly income, and self-righteously dismissed Rudy Wiebe as an 'academic' writer. Anyone familiar with Rudy's work would find this absurd.

NOURBESE: This question brings us to the other argument Brian Fawcett made in his *Books in Canada* letter about publishers knowing that minority writers have a small market, and therefore are unwilling to publish them. This assumes that a writer writes only for his or her ethnic group, so as a Black person I'm only writing for Blacks and Whites are writing only for Whites. At the same time, the argument also says that Whites have the right to go into those very minority cultures, take the raw material from those cultures, and write for a White audience. So why is it OK then? Why is it suddenly that the very same material a Native writer might use in his or her work limits such a writer to a 'small market,' but suddenly becomes relevant to a much wider market because a White person has written it? The White writer then becomes the mediator between the dominant culture and the marginal culture. And this attitude and approach I consider to be profoundly racist.

JANICE: Your last two books were originally published outside of Canada. *She Tries Her Tongue* ... won the prestigious Casa de las Americas Prize in manuscript form and was published in Cuba; you published *Harriet's Daughter* in England. The Cuban publication was part of the literary prize, but why did you go outside of Canada with your novel?

NOURBESE: I had an agent who tried to get it published here. She was refused by two publishing houses, who told her that they weren't interested in work with Black kids. Period. They didn't even want to read the manuscript. That really put me into a tailspin actually. I went to see a therapist, because I thought, my god, if they tell me the writing's not good enough, I can work on it. But this response was like telling *me* that I had to go and change myself. Then I sent it to McClelland and Stewart myself and eventually called them. They said that the readers' reports were all very good but that the manuscript wasn't marketable. I sent it to Heinemann and the Women's Press in England (no connection with the Women's Press here in Canada); both wanted to publish it. I accepted Heinemann because I thought that they might keep it in print longer. Also because they're into the educational market, there's a possibility it might get onto the exam curriculum in the Caribbean. Then the Women's Press in Canada bought Canadian rights to it here. It was ironic to receive the cover proofs from Heinemann with an image of the CN Tower – prepared in England! Herein lies a certain story about publishing in Canada – at least of writers like myself.

JANICE: When you use a collage form in your language poems in *She Tries Her Tongue* ..., I appreciate the analytic and sensual intelligence of what you're doing. I don't know whether it is your legal training or more likely the work of a creative female intellectual.

NOURBESE: I don't know how much of it is legally based. The negative part of it, Janice, is that sometimes there's too much going on in my head, so the blank page is never my problem. I need to turn certain things off, and I have techniques to do it. I think I tend to feel more the negative part of it because it can become so burdensome sometimes. My poems have become impossible to read as a solo person. How do you read something in which three voices are happening at the same time? And I sometimes wonder if, in trying to subvert the colonial project, I haven't hoisted myself on my own petard. One possible danger is that I have made the audience for my poetry even smaller than it already is. I wonder if these esoteric, complex things going on in my work don't reduce the potential audience even further. The problem is how to speak these poems when they have become unspeakable? Or is it just that the work is entering a community where I as the poet can no longer speak alone but need other people to help. The CBC did a recording of 'Discourse on the Logic of Language,' which is very good because they were able to use radio technology. They had a male voice saying some of the parts, and they were able to weave it in and out.

JANICE: So you've become a chorus.

NOURBESE: No, I need a chorus!

JANICE: What is your writing and editing process? How have you come to write the fragmentary bricolage out of quotes and other texts?

NOURBESE: I'm an inveterate note-taker, so poetic ideas or an idea comes and I'll jot it down and slip it into a file. I've got stuff sitting there from years ago. I was just thinking the other day that I had had that material that became 'Discourse on the Logic of Language' for a long time. I remember seeing it and thinking, that's so stupid, that's really crap. [Laughter.] But it was in the file that I was working on and just kept coming up. I can't tell you when it moved from that file to these poems. This is why I started off by talking about wanting more time, Janice.

JANICE: Your poetry is filled with body language. You talk about 'the profound eruption of the body' into your writing in your essay 'The Absence of Writing or How I Almost Became a Spy.'

NOURBESE: The body appears throughout the poem: tongues, penises, blood, you name it. It seems to me the only time that we – as women – legitimately take up space physically is when we're pregnant. The fat woman is still not seen as quite legit. I used to dance at one point, and I continue to be interested in the body. I often find myself looking at how men and women move differently. Some time ago I was up north, and I observed a man walk across a patch of sand to his boat, and there was so much in that apparently simple act of walking from here to there. His movement carried a world within it, and I don't think he was wealthy or anything like that. In the journal which I kept I would record my observations and concerns such as these. A very strong desire was my wanting to take up more space – that phrase, 'I want to take up more space,' came up many times. So the poems began getting physically bigger and bigger until I could no longer deal with them, and I had to leave them aside. And I began to work on poems which were more manageable, which eventually became *She Tries Her Tongue* ... When I finished that manuscript, I could identify the area of my body – the right side of my abdomen – where the poems had come from. It was actually a physical sensation which lasted for quite a while. I don't feel it any longer, but for several months I really felt like the writing had come out of that part of my body. That experience or sensation was very important for me because it really rooted me in the body in a very important way that hadn't quite happened in the two earlier books of poetry. Along with what I've just said, I should talk about the sense of play which played (if you'll excuse the pun) an important part in *She Tries Her Tongue* ... – something that I have taken into other work, I don't mean play in a dismissive sense, but in a very serious way. It sounds paradoxical – 'serious play' – but I am now convinced that play is an important element in art.

JANICE: A few years ago I heard San Francisco writer Ron Silliman read from his novel *Paradise*, which ends with the male narrator's penis in a women's mouth. As he read this, I remember thinking, whose paradise is this? [Laughter.] The woman doesn't have much to say. Feminist writers like Lola Tostevin have tried to rework the heterosexual erotic with a less male-identified script. In a White racist culture the Black female body is endowed with all kinds of exotic qualities. How do you as a writer revise the erotic?

NOURBESE: As you were talking about the erotic, I realized that the erotic, in terms of the body, doesn't play a major part in my writing – at least until very recently. If anything, the Black female body – at least for me – is still trying to get out from under the oppressive weight of various myths – highly sexed Black woman; matriarchal Black woman; asexual Black woman; castrating, ball-crushing Black woman. In the manuscript 'Looking for Livingstone' I flirted somewhat with the erotic; that flirtation has become a full-blown involvement in the work of fiction I'm presently engaged in.

JANICE: Some of your poetry is very sensual.

NOURBESE: In the 'Livingstone' piece there is a section where the female protagonist travels through several tribes of people. The names I've given them are all anagrams of the word *silence*, and she's tested at each place she arrives at. I was trying to grapple with whether silence comes before the word, or whether silence has any validity. I think to be silenced is a bad thing; I'm not sure that silence is necessarily a bad thing, particularly if you impose the silence on yourself for your own reasons. Many of the tribes the woman encounters are female, and she does become physically intimate with a woman from one of these tribes. I suppose I may be criticized because I'm not lesbian myself, but because it's set somewhere outside time, I felt I could get away with it, without having to deal with the whole reality.

JANICE: Even though it's been critiqued as too inclusive, you have Adrienne Rich's 'lesbian continuum' to fall back on–

NOURBESE: True! But there certainly is eroticism in that work. While I agree there is sensuality in my language, until very recently I really can't say that I was aware of a conscious attempt on my part to involve myself with the erotic. I think there are any number of reasons for the absence of the erotic – maybe because I believed it to be a luxury. There is an anthology of Black erotic writing, *Erotique Noir*, which will be out sometime next year in the U.S., and I have a piece in that which I'm very pleased about.

JANICE: Who are the writers who have instructed your writing?

NOURBESE: I'm hesitating because I suppose as a woman one ought to say a woman poet – it has to be politically correct, but I won't be politically correct. The poet who continues to give me the most is an obscure poet – though Nobel laureate – St John Perse. He came from the Caribbean, from Martinique, and eventually went to France, where he lived for several years. He wrote several books of poetry – the one I keep going back to is *Anabasis*, which was translated by T.S. Eliot. 'Looking for Livingstone' is probably the poem which reveals something of his influence – maybe in the imagery. His work is often set in timeless landscapes, and he's the poet I go back to time and time again. Césaire's work, as well, in particular his *Return to My Native Land*. In terms of fiction, Tony Morrison is a writer who moves me profoundly and for whom I have tremendous respect. I like Alice Walker's essays, although I don't think her fiction ever quite lives up to the intelligence she displays in them. Sarah Maitland and Angela Carter – English writers – both impress and excite me, particularly in terms of the short story.

JANICE: You've been writing for a long while. When did you begin?

NOURBESE: I started writing when my first marriage broke up some twenty-two years ago – I began to keep a journal. I was really a closet writer. And through writing I think I actually kept my sanity during that difficult time. Then over the years I continued, but it never occurred to me that writing would become a career or a vocation in any sense of the word. I was never that happy in law, particularly private practice. Early in my career I worked at a legal clinic and there was a very overt political context to the practice of law which I enjoyed tremendously. But private practice never engaged me in quite the same way. After *Salmon Courage* in 1983 I began to think more about writing as a full-time occupation.

JANICE: Your writing work has a double focus. On the one hand, it's an exploration and language research; and, on the other hand, along with others, your essays and activism have had a very powerful impact within the Canadian writers community. Your intervention with Vision 21 at the PEN international meetings is part of this work – although the most controversial in its reception.

NOURBESE: Vision 21 is multi-disciplinary, not just writers, but from all backgrounds, and not only Black. We're committed to making sure that the practice of art in Ontario is free of racism, sexism, and economic disparity. I am surprised our intervention, as you call it, has had this impact because as a group we went back and forth – should we do it – that is the leafletting – shouldn't we do it, a lot of laughter about what to do. First we thought we'd have a demonstration. The younger people, those who didn't come from the sixties, didn't want to demonstrate. So we teased them about not having come through the sixties and so on. Those ten years are really important. Then someone said, why don't we do a leafletting, and everyone agreed – it seemed harmless enough. Just like the argument about voice, a surrogate debate happens about censorship when in fact the problem is not censorship; the surrogate debate around the Vision 21 challenge was about whether PEN did or didn't do wonderful things by inviting people from the Third World. Our leaflet said that the composition of the Canadian delegation showed exactly how the Canadian literary scene operated – it wasn't sufficiently representative of African, Asian, or First Nations writers. We supported the fact that the people from the Third World were here, and we said that in our leaflet, but we thought we would also educate the delegates by handing out that leaflet. And you now know what happened: some people were pissed off with us, some people supported us, and some people challenged us to prove our allegations. It was fun until this thing happened with June Callwood. Our main intent was to raise the profile of the debate over the issue of voice that had begun with the split of the Women's

Press. We felt that by giving out our leaflets we would help to bring the issue to the fore once again, of course never expecting what happened. Had June Callwood not said what she said, the issue would have died. It would have got maybe a newspaper paragraph, and that would have been it. The only reason it got the attention it did was because she said what she did. Even after it hit the press, had she immediately apologized, then the matter would have died down very quickly, because she has a lot of good will in this country. None of the individuals in V-21 feels that this is something to do with June *per se*. I do, however, believe that her attitude, in first telling us to 'fuck off' and then refusing to apologize, is symptomatic of how many well-meaning individuals fail to understand how systemic racism works. It's too late now, I think, but it would have been important for her to have made a public apology, because it would have given us and the public the message that they – the executive of PEN – considered the issue serious enough.

JANICE: I thought June Callwood did say she was sorry.

NOURBESE: No, she never has. In various articles she's quoted as saying, she regrets saying what she did. But I don't think that that's sufficient. I'm sure she regrets saying what she did – that is not the same as an apology. But I think it's too late now in any event, and I suppose they just dug in their heels. I do think, however, our actions pushed the debate on racism in the Canadian literary scene to another level. Vision 21 sent out letters, you may have heard this, to all the people who funded PEN and asked them to make sure that in future, if they're funding something, that it reflects the ethnic and racial make-up of the province. And we've also asked these funders to support a call for a public inquiry into racism in the arts, across the board, not just in writing. The responses we're getting back are very interesting: with the exception of one, the Metro Library, none of the funders have supported this call for a public inquiry; they're all, in fact, being very defensive. Someone sent our letter to the *Globe*, which then reported that we were renewing our call of racism against PEN. Which was somewhat unfortunate because the *Globe* totally ignored the fact that within the body of the letter we were calling for a public inquiry into racism, and once again focused on PEN. We then had to write a letter saying that we were not interested in PEN, but in these larger issues. We've had to struggle to avoid getting bogged down in this issue of PEN and June Callwood.

JANICE: Developing a demonology rather than an analysis of systematic racism.

NOURBESE: Sure, excellent word for it. That's where it's at. I think we have succeeded in what we set out to do. I could have done without the harassing phone calls, but I suppose that comes with the turf. I must, however, confess to being amazed that PEN didn't strike a panel during the conference and invite us to come on in and discuss it. That would have taken the wind out of everybody's sails and moved things forward much more positively. In fact, even the *Village Voice*, in its coverage of the events, said that they should have had a panel addressing the issue of racism specifically. That's where they made their big mistake. But it's so deep-seated you know, so deep-seated, and sometimes I do grow tired of it all. But living has never been easy and more so today; a writer needs to be fully cognizant of her responsibilities, of the privilege and blessing that being a writer brings in its train; and of those many responsibilities, the most important is being a witness to the truth in one's writing, which is often a difficult undertaking. I believe, as James Baldwin said, my job as a *writer* is to disturb the status quo.

Toronto, December 1989

Gail Scott

Excerpt from *Heroine*

The telescope cuts out a circle. Whitening fast for after midnight tis November. At one edge of the lens, a string of car wrecks. On the other side a low green window where light won't shine until next spring. That's okay. I'm lying in the bath, feeling fine. As long as I can be alone. An artist needs solitude to create. If that Dr. Schweitzer comes on the radio, I'll turn him off. Yesterday he said modern women, despite their freedom, have a great difficulty of personal synthesis. Suffering as we do from terrible restlessness. Due to overly developed expectations in life and love. The pimp. What does he know? It's either happiness (where for a moment the world is your oyster and the possibilities so phenomenal you can't stand it) or unhappiness. The rest of the time it's floating along in the middle enjoying the little consolations. The bath, the warmth, the television in the corner of the room. One thing about the Waikiki Tourist Rooms is they supply everything. A person doesn't have to worry. She can focus on her work.

What inhibited me was Marie's visit. For earlier, I'd been sinking into a jazz afternoon at the Blue Café. Very moving. The spoons strung high against long-stemmed glasses. Se-i-i-i-i. Above the winter clatter of dishes the wait-ress's voice singing in treble broke so you could feel the pain. The café has a blue floor. Over the strains of jazz snippets of conversation. C-cocaine. My eye fell on the straight back of a Sephardic woman. I could tell she was a dancer by the way she kept bending over in ballet stretches. The skin was a particular olive, so different I'm attracted. On the other side of her a younger version of Jagger, smiling vaguely, aware of his charm on women.

I got up to go, concentrating on how to put the whole symphony down on paper. With the heroine a free spirit (although you can taste the fragility of her chances, for self, for love) radiating from the middle of the story. Out in the grey air I walked like a careful drunk, looking neither right nor left so as not to confuse my creative radar. Except what to my dismay do I see in front of the Waikiki Tourist Rooms but Marie? She's standing on the steps. They have artificial turf carpeting. Bright green under the old wooden door with its turquoise paint chipped off. I didn't know what to do. On one hand no one ever comes. But on the other hand I wanted to be alone.

I had to admit, in that black wool coat, 40s style, she was looking really good. I think she got it from an aunt. I open the door. We descend the inside stairs, a little slanting, down to my semi-basement room. True, this place smells slightly greasy. True there's the odour of garbage, faintly. From behind a door, you can hear the voice of that former steno who can't stop talking. Back when she had a job it got so she could hear everything. Earphones on or off, she couldn't help listening. She had to stop eating in restaurants because she could hear every conversation at every single table. *Political situation prostituting fascist referendum wife of Frank's girl's legs mufflers getting expensive four-to-one the Expos under conditions for selling stocks on St James' the church over the bridge at skis in the oracle ha ha that's what you get for being a nose-and-throat man.* Now everything that goes in her ears comes out her mouth. Shrugging it off, I stick my keys in my lock and open my door. Marie looks in. Then she says, fixing me with her sad brown eyes that have kohl around them and dark circles under them:

'Dis-moi pas que c'est ici que tu restes.'

Sepia, that's the tyranny of intimacy. My mother made the same mistake. Always waiting on the verandah after dances at the crossroads back in Lively. Her moon was in Cancer. Once She was stricken, She smelled of soaked Kotex. At night the dogs spread the black napkins over the snow. Anyway, following the love in the parked car, we kids hurried home beetling down the dirt road. The girls in the front seat, the boys in the back. I knew at that speed we'd never make the corner. The wind wobbled on my cheeks. The cows mooed lazily in the cool green grass by the river. *Roll me over in the clover.*

'All I got was a rip in my skirt. Honest Mom.'

But from the verandah She looked at me sadly with brown eyes that were growing a white haze over the pupils. I felt so terrible I couldn't make Her happy, I started planning my departure. When, at dinner, I said 'Montréal' the whole family winced. Then Lucie McVitty, the old maid across the street who watched me coming home at night through her lace curtains, gave me the address of a niece in Westmount. As she handed me the piece of paper torn off Boyd's General Store calendar with the cute little red-cheeked girl biting on an apple, she whispered:

'Watch out, white iris stems fade quickly, when uprooted.' Then she shut the door.

From *Heroine* (Toronto: Coach House 1987)

Gail Scott

'a very rhythmic and almost conversational surface'

JANICE: The reader is invited to engage actively in your work. Could you talk about the process of reading texts like yours?

GAIL: It's very difficult for me to really put myself in the place of the reader of my text. But I think that when women address other women in their writing, the body and the mind are both involved in a seductive process which is, as you say, performance. In other words, the whole process of using language, of learning new ways to use it, is linked to a disrobing, self-exposure. We present ourselves – when addressing the imagined female part of the audience – in a way we may not think of doing for a male reader – where there's a greater risk of hiding, quite subconsciously, behind the images or masks women are socialized to adopt when addressing males. This issue penetrates language deeply. Besides the male / female polarity, another of my big agonies as a writer is being caught between Québécois and English writing, and knowing full well that my francophone readers expect very different things of me than anglophone readers. I only feel it works when I've written something that I think both audiences will enjoy. Despite the fact that I live in a francophone milieu where people are not into anecdotal or straight narrative writing, I've always hung onto the anecdote in a funny kind of way, although I use it as language material as opposed to an element that makes a story move along. My novel, *Heroine*, is full of hundreds and hundreds of little overlapping stories, so that the narrative in that sense is very fragmented, but I think there's a pull all the time between the francophone preoccupation with text and the English lust for story in that fragmentation. There was discussion yesterday about accessibility to new women's writing and how sometimes people find it strange and therefore difficult to read. I work very hard to give my writing a very rhythmic and almost conversational surface, so even though sometimes it looks funny on the page at first glance, I think it works very well orally.

JANICE: In your essay 'Virginia and Colette: On the Outside Looking In,' you write about your friendship and conversations with France Théoret. The friction between your culturally specific versions of feminism allowed each of you to unmake your respective mythologies. How did this unmaking occur?

GAIL: That goes back a while, so I'm going to have to draw the threads together. We went through a process of approaching each other a little suspiciously and with a great deal of passion, because we saw each other as a member of the other national group with its respective national ideology, anglophone or francophone. You have to remember that we got to know each other in the mid-seventies, when there wasn't much contact between anglophone and francophone writers. Francophone writers weren't going out to English Canada as much as now and there was very little translation going on. As we began talking, we discovered that our love for certain women writers of the other culture was a bridge over which we could walk in order to break down the boundaries of suspicion that existed around the national question. Just before the Parti Québécois won the election in 1976, I was very interested in Colette, and France was very taken with Virginia Woolf. We transposed our tremendous love and affection for these two writers onto the other person, so we had a very strange and a very exciting female literary relationship. We talked and talked and talked about writing, and we never, I don't think we ever, talked about fiction by men, well, virtually never.

JANICE: In your discussion about these conversations with France Théoret, you described how you came to recognize what it was to live in a Protestant culture. For you, the repression of the female body is central to your Protestant heritage. You problematize this very clearly in *Heroine*, from the first page when the reader discovers a woman in her bath masturbating. Both her body and her pleasure challenge the reader. In Protestant culture there's no female figure like the Virgin Mary. As problematic as she might be, you point out she is at least a representation of women in Catholic culture.

GAIL: I grew up in a bilingual village in eastern Ontario that was half French, half English. On one side of the street you had my family, and my mother particularly, who was a fundamentalist Christian. Across the street, a large French-Ontarian family. I watched the women from my veranda as they watched me from theirs. They had a very, very different relationship to their bodies, to each other, to life in general. I had an early realization that culture is not only an intellectual process, but is experienced as a whole physical being which gets coded very early on. Not predetermined in the sense that one can't alter that relationship, but it is very different from culture to culture. Québécoise women started talking in the mid-seventies about the relationship between body and text as a way of getting at a woman's voice, that is, as a way of contesting our minoritized (as women) relationship to language. I started reading texts like Hélène Cixous's 'Laugh of the Medusa' and felt that this relationship or awareness she had of her body and her relationship between body and language were very different from mine. In Anglo-Protestant societies the body is mediated differently than it is in Catholic societies, where women, in fact, still have a symbolic presence, even if it's negative.

JANICE: Modernist writers like Woolf and Stein made different spaces in writing by shattering syntax and form; by challenging notions of narrative, and confusing the boundaries between what is poetic language and what isn't. In order to embody the differences within female desire our prose drifts towards poetry. How do you account for this?

GAIL: I pay a good deal of attention to poetic language. I'm very much concerned with the relationship between music and language. My novel actually is a kind of urban jazz piece, inasmuch as sound and density of language are crucial. I really get bored reading prose that has any slack in it, as even very good prose that has a lot of description in it usually does. If you're looking for a feminist reason, it's simple. When you listen to women talking in the most ordinary situations of their everyday lives, they don't talk like we write prose. The content of everyday language is not necessarily interesting, but if you sit on a bus and listen to the voices, particularly in a neighbourhood like this, where you hear accented English, it's an incredible, fantastic chorus. The voices of women coming home from textile factories, shops, offices – women who are multilingual.

JANICE: When I read Arthur Kroker's book *The Postmodern Condition*, I was distressed by his discussion of women's cultural production. His single chapter on a woman artist focused on a photographer whose work evoked, according to Kroker, the suicided body. The pleasure or 'jouissance' in French feminist writing was described as naïve utopianism. A sceptic might imagine this as a convenient definition of postmodernism that effectively kills off women and makes it unnecessary to pay serious attention to their cultural production. Your essay 'Spaces like Stairs' addresses a similar problem and imagines 'two postmoderns, one for women, one for men.'

GAIL: On this, I should make it clear, I'm speaking out of my relationship to a very particular Québécois experience. The appearance of the 'text' – a pivotal form in postmodern writing – was crucial here for the development of what some people call *la modernité au feminin*. The text, precisely because it broke down the genres, notably between fiction and theory, became a very important vehicle for women. If women are interested in breaking down the genres, it's partly to get around this silly separation that constantly happens between the mind and the body. Knowledge is specialized in advanced capitalist society, and men can participate very easily because they only have one job, whereas women do many things and have to specialize in everything. Maintaining genre distinctions doesn't really correspond to our experience. Our lives are full of so many things. You're cooking dinner, and you're thinking about the text you're going to write for tomorrow; you're waiting for a teenaged kid to come home, and you're trying to figure out how to write a story for women. Even our sexuality functions in a much more complex way than male sexuality. I'm thinking here of Luce Irigaray's image of the two lips corresponding on and on and on with each other. So, the text became the form for women to express their relationship with language through the process of theorizing their fiction within their *fiction*. Only using the imaginary part of your mind when you're writing *fiction* makes it very difficult to make a qualitative leap forward. Because dealing with the 'suicided body' is collective, political, it ultimately involves 'theory.' In straight prose your process is hidden and you know what your process is, but you haven't shared it with the reader. And, again, it's the whole idea of how a relationship can be shared between reader and writer in a community. It outrages me talking to writers who are suspicious of fiction-theory or theory within the context of a fiction piece. After all, we writers do theorize, in a sense, in our minds as we work. We think about our processes, our poetics, whatever you want to call it. If we refuse to share this with the reader, the reader cannot respond; the reader can't play back, the reader can't say, 'OK, you did this and I don't like the way you approached it.' The reader doesn't see the intention. This attitude is parsimonious and elitist because it's hiding knowledge, although, oddly enough, people who are interested in fiction-theory are accused of being elitist.

JANICE: When you talk about *la fiction*, you're referring to a mode of writing that is difficult to translate. In 'A Story between Two Chairs' you discuss this difficulty in translation.

GAIL: *Fiction* in French means prose or poetry; it's imaginary writing. In English, fiction tends to mean prose. It's interesting that in English the words in their common usage have become limited. Were I writing in French, I could write *fiction* and I could choose between a whole realm of modes: I could write prose, I could write poetry, or I could move in between or through the texts. Whereas in English, if I present myself as a fiction writer, very precise things are expected of me.

JANICE: Would you elaborate on *Heroine*'s anti-utopian ending when 'Gail' asks, '... is it possible to create Paradise in this Strangeness?'

GAIL: There are two things going on there. One is intertextuality: when I wrote this, I was playing with Nicole [Brossard] in a way, because Nicole is always so positive, always the bright one, the one who's looking towards the wonderful future. I think the character is asking Nicole that question as she walks along. On the other hand, she's being a very typical North American revolutionary, a left-winger of the seventies. If you recall in the passage just before, 'Gail' is walking along the street and has two desires: one of them is to blow up a building which is far higher than all the other buildings and is therefore ruining the street because no sun ever shines any more; and her other desire is to buy a nice espresso coffee machine that she sees in one of the windows. I think that sums up our generation quite well.

JANICE: I thought this passage was also an affront to American writer Ron Silliman's paradise, portrayed as a woman with a cock in her mouth.

GAIL: [Laughter:] It might be an unconscious reference. I had forgotten that.

Montreal, December 1986

'Writing starts in trying to create a text that listens.'

JANICE: When we first spoke in 1986, I had read parts of *Heroine* in manuscript form. Since its publication in English Canada, it's had a very positive response.

GAIL: One thing that's really moved me about the reception is the response from younger feminists, many of whom have told me how liberating they find the book. Because it's a book that doesn't gum over the tension between thinking and feeling, that doesn't deny or repress that contradiction between an ideal construction of self – as mask or public face – and what's really going on inside. It permits an ironic look at our foibles as we try and move forward to some new vision. It permits us to make mistakes and be silly. Women have told me that it's opened a space for them in their writing, and for me that's the most wonderful thing about the reception. Some older feminists have been very defensive about it.

JANICE: How do you count for that defensiveness? It's a generational gap, an ideological gap, an aesthetic gap ... ?

GAIL: I think it's all those things. The older end of the age spectrum of the second wave of feminism insisted on putting forth a positive image. That was a necessary period, and I think that women who have been working really hard on that, as we all have at some level, do a double take when they see a book where the woman protagonist admits to her melodramatic propensities, her tendency to hysteria. But I feel strongly that you cannot engage in writing-as-exploration – and at the same time be involved in some kind of positivist cover-up. It's the old problem of the relationship between art and politics, which is more complex than getting across a certain message or type of female image. Writing over those spaces, those semantic gaps that are, among other things, the places where we are not heard in culture, is bound to turn up contradictions that some people serious about their politics would prefer to forget. The relationship between political ethics and poetic process is necessarily oblique. I am uncomfortable with the term 'feminist writing' because I believe with Walter Benjamin that work endures 'whose truth is deeply embedded in the subject matter.' In other words, the 'truth' of a text (somewhere else he calls the text's truth its secret) is probably unspeakable, indescribable. I am, however, most of the time, conscious of writing in a female voice. I have felt I had to be in touch with that desire, so as not to give into dominant patterns – and male dominance is only one take on how people are dominated in society, albeit crucial for me, since I'm a woman. But even awareness of what this means is constantly changing and does not preclude anything. For me writing is a desire to displace discourse, step out of frames, rather than speak within them. A desire that starts with listening harder to women, often, than I do men. But getting back to the question of how different generations of feminists read / write – for ten years we have been talking about the relationship between our lives, our writing, and contemporary philosophical currents such as post-structuralism – which have turned traditional ways of thinking about writing on their heads. A lot of younger feminists have absorbed the semiotic / feminist conjuncture as if by osmosis, which surely opens up different possibilities for reading / writing texts.

JANICE: Have there been different responses to your book from socialist feminists and radical feminists?

GAIL: I've had letters and comments from both women and men who have a similar background to mine in left-wing politics and like *Heroine* very much. They do not see it as a rejection of political experience, for example. But no doubt there are some who object to this work as well – people are more likely to tell you to your face that they like your work, than that they do not. One radical feminist writer has told me directly my book is not feminist. And I've heard of other feminists (of both persuasions) who feel the same way. I think the real problem is that *Heroine* is written in a way that gives one a sense of losing control – of moving close to the edge. This makes some people very uncomfortable.

JANICE: How did your essays develop into the publication of your *Spaces Like Stairs*? What different process do you undergo in writing a work of 'theory' versus a work of 'fiction'?

GAIL: The essays were written over a long period, and all of them, except the diary, 'Paragraphs Blowing on a Line,' which accompanied the writing of *Heroine,* and the essay 'A Visit to Canada,' came directly out of situations of dialogue, mostly with other women – usually francophone women. Either they emerged from discussions in my writing group, or took off from texts initially prepared for public forums, debates on the subject of writing. The addressees are therefore virtually always women in struggle – feminists trying to come to grips with issues of language and culture. But this immediately set up a context somewhat different from that in which essays are normally produced in our society. I think it accounts partly for the fluidity of the essays, the sense that there are spaces left open wherein the reader can intervene. It also permitted me to blatantly present these essays as writing in search of something as opposed to writing seeking to prove the author has already resolved something, as an authority. The feminist context being ideally more dialogic than competitive – unlike universities, or certain political contexts. The tentativeness has nothing to do with false modesty on my part or lack of theoretical rigour. I know what I want – which is a movement always against closure – every answer raising another question. Among things that underscore this writing are: things I learned reading Freud, on seeing how he wrote about the process of psychoanalysis (I'm talking about form rather than content), and the feminist insistence on plurality.

I'm never happier than when someone tells me she had a good argument with one of the essays. That was my intention. The men who can relate to them seem to be those who have reconsidered issues of reading/writing via a connection with postmodernism. Some people seem quite irritated by *Spaces Like Stairs* – think of it only as notes, of being too tentative. Again, that lack of reassuring authority, the feeling of less-than-total-control is apparently scary. But I think this approach is part of a movement towards a progressive way of reconsidering not only aesthetics – but also the whole realm of politics. And above all the relationship between the two.

But you asked me about the relationship between the essays and the fiction. They provided a space of self-reflection between works of fiction, a space shared with other women, which also spurs me on, prepares me with new insights for writing the subsequent work of fiction. That space involves the 'first circle' I talked about in 'A Feminist at the Carnival' – women I can talk to in my own language, as it were, who provide both intellectual and emotional support but who can be highly critical, too. It is at this point that the most direct contact between feminism and aesthetic questions takes place for me. The process of the fiction-writing itself is somehow in excess of the rational – where political discourse functions.

JANICE: I was in psychoanalysis when I first heard you read from *Heroine* at Westword, in the summer of 1984. I remember telling you afterward that the bath was a perfect place for a hysteric to tell her story, comforted and contained within the walls of her porcelain womb.

GAIL: Hysteria, be it hysteria represented in a novel, or the way hysteria surfaces in everyday life, is a mask. The stronger a woman is, the more hysterical she can end up, if the conditions of her life are bad enough – because the effort of self-repression of her potential becomes a full-time occupation. The character in my novel is hysterical inasmuch as she has a series of masks that she presents to the world. She also has a very perturbed relationship to reality, whatever reality is. I like to think there's a movement through the novel out of hysteria towards something else, which happens, actually, through the writing in her diary. But again, I didn't want the novel to be a movement from A to B; I didn't want the novel to be a resolution in the sense that one often expects of a political novel. I wanted to posit the issue of politics in a different way, so you've got two contradictory elements right from the beginning. On the one hand, her tendency towards classic melodrama: this heterosexual love affair that she can't get over. And, on the other hand, a feminist consciousness and *her* desire for a woman who counterbalances and is often in conflict with the melodramatic part of herself. Rather than a resolution at the point at which the novel ends, it's a circling around; she's finally got out of the bath and she's alone and in the street, but she's not necessarily on her way to a great career or to a terrific lesbian love affair, or to any of the other things which I think have become the classic happy endings in 'feminist writing.'

JANICE: The resolution isn't the ultimate of happy endings, and the novel begins in the suffering of depression and breakdown; after all, your heroine is recuperating in retreat from the world in the Waikiki Tourist Rooms. Perhaps this movement from despair to possibility is no small step for womankind. *Heroine* is written in pain and also in the possibility of healing. Can you talk about pain and your writing?

GAIL: What is pain? Despair? I don't know how to say it any other way than to say that pain only begins to be healed when you can start to talk about it and put it in a context that means something to you. All writing is about that in a sense, isn't it? I mean we're doing it 'in-the-feminine' because that particular part has been suppressed for so long. At least, suppressed as an ACTIVE agent. I think until you can construct the body (which is also the 'text') in a non-alienated way, in words and images, you're stuck with that repressed pain which is really crippling. Earlier we were talking a lot about incest. So many women who've had incestuous experiences have said, 'Until I began to deal with this, I was completely blocked from doing anything creative. I couldn't write. I couldn't speak. I couldn't live.'

JANICE: When you talked about the healing listening, I was thinking about 'A Visit to Canada,' which opens with you listening to Erin Mouré read an Olga Broumas translation of a Greek poem. This is a complicated multi-layered series of voices and listenings. Can you talk about the communicative process which translation becomes in this essay?

GAIL: I was concerned in 'A Visit to Canada' with discussing my problems with translating ideas, experience, from French to English when I visit Canada. I wanted to frame the text with translation as a positive experience as well as an experience of loss. When you translate, you always lose something, but you gain something as well. I like the chain of events which begins with the poet Erin, who's a very important part of my personal life, reading a Greek poet who means a great deal to her but not necessarily anything to me. I was interested in how that was communicated to me by a series of things – by her voice, by the work of a Greek woman translating into English, a lesbian translating into English. So there was a female connection, as well as a language connection, a love of language going through all of it which is the bond between Erin and me and other women. Then there's what gets lost in transmission from one culture to another – an underscoring of pain that often accompanies these attempts to communicate. A good part of the responsibility for this difficulty lies with the reader / receiver, who often has difficulty getting rid of her biases in order to hear well. I'm often amazed at what gets lost in terms of depth when French-language writing is discussed in English. It becomes something quite different. And French is relatively familiar territory, compared to Native cultures, for example. I hate to think of what we fail to hear as White people in those kinds of transmissions. The pain of loss involved ...

I also wanted to talk about the space translation opens up in my writing – or in any writing that spans more than one culture. An essay germinated in French, then written in English by the same author, to speak of my own experience, is necessarily full of semantic jumps, leaps of faith between two modes of thinking. The sense of the abyss over which we write is reinforced by this process, positing another resistance to closure. I think this is another element that invites dialogue in *Spaces Like Stairs*.

JANICE: You conclude 'Red Tin and White Tulle' with a response to Sheila Rowbotham's comment 'As soon as we learn words we find ourselves outside them.' You suggest that we don't and disagree with this alienated sense of language, insisting that 'one just has to get over that fear of sounding ... different.'

GAIL: Again, it's a question, in part, of the space you write in. Language doesn't belong to anyone, but conventions of usage reflect traces of dominance. You have to have the space to differentiate from that. You get blocked at that point of sounding different all the time, until you take the fear by the horn and say, OK maybe this is going to sound really crazy or ridiculous in the beginning, but I have to do it. When you start doing it, you realize that maybe the best thing about your writing is exactly that point where you deconstruct the fear and reconstruct something else. In fact, getting over the fear is still very much part of the process every time I write. I think writing is a tremendously painful and difficult process, but very joyful, too, when you manage to do something you feel is OK. But you're always confronting that fear. I think this is true for good male writers as well.

JANICE: I taught *Heroine* in my class, and my female students in particular really connected with it. One of the assignments over the year was a journal project, and one student, a visual artist, had written sections of her journal in the bathtub. By the time we read *Heroine*, she was just *ecstatic* because throughout her journal she had been talking about the process of writing and the body and why the bath was the place for her to write. With *Heroine* we were all intrigued with how the continuity of setting, the bath, seduces the reader in spite of the novel's radically fractured perspective. Why did you choose the 'black tourist' and the 'grey lady' to displace any possibility of omniscient narration?

GAIL: Well, I was trying to play with a lot of contradictions that I remembered from the period when I was a young radical. One of them was that you couldn't really be radical if you weren't a member of a minority group. So the Black tourist became a figure for that in a way. He is completely outside the woman's consciousness, as is the grey woman, although she fears ending up as a homeless woman, just as many, even relatively privileged women fear that if they slip they're going to go over the edge. But I wrote a whole draft of the novel where the grey woman was the main protagonist, and it didn't work. The protagonist realizes that there are all these people peripheral to her experiences whose consciousness she can't get into. She has to acknowledge that their vision is outside hers and that she can never really connect with it but only sense and acknowledge it. The Black tourist on an earlier visit to Montreal has met a Québécois radical who does 'tours for revolutionaries,' and they communicate with each other during the tour. The anglophone woman in the bath seems unable to step inside that experience.

JANICE: There is another 'other' figure in your writing, that is, the mother whom you describe as a gothic figure. How do you write this Möbius loop of mothers and daughters?

GAIL: Mothering is something we've scarcely begun to look at in literary terms. In 'Feminist at the Carnival' I wrote that one of the dilemmas for us in terms of our identity is never being able to find the woman in the mother. We can find the man in the father but not the woman in the mother. The father, 'a real person,' is also linked to, representative of, the symbolic. While what we have in the mother, as figure, is the murdered woman (as person). Talk about over-determined presence and absence. Is it any wonder women's writing at its best is so radical? There is so much at risk, stalking death, to find the connection with life. The tables are completely reversed when you're a mother, since it's very difficult to be a woman and a mother at the same time. I certainly experience that constantly as a mother, slipping into behaviours (like constant worrying) which I know are completely and totally ludicrous. I've done it all winter long and seen myself doing it. How does someone who's a fully constituted person take up a role where she has all this responsibility as well as incredibly subliminal ties, ties which seem impossible to separate properly because of the way mothers are inside. I use the 'gothic' mother because all of our mothers are gothic in some sense. The mystery of the murdered woman that dogs the mother figure. I don't know if Daphne [Marlatt] would consider her *Ana Historic* mother a gothic mother, but she is to me.

JANICE: What are the characteristics of the gothic mother?

GAIL: She's a ghost for one thing; she's terrifying and terribly attractive, full of darkness and mystery. In a way, she's the feminine, with all its question marks.

JANICE: You have worked closely with other women writers. Have you had mentors?

GAIL: Oh mentors ... [sigh] I don't know if the word *mentor* really works except as a certain body of fiction by women writers of a previous generation of modernists, writers like Gertrude Stein, and

Djuna Barnes, Jane Bowles, and Virginia Woolf, who really opened the way for the kind of work that's being done in feminist new narrative prose today. I've been greatly influenced by what's happened in Quebec. But I think there's been a process of give and take that's gone on between myself and certain Quebec writers. I've brought something to the discussion from what I know about writing in English, as well as learned from the context. I greatly admire the work of Louky [Bersianik], Nicole [Brossard], and France [Théoret], Louise Cotnoir, Louise Dupré. Our mutual affection and respect is part of our strength.

JANICE: As a group you have recently published *La Théorie, un dimanche*, a selection of some of the theoretical results of your collective meetings, which I understand were both intellectual and culinary.

GAIL: We have a writers' group that's gone on for about five years, which has been a wonderful process of meeting every so often with texts which have to do with theoretical questions about feminism and writing. We very seriously discuss each other's texts and then have wonderful long dinners where the discussion sometimes continues late into the night but in a less serious way – due in part to the endless bottles of wine we consume. In the whole Quebec context the impact of politics in writing has often been very immediate. In the sixties and seventies there were events like Les Nuits de la poésie – whole nights of celebration of Québécois culture, sometimes at serious risk of harassment from La Gendarmerie Royale (RCMP). Notably, the one that took place during the War Measures' Act. In smaller ways in the seventies and eighties feminists have taken up this kind of activity, organizing public forums, readings, discussion, which are both very literary and political. For example, Le Forum des femmes in 1985. A whole afternoon where each member of our group gave texts that were responded to by other women from very different milieus, including journalists and academics. This was preceded and followed by performances by other women and by exhibitions of women's art. An ambiance of celebration and questioning really is part of a Quebec tradition of publicly manifesting a relationship between art and politics.

JANICE: Is feminism becoming less central in Québécois writing?

GAIL: There has been a critical backlash against feminist writing with angry reactions by some male writers about the central place women have had. The yuppie decade has created a certain amount of fallout, for sure, and not only from men. But I think other things have entered into the picture as well. There is new awareness about how complex the whole concept of feminism is, including the necessary criticism of failure by White women born here to hear the voices, needs, of women from other cultures, and notably, visible minorities. There is the constant need for renewal, for subsequent age-groups to distinguish themselves from what has gone before.

JANICE: You have a liminal position *vis-à-vis* Québécois writing and also within the anglophone-Canadian community. How have you managed to develop a sense of your own cultural space between these different communities?

GAIL: The process has been to find a voice that is as close as I can get to my own experience, a voice which reflects in the very texture of the text, in the way the sentences and language sound, the point where the cultures cross. I was very conscious writing *Heroine* of contradictorily opposed audience expectations about everything from notions of text to interpretations of history. And the space my own writing might occur in. Even the word *fiction-theory* might mean different approaches in French and English. On top of this, for many Canadians who are not anti-French, Quebec is something exotic. So that coming from Quebec as an English-language writer was like being a nonentity, a subspecies. It's hard to convince people that one can be Quebec anglophone, yet have a culture quite distinct, quite unlike, anything beyond the borders of Quebec, due to the impact of French language and culture. I wrote 'A Visit to Canada' partly to discuss that, and also to air some of my suspicions about how Quebec had gone from being nothing to being this object of exoticism among Canadian intellectuals. The latter position seemed to me also to conceal bias, prejudice. It's like when a man puts a woman on a pedestal: it's entirely his text. And if she doesn't live up to it, if she falls off, she kind of disappears from sight. Again it has to do with really hearing the other. One has the impression that all minorities in this country have to live up to a text generated above all in Toronto. With no regard for the fact that if you come from Quebec, the dominant influence might be French, not Ontario English. While the dominant influence in the far North is something else again.

JANICE: Or Alberta!

GAIL: Or wherever! If we can hear each other's differences, we're really being pluralist in the way we mean it when we talk about feminism. To do this, we have to constantly look at our prejudices. I'm not pretending that my difference, my little sense of *malaise*, has been as great as if I were from a Black or Pakistani or Native community living in any Canadian city. We have to be careful about the kinds of generalizations we make, and I think that women of visible minorities have really brought us up short and made us realize, in fact, that we haven't listened.

JANICE: Critics like Gayatri Spivak have criticized pluralism as a liberal concept which doesn't allow the marginalized a legitimate voice. Since everything is not equal, the liberal pluralist speaks from a position of privilege. How would we develop a sense of multiplicity which genuinely privileges marginal voices?

GAIL: Well, that's a really good question and that's why I emphasized just now that I don't want to co-opt the question of difference in any way. For one thing, I'm here by choice; I can live in English perfectly well in English Canada, and I don't have to stay here and live in French. The Canadian concept of multiculturalism strikes me as having the problem of hypocrisy I think Spivak was getting at – which is one reason why people in Quebec are so much against it. In political terms, pluralism has a liberal dynamic inasmuch as it loses sight of the fact that everybody does not start from a level playing field. I had something more literary in mind: the textual figure of continual opening towards the female other, which has its source (and also its limits) in the work of Irigaray. But, again, can we talk about both politics and text in the same terms, exactly? The writer's way of consciousness-raising around issues like race, class, is in part by keeping her pores constantly open to the pain around her – with one eye turned critically, ironically, on her own responses to things. But liberalism is always a possible pitfall if she isn't involved heart and soul in some kind of struggle. Be it the struggle to contemplate the nothingness at the centre of things – a struggle in which politics and other narratives become allegorical. Writing starts in trying to create a text that listens. I know everything is ideologically charged, and that no matter what I do, my listening text will listen to some things better than others. That failure has to be constantly addressed.

Montreal, June 1989

Lola Lemire Tostevin

Excerpt from *Frog Moon*

My first memory is of my mother telling stories.

'By the time you were three months old you answered to the name of a frog.' Not unusual for a French Canadian except my frog was Cree. Kaki. Shortened version of Oma-ka-ki, second creature born to Oma-ma-ma, earth mother who birthed all spirits of the world.

Because my mother was very ill when I was three months old an Algonkian woman who lived in our neighborhood helped my mother wean me and she nicknamed me Kaki. Undoubtedly because we were French Canadian but also because I was born in the month of June, month of The Moon of the Frogs.

I often wondered what my mother meant when she said an Algonkian woman had helped her wean me but I never asked for details, preferring my own, almost certain they weren't the right ones. Like most stories there are those that are so factually accurate that the names of the main characters have to be changed to protect the innocent while there are others whose facts are so irrelevant only real names should be used.

Kaki. Shortened version of Oma-ka-ki, second child of Oma-ma-ma. My first memory is of my mother telling stories.

'When you were three years old you wandered away from home one day, strayed away on your new tricycle. We lived near the Temagami River and by the time your father came home from work that afternoon the whole neighborhood was frantic in its search.'

According to the story, my father, before setting out and in a voice meek with embarrassment, turned to my mother and asked 'but what's her name?' Inside our house or with relatives and friends I was known as Kaki but in front of strangers and within earshot of neighbors my father must have thought it inappropriate to call his daughter by a name that was not hers, a name associated to an element even less desirable than French Canadian. In the presence of strangers he felt compelled to call his lost daughter by a name she wouldn't recognize as her own. Kaki was not a proper name. That would be retrieved at the age of nine when I was sent to the convent when the time had come to be proper.

All my life I've had to move from one place to the next but the names of childhood are where I continue to dwell. Temagami River. Algonquin Boulevard. Iroquois Falls near Lake Abitibi where, on Saturday afternoons, you could hear the rumbles of angry Iroquois being led down the Falls by an old woman from an enemy tribe.

Two or three times a year, to get to the *Pensionnat* we drove from Iroquois Falls through Mattagami, Gogama, Temiscaming, lunched at Lake Wanapitei or Powassan, drove on to Mattawa, Chippewa, Kanata.

In my father's early model Plymouth, my brown metal trunk full of crisp clothes in the back hatch, we coursed through a geography of foreign names that were no longer foreign, oblivious to their history while they coursed through our veins and became part of our geography. Each line on the map a seam that connected us to something larger than we could grasp or understand. Maskinonge. Nipissing. These were the names from which I was weaned, their sound as sharp as wild berries on the tip of the tongue. That's where they carry their history as well as my own.

My first memory is of my mother telling stories when years went by like turtles but now they jump around like the proverbial hare. I am a middle-aged woman with a phantom body of old age that hovers and dreams of the agile body of its youth. The long back legs of the frog that leaps twenty times the length of its body. The frog mouth that lodges for days and weeks its unhatched eggs. The long tongue that shoots out and captures everything in its path. It yearns to change its skin. Pull it over its head like a dress, place it in its mouth, chew it, ingest it so that the fiction of that body is never lost.

From *Frog Moon* (Toronto: Coach House 1993)

Lola Lemire Tostevin

'inventing ourselves on the page'

JANICE: Lola I've been thinking about how productive you've been in the past few years. Beginning to publish later in life is specific to women's lives in lots of ways. What advantages were there in your delay?

LOLA: For me it was very good because I had worked out many things in my life, both at a practical level and an intellectual level. When I started to write, I knew exactly in what direction I wanted to go. Of course that always changes; it never goes how you've planned it. But I knew what the issues were that I wanted to deal with, and that was very helpful. I've been able to publish four books and many essays in seven years, as well as a forthcoming novel and a fifth book of poems. When I realized what it was that I wanted to do, what I wanted to say, much of it had been worked out; it just opened all these gates for me. I'm not saying that somebody who starts writing at eighteen or twenty doesn't have this; I'm sure that many writers do, and I'm very envious. But in terms of my life, at twenty I didn't have the feminist consciousness, and I didn't have things worked out around my two languages – that only came in my late thirties. I really felt ready to work then. Before this I was very busy being a mother and following my husband around because I didn't realize that I had choices.

JANICE: At that time weren't there fewer choices?

LOLA: Yes, feminist awareness had not reached Canada. We had Simone de Beauvoir's *Second Sex*, which we all read when it came out, but that was so foreign still; it wasn't immediate to our minds.

Most women who went to school in the late fifties and early sixties did not realize that we had choices – and there *were* fewer choices for us. I desperately wanted children, so I got very busy having children and following my husband, and it was only in my mid-thirties that I felt something was wrong. I wanted to do more. It's worked out well for me, I don't regret – sometimes I think, oh well, I would be so much further ahead if I'd done it like a Margaret Atwood or Alice Munro, or whoever. But I didn't, and the alternative is not having done anything at all.

JANICE: What role did mentors play in the development of your writing?

LOLA: I think my mentors were mostly women writers, especially the French feminist writers I became aware of when I was living in Paris in the early seventies. One of my mentors was also bpNichol, mainly because I told him once that I wanted to write. He was one of the few people who encouraged me and the first one to phone me and say we're gonna publish *Color of Her Speech*. He never gave a prescriptive type of encouragement, just left you alone. If you wanted to show him something, that was great, and if you wanted to discuss it with him, that was great, too. He was very generous that way.

JANICE: I was rereading *'sophie*. The prose texts about the International Semiotics Institute function as an interruption of French philosophical discourse in a way that is similar to Irigaray's interruption of Derrida. Can you talk about this rhetorical strategy of interruption?

LOLA: All of *'sophie* was written from the point of view of the thinking muse; 'The Muse Has Learned to Write' is the last poem of that book. Most of the poems deal with philosophy, and 'the thinking muse' became a way of blurring the boundaries between philosophy and literature. I'm not a philosopher, so I'm doing this in a very abstract way, but philosophy was always such an exclusive area of patriarchy, and whenever patriarchy talked with the muse she was always a non-thinking muse. The pieces around the Semiotic Weekend on Eroticism are there as an extension of breaking down what's happening in philosophy and also in theory. Although I love theory, I realized in some of these seminars how marginalized literature is to a lot of theory and to philosophy; I think it's important for us to break down the borders. To me philosophy is just another genre.

JANICE: Your thinking muse has bad girl intelligence; she revels in a certain kind of mischievousness. Your 'sophie is a reversal of Jean Jacques Rousseau's construction of a R.E.A.L. right-wing woman. How do you reconcile the seriousness of your subject matter with your ironic mode of thinking?

LOLA: I think I've always had a sense of irony about myself. As a young girl, I knew I was desperate being locked up in this convent for eight years of my life, but somehow it was such an absurd situation. Once I got over the shock of being there, I couldn't take it seriously. Even at the most crucial moments in life, I always see the other side. Perhaps that's why Derridian *différance* appeals to me. I like the fact that there are so many sides to so many issues, we have to explore them all. Philosophy doesn't have a sense of humour, so I took great pleasure in some of the poems in 'sophie in injecting a certain humour into serious concerns.

JANICE: The epigraph to 'sophie is from H.D.– 'she carries a book, but it is not the tome of the ancient wisdom.' What is the book?

LOLA: I'm not sure which book H.D. is referring to; the book that I'm describing is the space of my own writing. In 'sophie there's a section called 'Espaces vers', which is 'espaces d'écriture,' of writing. The book that I'm writing continuously is not the book of the ancient wisdom; it's a book wherein women look at ancient wisdom and realize they have to write their own book. Mine is my own space of writing.

JANICE: I would like to consider the differences between women writers in terms of your wonderful series of erotic poems, the 'Song of Songs.' In Canada, recently, there have been a number of lesbian love poems published, and yours are very much heterosexual love poems. Can you talk about the pleasure of these texts as well as the problems of writing heterosexual love poems in a heterosexist culture?

LOLA: It's something that became urgent for me personally and because of conversations that I've had with lesbian feminists. Some women feel they can no longer write about heterosexual relationships, first, because they don't live them any more, and secondly, because heterosexual relationships have been overdetermined, so that there's nothing they can write about them that is new. I would like to write about heterosexual relationships in a way that isn't overdetermined and predetermined. There's a great challenge for us to find new ways of relating to the other sex and new reciprocities to explore. I'm married, I have a son, and it's urgent for me to find new ways of relating to men. I wanted to write love poems. I wanted them to be heterosexual, because that's what I live; on the other hand, I didn't want to write heterosexual love poems where women are passive. It was very difficult. Again, it was a rewriting, I suppose, from the 'Song of Songs.' As much as I like 'Song of Songs' – it's the only occasion in the Bible where a woman is given *la parole*, speech, where a woman speaks – we can't overlook the fact that it was probably written by a man. So I wanted to write my own 'Song of Songs,' where the woman becomes as active as the male, and I wanted to examine desire from a heterosexual perspective. I'm penetrating the language as much as being penetrated. It is also the penetration of the muse, who is herself erotic and looks for eroticism in the other; she is not passive but an erotic muse, a thinking muse, an emotional muse. The 'I' in 'Song of Songs' is not always the same 'I,' it's not always the same woman, and it's not always the same lover. So it's not one 'I' writing towards one 'you.' It's not lyrical in that way.

JANICE: Your sliding subject differs from the beloved of a traditional love poem, where the female body is often fragmented in order to construct the erotic other, a strategy used in pornography. The shift is from the fractured body of the woman to embodied subjectivity.

LOLA: Yes, but subjectivity can never be one subject or static because immediately we become defined into that one subject. The 'I' in my book is an ongoing 'I,' an ever-changing 'I'; the 'subject-in-process,' to use Kristeva's term.

JANICE: Your French and English gives you a doubled linguistic consciousness. Your own writing enacted certain theoretical insights. Do you see your use of theory as a process of translation, from one genre to another, as an extension of your doubled consciousness?

LOLA: All of writing is a process of translation. It's a process of translation from experience, from one writing to another, from theory, from all different sources. Translation is important to me because often when I'm writing I find myself translating either from English into French or French into English. Plus it's also a matter of degree; we're always translating something that we have lived, either through another book, or through experience, or through language. So to me writing is an ongoing translation process. The fact that you are forming these letters on the page is a form of translation. You're translating your body into these forms on the page, your hand is translating some sort of calligraphy. You translate your body into your writing, your intellect into your writing, your perceptions, etc.

JANICE: 'sophie's opening poem invokes Billy Holliday's voice. Is this part of your translation process?

LOLA: Oh absolutely. The poem begins with me listening to Lady Day, Billy Holliday, in the same way that she must have listened, so closely 'no sound must have gone past her.' I'm listening to her listening to the sounds that she had to capture and translate into her songs the way she did. So in a way I'm translating – what's the word that Kristeva uses? It specifically applies to music, but she uses it all the time as a poetic process. Transposition. It's the signifying process's ability to pass from one system to another via an instinctual intermediary common to both. In a way I'm transposing Holliday's process to my own through an instinct I think she and I and many women have come to understand.

JANICE: One of the concerns in my interviews is identifying differences between women writing. What is lost in translation between you listening to Lady Day and your writing?

LOLA: Translation always means loss. You read a poem and you're translating it in the act of reading it and losing something, of course, because you're not reading exactly what the poet wrote. In a way that's a loss, *but* there is also a gain, because you translate yourself into the thought of an other.

JANICE: What sense of connectedness do you have with other women writers and what differentiates your awareness?

LOLA: Well one of the common things is that we are all women, we all breathe, and write as women. And we have a lot of common experiences at the cultural level. As far as our culturally defined gender is concerned, it's exciting at this time in our history because how are we going to translate *that* into the page? How are we going to construct, invent, reinvent ourselves? I find that quite a challenge. The moment you define yourself as gender, you're boxed in again. There's a wonderful line in the film *Les Liaisons dangereuses* where the man asks the woman, 'How did you invent yourself?' and I find that fascinating. How are we going to invent ourselves on the page? I have this in common with all the women I'm interested in as writers. Our differences are differences of ideology. Some women think that if you're not radical enough, you're not feminist, and I find that a problem. We live in a time where all differences should be encouraged and not judged. We're very tribal people; we form all these groups, tribes, and while we support each other within those groups, all our aggressions are projected outside the group, much as men have done over the centuries. I become nervous around that.

JANICE: Women's Press has recently been one of the only presses in Canada to aggressively raise the question of race as a serious problem in Canadian publishing. While you talk about common experiences and cultural similarities between women, how do you as a writer relate to women with different cultural histories? How do you relate to Québécoises feminist writers who share your language and culture but with a difference?

LOLA: I have great admiration for the work of Québécoises feminist writers, how they picked up what was happening in France, which has proved to be an incredibly fertile and important time for women's writing. And they made it their own. In spite of what some people are saying about French detritus contaminating our *Canadian* literature. What nonsense. I often wished I'd spent more time in Quebec, although even there I feel like a franco-ontarienne who doesn't quite belong anywhere. Perhaps that's where the difference lies, not having one language, one culture with which I can identify. Which is fine, I like to be in that position and I'm sure that the feeling of not belonging is not peculiar to me or my situation. I was just reading Jean Genet's *Prisoner of Love* and Edmund White's introduction, which claims that Genet's political neutrality represents a rejection of over-determined values and an affirmation of independence and passive resistance against forces of order. That appeals to me, although I don't think my writing is that neutral. The way I write is political, although I don't address specific issues directly, I like, for example, the idea of what Barthes referred to as *le neutre*, which allows us to escape the constraints of bipolar gender differentiation. Not so much as neutral but as sexually indifferent to ideological wars between men and women and in some cases even between women. As Jane Gallop points out in *Thinking Through the Body*, sexual indifference doesn't mean indifference to eroticism but to the bipolar gender differentiation which culturally defines us. Both Genet and Barthes achieved this through homosexuality, but it would make things easier for heterosexuals if they could also achieve it. Find their eroticism, their pleasure, outside the dichotomy of reproduction, of power over the other, and introduce women to pleasure that exceeds their traditional roles and as such displace those roles. How do I relate to women of different cultural histories? My first concern is to respect everyone's differences, but that doesn't only apply to women of different cultural or racial backgrounds. As women we may share certain experiences, but each and every one of us is different. I don't believe in essentialism to the point that it determines who we are. Each and every one of us has a mediating faculty with which to make choices and shape our lives as long as we're aware of those choices. As for the recent problems at Women's Press, I've discussed this issue around race, writing, and appropriation of voice with Women of Colour who make a lot of sense when they explain their views. But when I listen to those who have opposed the Press's policy, their views seem valid too, it does sound like censorship. So where does one draw the line? Again we get stuck in these extremes where one group is supposedly right and the other is wrong. And we always box ourselves in like this, when in fact the truths, the answers, lie somewhere in between. I just came back from Thailand, where a guide in Bangkok explained to me some of the teachings of Buddha. I thought, my god, this is where Derrida got his concept of *différance*, although he doesn't call it a concept. In the Thai Buddhist religion they don't have a concept of binary oppositions. The third most important element is a relationship between the two. I find this necessary.We have to stop thinking of one section of the population being right and the other section being wrong and more about the possibilities between the two.

JANICE: What are you writing now? You're moving into prose. Why the shift in genre?

LOLA: We need to express ourselves at different levels. If we only express ourselves in a fragmented way, we define and limit ourselves, which is a real loss. I've been working on a book of short stories which are interconnected to form a novel.

JANICE: Does your concern with story signal a thematization of language in narration?

LOLA: Well, there is certainly a more narrative line in these stories, and how can you move away from language when using language to write the stories? I may not play so much with language as I did in my poetry, but the centre of many of these stories is often language itself. Yes, I need to tell stories too as well as work around poetry.

JANICE: The realist tradition in prose writing in Canada has been critically dominant. How would you see your prose narratives in relation to that tradition?

LOLA: Art that breaks new ground never gets critical attention, at least not initially. Since I'm still working on this book, I don't want to talk about how the realist tradition relates to my work just now. It's not up to me to compare, articulate my writing against any tradition. It's too much like placing writers each in a slot in order to define them. The fact that my novel will be divided into many stories already fragments the traditional view of what some people think a novel should be. I don't work within a framework of completion or closure, which will probably be a problem for traditionalists, or realists, whoever they may be. Not only is it time to displace the 'realist tradition,' but it's time to displace the term 'realist.' It's a very subjective concept.

JANICE: This interview is very different from the first interview we did a few years ago. There is a different moment in women's writing, and also a different moment in each of our lives.

LOLA: Well, maybe your questions were different. I think probably both questions and answers a few years ago were more theoretical.

JANICE: I was an earnest graduate student.

LOLA: And I was an earnest 'interviewee.'

JANICE: Also that cultural moment was the exciting flowering of feminist theorizing, a new beginning again.

LOLA: Yes, I think women now are more aware of the different opportunities and potentials existing at different levels, which I certainly want to explore.

JANICE: The interaction between different levels of being and the embodied emotional intelligence of 'sophie moves me as a reader. There is one line in your prose piece 'By the Smallest Possible Margin,' where you refer to the film *Shoah*, which interviews Germans and Poles about the Nazi extermination camps. You comment that 'each person is aware how words and pain always derive from the same source.' I'm always struck by the pain in so many women's texts.

LOLA: Yes. You know Samuel Weber pointed out that theory is not written by the unconscious self but by a conscious subject. That is one aspect of theory which appeals to me. Through it we become aware of the framework through which we write. It's not a matter of writing poetry or fiction from a theory; it's just that there can be no writing act without a theoretical framework, whether we are aware of the framework or not. Language with its structures is *always already* there. For example, so-called historical realism is written from a concept that the language used to access facts stands for reality. That is one theory. Another aspect of theory which appeals to me is that once a woman acquires a feminist consciousness she loses part of the framework that culturally defined her. She must now re-define herself, become her own subject of inquiry, discover new frameworks through which she can access what she has repressed. She needs new frameworks from which to write and, ultimately, live. As much as I love theory, however, a film like *Shoah* did more, as far as I was concerned, to place certain events into a context than two weeks of theory in Derrida's course. People who had experienced the horrors of the war had hopefully buried these stories and continued to lead their lives because it was too painful to live with the memories. In the film's interviews, a lot of the survivors have taken a position distanced from what happened. And it's through the words and the questions, through their verbalizing, that you could see everything rising to the surface through language, until several of them couldn't deal with it. They would talk about it and talk about it, and then you would hear the language becoming more and more disconnected and they would break down so that the pain and the words came from something that had been repressed for so long. It was amazing how ·the language and the pain came from the same source, that pain came through the language, through verbalizing the horrors. What happens with women to a lesser extent is the same thing; you have repressed so much for so long, and suddenly you are writing the book, your book, and, through language, pain starts rising to the surface. The language pulls it out, fishes it all out. The pain and the words all come from some level of repression we just have never dealt with. And that's why language is so important to women. And that's why Kristeva's theory of semiosis and so much of writing today is connected to a certain rhythm of the body because it's as though women have to start all over again and bring all these repressions to the surface to envelop ourselves with the language and rhythms of the mother because you need some support, you need some caring, you need some love. And language, with its bodily maternal rhythm, will do that if you let it.

Toronto, May 1989

Bronwen Wallace

Koko

Only now it is our terrible labour
(or what we thought was ours, alone)
unfurling from the root-black fingers
of an ape. Koko, the talking gorilla.
In Ameslan, her hands are muscular
and vibrant as vocal chords, name
colours and distinguish *had* and *will*,
can make a metaphor; they choose
a tailless kitten for a pet
and christen him *All-Ball*, lie
when they need to and insult their trainer
Penny dirty toilet devil, a repertoire
of over 500 words that upset
Descartes, Marx, our known,
human world. Not to mention fellow linguists
who say it's all a trick – Polly, Polly
pretty bird or Mr. Ed. They point
to her IQ score, a meagre 85,
though when they asked if she'd choose
a tree or a house for shelter
from the rain, she chose a tree
and got marked wrong.

Who says
and what
is what it comes to, though,
the sky filling up with satellites,
the cities with paper, whole stores
of greeting cards for everything
we can't spit out ourselves,
like the scratch at the back of the brain
we no longer recognize as memory.

On the TV Reagan and Gorbachev in Geneva,
though their names don't matter much,
just two more faces over shirts and ties
discussing missile size, the 'nitty-gritty'
as a spokesman puts it, while
'women are more interested in peace
and things of that nature ...
the human interest stuff.'

The human interest.
Kinda like the swings in the park
across from here, how they always
squeak, day in, day out.
The guys who trim the grass
and keep the benches painted
don't even try to fix them anymore;
they know some things are like that,
stubborn as hell, no matter how much
you make an hour or what kind of government
you get. So that what we have are humans
in Oslo, Leningrad, Peking, Thunder Bay,
Denver, Cordoba and Rome pushing their kids
on swings that *squeak   squeak   squeak*
like the creaks
and farts and stutterings the body makes
to say *here* and *here* and *here.*

After living with them,
Jane Goodall found that chimpanzees
use tools, which leaves us language
as the last thing
we've got, we think,
and at the compound, Koko looking out,
a reporter tries to keep it:

'Are you an animal or a person?'

The hands coming up, almost
before he's done: *Fine animal gorilla.*
Close to the chest, showing him

familiar palm and fingers
sing *fine* caress *animal*.

From *The Stubborn Particulars of Grace* (Toronto: McClelland and
Stewart 1987)

Bronwen Wallace

'... I couldn't separate the landscape from how I see my poems moving.'

JANICE: Your work focuses on women's lives. How have you developed an understanding of the community of women and the daily language which women speak?

BRONWEN: Some of this just comes from my own experience. My parents came from the farm, so I grew up around rural people and working-class people who tell stories. Some of that language comes from what I remember of all those conversations and people telling stories. The other big influence is that I've been a feminist since 1969. Some of what happens in my poems is an attempt to capture how women's conversations work, which is never linear but circles and moves around things. It's really important for me to try to capture conversational English, to make the poem as accessible as possible, to make it seem as though what's happening is really mundane. I started out thinking that story was all that mattered, that what happened was all the poem was about, and now what I see is that the story is an extended metaphor for the voice of discovery and mystery within what happens. That's how the poems have changed in terms of that narrative.

JANICE: You've lived and worked in the area around Kingston in southern Ontario all of your life. How much of that region is in your work?

BRONWEN: A lot, a lot. I personally could not separate the landscape from the way people talk, and I couldn't separate the landscape from how I see my poems moving. In my head my poems try to replicate the landscape of southern Ontario, which appears mundane, straight, and ordinary, though I think it's quite surreal and magical.

JANICE: Are there other writers in the area whom you identify as having a particular regional aesthetic?

BRONWEN: The person who had the most direct influence on me was Al Purdy. I went all the way through to half of a PHD in English and never, ever read Canadian writing, never, ever read a Canadian poem. I spent all those years at Queen's hearing people make fun of the way the people where I came from talked, hearing those people put down as unimportant. So when I first started to write, I wrote bad T.S. Eliot. Then in 1970 I quit school and hitchhiked around Canada. I was in a Vancouver bookstore and found a copy of *The Cariboo Horses*. I remember reading 'the Country North of Belleville,' and it was like one of those kind of intense – like it was a religious experience! I remember I was actually crying, because it never occurred to me that it was possible and OK to write about those people in that kind of language. My poems move in a different way than Al Purdy's. His move very conversationally; the associations or leaps that I make are different. Another important person for me was Alice Munro, obviously, in terms of respecting the landscape and the way people talked.

JANICE: This is a similar question, but from a different location. You've been thinking as a feminist since 1969 and writing seriously since about 1975. You've participated in the women's movement during an incredible cultural explosion of women's writing, of women thinking and writing about women writing. How do you locate yourself as a writer in this new feminist landscape inhabited by women's bookstores filled with provocative ideas and a sophisticated critical vocabulary?

BRONWEN: Personally, as somebody who's also an activist, it's really exciting to see this happening; it's really exciting to be part of that history in the present. There is also an increasing feeling of support and safety to try different things, a certain real sense of community. In the last ten years I've become excited by the range of voices from Daphne Marlatt or Di Brandt to someone like me, whom you might regard as a much more conservative writer in terms of the kinds of experiments I'm willing to do with language. I see this as a big choir; everybody has her part; I'm really excited by all the different and valuable ways women are writing. I know that I couldn't do what Daphne does, but obviously she can't do what I do. I'm also interested in the development of feminist theory, because writing is very, very lonely. You put out this stuff, but with theory it comes back to you connected to the world in a different way.

JANICE: Your notion of a choir, of a politics of difference and diversity, has been enriched by Black women and Native women speaking out and saying, 'You White women, whether you're working class or middle class, have not enabled us to speak, and you have not heard us.' How particular is your voice coming from rural, working-class, White ...

BRONWEN: What I've got to say comes out of those roots, but it's from someone who's also had a lot more education than my parents had. I had really strong feelings about the Women's Press debate. As I understand the debate, Women of Colour are saying, we don't want you to write in our voice because we don't get a chance to write in our own voice because this is a racist country and we don't get published. This is a real world issue, not something in our heads about our imagination. It's about who gets published and who doesn't. I don't see it as censorship; we're being asked to stand in solidarity with Women of Colour. It particularly bothers me when White women equivocate on that issue because we're always talking about the same issue. Henry James did such a great job in representing a woman's experience in *Portrait of a Lady*. *Portrait of a Lady* is certainly one of my favourite novels, but why didn't Henry James bring all that sensitivity to bear on the character of Gilbert Osmond and look at what it was like to be all of the things that he knew how to be – male and upper-class in that society? What would have happened if he had? We don't have a portrait by a man that has the kind of accuracy and the wholeness that Jane Austen brought to bear on somebody like Emma. Why do we see limitation as something negative rather than as what we are?

JANICE: Your concern with violence against women is carried into some of your poems. Elly Danica and Sylvia Fraser have recently written very difficult accounts of their own experiences of child sexual abuse. How do you write about violence against women?

BRONWEN: I can only write about my own experience of it, so I was very careful in the 'Bones' poems to write as a shelter worker. I don't have the right to write as someone who was battered. I don't think we should kid ourselves. As it becomes more socially respectable to be a social worker who works with abused women, the language is starting to change. Now social workers talk about 'conflictive' families or 'spousal abuse' and, once again, feminist language is going to get co-opted. Just telling the stories is essential – one novel is not enough.

JANICE: Your beautiful title *The Stubborn Particulars of Grace* ranges over just those contradictions between a language of transcendence and a concrete apprehension of the everyday. The everydayness of things provides a poetics and politic in your work.

BRONWEN: Essentially it's how I see the world. George MacDonald wrote a children's story called 'The Shadow Dancers,' in which a man is taken to shadowland. When he comes back, everything looks different. MacDonald says that's how we know that this was a true vision because as he went by the true vision he saw that common things are wonderful, whereas if he'd had a false vision he would have found that common things are commonplace. That is how I really see the world. *The Stubborn Particulars of Grace* is an attempt to begin to talk about spiritual matters in a political context and to say that if we're going to live in a state of grace, if we're going to live with wholeness or integrity in the world, we have to pay attention to the particulars and politics of where we are. You can't be the transcendent god who saves the world by getting out of it. I'm very interested in goddess worship and witchcraft, that sense of the godhead as immanent. I'm also involved right now in the Kingston Coordinating Committee against Domestic Assault on Women (CCA-DAOW), which sets up liaisons between shelters and police and men who are working with abusers and tries to do public education.

JANICE: How do you link these parts of yourself? Is there a relation between your writing and social change? You write the feminist column for the Kingston *Whig-Standard* and you work with women's groups and write poetry and fiction. Are these separate activities?

BRONWEN: No, I see them as connected. Others have asked me this question before so I can quote W.B. Yeats who said, 'The arguments I have with others I call rhetoric. The arguments I have with myself I call poetics.' When I'm writing my column or doing public education, those are the arguments I have with others, the places where I take a certain position and I'm rhetorical and persuasive. That's one of the things language can do for us. At the other end of the continuum are the internal arguments, which are in many ways more complex and may not come up with theoretically correct answers. In fact, I think that if you try to write out of some purely theoretically correct stance, you usually end up writing really bad poetry, because that's a Stalinism of imagination. But both positions are essential to understanding my place in the world.

JANICE: Could you elaborate on the limitations of a 'purely theoretical stance'? I assume you mean something that isn't politically engaged in some fundamental way?

BRONWEN: Yes. The academic feminists who make me nervous are those who are not engaged in the world, who just sit and write some interesting papers about feminist thought but have never talked to a waitress in their lives. If feminism goes that way, we'll end up like Marxism. At Queen's University a few weeks ago there was a possibility of a strike, and according to my friend in the History Department, Marxist historians were the least clear about what they were going to do because they could do theory but no longer engage with the world – which is a choice. You've got two choices: one of them is to support the oppressed; the other one is to not.

JANICE: As an academic feminist, I imagine my engagement with the world as, in part, trying to change the academy itself. I want to work with others and make it a place where alternative programs like women's studies or alternative pedagogies within traditional disciplines can stimulate students and others to think critically about feminist issues, and to act, and to change. That's the ideal, though it's often not possible to touch more than a handful of students each year.

BRONWEN: I see academic feminism as important as long as it recognizes its class privilege, doesn't shut out other women, and recognizes what it's doing is not all of feminism.

JANICE: There is a really strong community of women intellectuals who focus on feminist theory in a very actively engaged way.

BRONWEN: That's great. There's also a very strong community of women who focus on pay equity. I'm part of a very strong community of women that is focusing on domestic violence and child abuse. What really burns my ass is when a few academics try to tell me there's only one way to write, or one way to think about the world, or that all my writing or thinking has to be post-structuralist. I react to this in the same way that when I was in the Left I reacted to male Stalinists telling me that there was only one way to read Marx. I say bullshit to that. Sometimes when I hear feminist debates about theory, I hear my days on the Left where a bunch of men sat around and talked about Mao versus Stalin. Who needs it?

JANICE: But with your interest in voice, and the source of the voice, aren't these different conversations in part because they have different relationships to authority?

BRONWEN: Yeah, except in terms of where they stand in relation to dominant society, there is some similarity between a White male radical from the sixties and a woman with a PHD in a university. There are similarities as well as differences. I only have problems with theoretical debates when they become prescriptive.

JANICE: In your most recent book you have a poem 'Joseph MacLeod Daffodils,' which is dedicated to another wonderful Ontario writer, Isabel Huggan. It begins, 'I'm planting perennials this year, you tell me, because I'm scared it's the only way I know to tell myself I'm going to be here years from now watching them come up.' And the poem goes on to address aging, and the conundrum of the middle-aged woman. I'm edging towards forty and that very strange location where we shift between a pre-written cultural text and the possibilities we imagine for ourselves. Can you talk about that?

BRONWEN: For me, the contradiction is that this is the time in my life when I feel the most powerful and the most together and the most on top of things, and it's a time when I'm also most aware of how incredibly misogynous this culture is, even in terms of how this culture treats aging women. It does happen to men to some extent, but not with anywhere near the same intensity. I have all these images of how women are disempowered and brutalized simply because they're aging, and I'm also much more aware of the kind of power that women have. It's an odd kind of balance. Another aspect for me is in my relationship to young women; I find that their hopefulness is both touching and frustrating. Seven years ago a woman who had been my closest friend for a number of years died of cancer at thirty-three. She was sick for five years before she died and left four very, very small children. We spent all of the available time we could together, and I took care of her during the last three weeks of her life. I learned an awful lot about living from her, but I also learned what I would call a feminist way of dying. One of the things I really notice as I get older is how much more I need the feminist community and how important it is to develop a feminist understanding of death and dying in the face of the denial and technological nightmare that the medical profession is built on – denial of the body. They try to control death in the same way they try to control birth. When I think about what they tried to do to me when my son was born, and what they tried to do with Pat when she was dying, there are so many similarities which come out of a denial of the body. There's so much power in the body. If we would attend to the power, we would learn not to fear what our bodies do. It's connected to how we see the body of the earth; by denying that we're part of the body of the earth, we're going to kill it.

JANICE: How do you as a poet represent the female body when it has been constructed in patriarchal language in traditional discourse and connected with the earth in a very objectified way?

BRONWEN: The voice in my poems is tremendously important; it's always very clearly a female voice. In using female anecdote as a metaphor for human experience, I see myself in a simple way assuming that a female view of the world could be a human view of the world. Underneath that is the belief that if we don't listen to this voice, we're not going to be here to have any view of the world. The book I'm working on now, which I have just barely started, is very different than my writing until now, much more public and much less personal. I have a whole series of poems called 'Everyday Science' based on 'scientific' facts from the tabloids or *People* magazine. So

I'm having a great time, because that's how people understand the world, I mean, that's where we get our facts, right? Another section has to do with our relationships to other animals. I'm a big Vicky Hearne's fan. She's a poet and animal trainer, and has a lot of really interesting essays. Her *Adam's Task* is about our relationship to other animals and our sheer arrogance in assuming what other animals understand of the world. The 'Koko' poem in *Stubborn Particulars* is a beginning of that. The whole debate, the ludicrous fact that intellectuals, like Noam Chomsky of all people, think that apes can't talk comes out of the sheer patriarchal arrogance that also strip-mines.

JANICE: These poems seem to provide a populist sociology of knowledge, to help us connect how people think through the popular knowledge they read.

BRONWEN: That's right. The first section of poems that I've already finished is a series of poems for – I'm a born-again country music fan. I listened to rock and roll for twenty-five years, and I just got real tired of men masturbating into their guitars. Somebody gave me 'Trio,' a great country album with Linda Ronstadt, Dolly Parton, and Emmylou Harris, and I fell in love with Emmylou Harris. I've been working on a series of poems for Emmylou Harris about country music. What interests me is the fact that country music uses a really traditional style; they don't deconstruct anything. But in country music you have people like K.T. Oslin singing love songs like 'I'm Always Coming Home to You' to a kid. In her video she's a mother who does not have custody and can only see her kid on the weekends. In another one called 'Child Support' a woman talks about how no matter what happens to her, she always has her child's support. The voices of these women singing about the world from their point of view and assuming that their perspective is going to be accepted fascinates me. That's what I try to do in my poems. I don't think I have the kind of talent to expand it very much with language, but I've consciously chosen not to draw attention to the fact that I'm just matter-of-factly assuming that a feminist philosophy is part of the world and to be accepted by my reader as common sense. That's what I want to have happen.

JANICE: The title of your recent book of short stories is *People You'd*

Trust Your Life To. How much of that world is informed by feminism, and how much do you think your poems appeal to 'traditional' values associated with community and rural familial values?

BRONWEN: You mean, who am I talking to?

JANICE: Yes, who are you talking to, and also I'm curious about the appropriation of feminist language by the right-wing.

BRONWEN: Anything can be appropriated by the right-wing; I don't see that as my concern. Lao-Tzu says that you have to treat every person as if they were wounded. I'm writing to the wounded part of each person, men as well as women. The power of feminism is the power of the victim who has recognized a way to use her damage. There's a great line in an Adrienne Rich poem about knowing that her wound came from the same place as her power. When you get in touch with your damage, recognize and care for it, you also discover the source of your power. We know that abusers, men who batter, or anybody who abuses children, have usually been abused themselves and have denied it. It's the denial of our damage, our limitations, our vulnerability, our mortality, that's got us where we are. The voice I try to speak is speaking to that person. I think we're kidding ourselves if we think there's any form of writing that can't be picked up by monopoly capitalism, and that includes any kind of experimental deconstructive writing. Look at what's happening in rock and roll on video, all that is being picked up.

JANICE: The process of writing for you seems to be a laboratory which feeds you with new questions and material for the next project. You talk about your poetry as narrative poetry. What's the transformation in working on your new short stories?

BRONWEN: I always thought there was a major difference. The poems aren't about what happens but what's discovered. The narratives in my poems are like guideposts towards a mystery at the centre of any story, the mystery of our existence or the mystery of our personality. In the poems the voice is trying to discover this as she moves through the poem. Starting to write short stories was literally a gift; I was standing in a line-up at Swiss Chalet, and a woman started talking to me in my head. I wrote that story, and once she told me her story, then a number of other women did and I became interested in expanding character. One of the things that makes my poetry strong is a very recognizable voice. In the stories I try to expand that voice. It's a first collection and has its weaknesses, but it has taught me some interesting things about voice that I'm now able to apply to the new poems.

[pause]

JANICE: OK, we're talking again after your reading at Common Woman Books.

BRONWEN: This plant closes up at night?

JANICE: Yeah, Shamrocks – no good luck in the dark. At the beginning of your reading tonight you read a Gwendolyn MacEwen poem and talked about how you like to evoke the memory of people who aren't here any longer. Why do you invoke other voices?

BRONWEN: I feel strongly that my voice is only one voice in a huge community. It's important to remember that this community includes the dead as well as the living, so everytime I read I start with a poem by someone who is dead. I started doing it last September as a result of Barry Nichol's death. I gave a reading at Western just after he died, and I began that reading with a poem of his. Gwen died and Raymond Carver died in the summer – people who had been really important to me.

JANICE: You seem to generate some of your poems through other voices in epigraphs or quotation. Could you talk about that procedure?

BRONWEN: That's something I started doing in *The Stubborn Particulars of Grace*, and obviously I'm moving on with that in the Emmylou Harris poems with quotations from country songs. But a lot of the references are not a direct quote but are echoed so that if you know country music you're going to know the quote. It's a way of deepening the poem for me and a way of evoking other voices. We do this in conversation. We say, I was reading so-and-so, or so-and-so said ... I'm trying to bring as many voices into the conversation as I possibly can. In *Stubborn Particulars* it's quite literary. Somebody who doesn't listen to country music read a rough draft of the Emmylou Harris poems and said that they couldn't hear the music. Sharon Thesen has a wonderful series of poems based on Matisse paintings; it's assumed when you read those poems that you know the Matisse paintings. This is in no way criticism, but reading is based on certain assumptions which are located in a particular class, in a particular relationship to a particular kind of art. In my case, not everybody's going to know country music but there are reasons for that and I think we have to look at the reasons.

JANICE: At the reading tonight a woman prefaced her question by a self-deprecating 'This might be an ignorant question, but ...' Then she asked a wonderful question which came from her immediate response to the poems. How do you respond to that?

BRONWEN: That makes my day. That's what I do it for, and it is much more important to me than, say, a good review, because I get the sense that in some way she's taken those poems into her life. That's what I want to have happen, and that really matters. It's especially great when somebody says, 'Oh, I don't like poetry' or 'I don't know anything about poetry but ...' I try to make my poetry popular and accessible, so when somebody finds it that way, I know I'm on the right track.

JANICE: You wrote what you call a love poem, but a male reviewer called it 'a feminist rant.'

BRONWEN: Anger is one of the stories we have to tell. We have lots to be angry about, and feeling safe or strong or sure enough to be able to reveal our intense anger is part of what the feminist community has done for women in our 'take back the night' marches or our speakouts. We can admit, like Robin Morgan says, to an almost intolerable rage of being female in North America in the twentieth century and know that we're not going to be ostracized for it, that we're in a community which recognizes there's a reason for our anger. My poems don't always sound as angry as they feel because I assume the anger is shared.

JANICE: How confessional are your books? How autobiographical are they?

BRONWEN: The separation is becoming greater and greater. The first two books are intensely autobiographical as well as confessional. But in Stubborn Particulars a lot is not autobiographical, but stuff I've made up or stolen from other people's lives. I'm creating a persona in Stubborn Particulars, a persona who is the best or bravest part of me. She does the talking and has more courage to explore things than I probably do in my everyday self. In the new book I'm exploring and I'm going to fragment and split up the voices. It's still confessional as voice in that someone will be talking intimately from the details of her life. Confessional poetry does not simply bear the actual autobiographical details of our lives, but it can be a particular stance *vis-à-vis* the reader, a tone of private conversation. When we tell the stories of our lives, we're confessing to each other. That may have religious or spiritual connotations. I was raised as a Protestant, so I don't understand the Catholic confessional as institution, but when we tell people intimate things about ourselves we are in some way asking for, if not absolution, at least support, inclusion, something, a healing gesture from the other person. That's why we confess. And so I see that it's part of what I was saying about wounds and damage – it's another way of opening yourself up to the other person. This goes far beyond the confessional as we've understood it in autobiography. When Lowell wrote 'confessional poetry,' he wasn't using it in this sense. For me, it's a request placed on the reader to stand in a certain relation to the speaker.

JANICE: Your humour works to position the reader within complicitous laughter. Is this a gesture which requires a similar kind of understanding?

BRONWEN: I like to make people laugh. Humour is obviously less intimidating, and I suppose it is another way of trying to set up some sort of openness between the reader and the speaker. When I'm writing a poem, my image of the reader is not like you and I sitting here talking. When I think of the reader, she or he is not on this side of the poem while I'm on the other side. The reader stands beside me, and we're reading the poem together.

JANICE: What about differences? Your side-by-side reading suggests a process of recognition. What about the spaces where there is no recognition?

BRONWEN: The image of two people looking in the same direction does not necessarily mean that they're seeing the same thing. We can be in solidarity and still not have the same experience of the world. I can be in solidarity with Salman Rushdie and know that we could be totally opposed on a whole bunch of other issues. In his essay 'The Storyteller' John Berger talks about storytelling in the peasant community where he lives now. Although the stories in this community do carry judgment, they're always told with the awareness that the person who's telling the story will live in the community with the person he's telling the story about all of his or her life. This affects all the individual responses to the story and not in a negative way; it's not censorship but a certain kind of tolerance, kindliness, a desire to withhold judgment which does not necessarily mean that you don't still marvel at the mystery of the story. This is connected to what I was saying about the confession; we can tell each other about our lives, recognizing that we're going to be inextricably connected as long as we're human beings on this earth. And in the best possible world, this affects how the story's heard, too.

Edmonton, February 1989

Betsy Warland

Excerpt from *Proper Deafinitions*

difference = invisibility:
the ground of our meeting

in the authorized world as we know it which is the wor(l)d as The Fathers
have told it, Woman is invisible – Woman has only been recognizable (that
is *noticed*) in her **caricatured, carricare, a kind of vehicle** difference; bull
shit, (as they say) ... a shit load

as women, it is *in our difference* that we perceive ourselves and each other;
this is the ground of our meeting – what we are not what we don't want to
be what we are (unauthorized) what we wish we could be what we are afraid
of being

it is *in our invisibility* that we perceive ourselves and each other: difference
= invisibility

it is here, at the locus of our greatest injury & distrust, that we make our
trembling attempts to *speak our names hear* one another here on this ground
of tears

is it any wonder that we feel such a frightening vulnerability; is it any wonder
that we turn away?

difference, dis-, apart + ferre, to carry. see bher-, to carry; also to bear
children/bher-: bairn, birth, fertile, suffer, burden, bort 'beast of burden'

difference is a gendered word/difference is a gender

so, as 'liberated women,' we 'celebrate our differences' – at conferences, events,
concerts, in publications, or is it salivate our differences (each celebrant leaving with her monosyllabic celibacy intact)?

everyone knows the adage 'never trust a women' or 'women never trust each
other'; everyone knows that's what's going on behind our nervous smiles

i fear for us, if we cannot come to grips with how deeply threatened we feel when we encounter differences among ourselves – i fear that our names will only be exchanged with those women most like ourselves

i fear we will continue to look to the face of The Fathers for our comfort (which is our forgetting), for in His Gaze we can slip sweetly into the Amnesia of Woman:* we will not see *our pain (which are our possibilities)* mirrored back

divide and con-her

as we encounter difference within the feminist communities we are enraged when our disparate names are denied; we are terrified that we will be rendered invisible yet again in the very place we had held out our hope of finally *being seen*

this is a well-grounded fear, for as women *our difference has meant our invisibility;* experience has given us little reason to trust it

and yet, if we cannot find other ways to respond to each other than with The Fathers' fear and dismissiveness – we will perpetuate our ghostly roles, police ourselves, never know the **bher-, euphoria** of our own substantiveness

we will persist in embracing our *invisibility as a decoy*, never knowing one another beyond the Fathers' caricatures of Women, or, can we take our *invisibility as a homeopathic remedy* for our fear, step out from behind our wooden smiles: own our creative **'burden'** as we move our hands across the blank page, the empty canvas of Woman?

*The amnesia of women is Louky Bersianik's concept.

From *Proper Deafinitions* (Vancouver: Press Gang 1990)

Betsy Warland

'a language that holds us'

JANICE: Your epigraph to *Serpent (W)rite* is from Adrienne Rich: 'Truth is not one thing or even a system, but an increasing complexity.' How does this epigraph relate to your participation in the women's writing community over the past fifteen years?

BETSY: There was a period at the beginning of this second wave of feminism when our writing focused on shared social-political concerns. After a few years we became aware of the flaws. We were bumping against differences and didn't really know what to do with them. There were basic misconceptions about our 'we,' which assumed that a feminist was White, Anglo-Saxon, and middle-class. This first surfaced in the United States, where a growing sense of betrayal and anger became apparent in the writing – such as Audre Lorde's critique of Mary Daly's anglo-centricism. In the last few years these concerns have also become increasingly crucial in Canada, particularly during this past year with the debates about racism within the literary community. There's a growing awareness of the need to understand, articulate, respect difference, and to avoid universalisms which have repressed women all along. Rich's statement has a real resonance in my work because I find that my writing has more integrity and fascination for me when I'm involved in an ongoing investigation of form, language, and content. What seems difficult for us all to circumvent is the desire to say I have the right point of view. While it's a very interesting time to be writing and living, it's not easy.

JANICE: I remember going to hear a reading of Adrienne Rich and

Nicole Brossard in 1973 that you organized with the Toronto Women's Writing Collective and the Toronto Women's Bookstore. The OISE auditorium was filled to the rafters with women. I was stimulated and provoked not only by the quality of writing but by the passion of the audience. It was a time of great optimism. The sense of possibility seems less acute now.

BETSY: Yes, On the other hand, I was at a LEAF benefit here in Vancouver recently [Women's Legal Education and Action Fund cross-Canada tour, February 1989], and I was astonished by the groundswell feeling. The Orpheum, the largest theatre in Vancouver, was packed with women in diamond earrings and mink coats sittings next to old-style lesbian dykes with plaid shirts. I have never seen such a disparate array of women in my entire life! And some of the performances were outrageous and politically challenging. All of these different women were laughing and absorbing it. I thought, 'There's hope,' even though, if you tried to make two of those women actually talk, they couldn't talk through the difference. But at least now we can sit in a gathering, believe in a cause, and respond to our repression and the complexities of our feminist culture together.

JANICE: In *Open Is Broken* you wrote 'in her textuality.' Is there an ideal feminist reader to make these female connections in writing?

BETSY: I think that the feminist reader who is attracted to my work wants to have a sense of vision. It is absolutely necessary for me to have vision as a writer; otherwise I would be full of despair and unable to write. I think the feminist reader who is drawn to experimental writing wants to be challenged, wants to see the radical impact feminist consciousness has had on our writing and thinking, and wants her presence as a reader to be changed as a result.

JANICE: A dichotomy has arisen occasionally in the women's movement between the 'intellectual' feminist versus political activist. Does this anti-intellectual schism reproduce itself in some responses to your work?

BETSY: Yes. The general feminist reader and a lot of feminist writers are still very attracted to realism and the concept of an all-encompassing reality. For those of us who question the concept and don't want to work within the constraints of realism, there is a profound gap. I've found that the word *intellect* goes back to the Latin word for intelligence, which meant to 'choose between.' It's sometimes frightening that while much of the impetus behind feminism is for women to have choices, we still gravitate towards patriarchal ways of dismissing one another's choices, particularly when they're choices that are unfamiliar. But I've found that more feminist and lesbian readers are coming to hear readings of experimental writing. Hearing the work read aloud seems to make a big difference. When you're not used to how it looks on the page, it can be difficult to read it. It's like music; once it's heard, all these lights start going off in people's faces who realize, 'This doesn't exclude me; I *can* understand this intuitively.' So I think that the feminist, particularly the lesbian feminist, reader – and this is perhaps a value judgment – is becoming more adventurous, probably because she has to.

JANICE: Why does she *have* to? What is the advantage of writing or reading 'experimental,' for lack of a better word, or language-centred writing which challenges realist conventions?

BETSY: The lesbian reader has to become more sophisticated because she doesn't want to be constrained by what comprises the existing official reality, whereas the heterosexual feminist reader still has an investment and location in patriarchally defined reality, so she can imagine it embraces her. On a day-to-day basis, as a lesbian, you know that any of your basic rights are vulnerable. Our sense of reality is profoundly changed by our unauthorized life. I know lots of lesbian readers who aren't interested in experimental writing, but I feel a growing desire for a visibility and presence in the text which is more than a matter of inserting lesbians into a heterosexual, and most often male, defined reality.

JANICE: Jane Rule has been a wonderfully important lesbian writer of realist novels which have a wide readership. How do you read Jane Rule's work in relation to yours?

BETSY: Jane and I have actually had some debates about this, mostly through letters. Jane has conveyed to me some strong ambivalences about feminist experimental writing, and I certainly have some reservations about realism. Our sense of reality is shaped by the contexts in which we have lived. The times during which Jane and I developed as writers are so dissimilar. I imagine what appeals to the lesbian reader about Jane's novels is that she places lesbians within the familiar, daily world. You know – we don't hate children or men or our mothers, and I think that is one of the great integrities of her work. The era in which I developed as a feminist has been intrigued with the significance of the body: the body (and gender) has been a major focus of psychology, sociology, linguistics, politics, and literature. As a lesbian writer, it has been important for me to articulate the particular sensuality, eroticism, and language of my body. Because this is a language that has not been articulated, it can seem very unfamiliar – even to ourselves! And it doesn't stop there – it impacts whatever I write about.

JANICE: How did your own time and history affect your aesthetics and writing?

BETSY: I learned English as a second language but didn't know this till I was thirty years old. I grew up in a Norwegian community and everyone spoke English as a second language. All important conversations happened in Norwegian. So the important things happened in a secret language, my first language, which I wasn't allowed to learn. It's as though I have this Norwegian sensibility of language and sentence structure imprinted on my brain. I have had a skewed relationship to language right from the beginning. Then when I became aware of my incest, that really deepened my understanding of my relationship to language. Right from the beginning there was a deep message that language was not truthful; that language was often used to erase the reality of another person or exclude them. Consequently, as a writer, language will never be a 'given' or neutral medium for me.

JANICE: Your first books focused on etymology, on cliché, and on received meanings in language. You ask at the very beginning of a recent piece, 'How do I write to you? I have protected myself from you for so long, even in my crib, listened intently, how you move from room to room, not wanting to agitate, turn, turn, tension tighter. You were my m/other.' This appears much more a direct address to your own history.

BETSY: Yes, I suspect the reason I'm a bit more interested in working with autobiography is because of my incest recovery, a process I'm in the midst of now. My incest experience profoundly cut me off from my own history. I moved to Canada from the United States and just began a whole new life here. My friends here are my chosen family, and most of them have never met anybody from where I grew up; it was another planet. Now some bridges between those two worlds are beginning, but I think that's partly why autobiography's coming in more. I doubt if I'll ever write a great deal out of my own auto-biography. While someone like Daphne mines her autobiography in a remarkable way, I tend to agree with Nicole that autobiography isn't in itself particularly interesting; for me it is only interesting in terms of how it replicates patterns and forms and structures which are much larger. On the other hand, I am beginning to think that it may be important for English-Canadian experimental feminist writers to reveal more about the context out of which we each write. Unlike Quebec, we come from disparate cultural and racial backgrounds, and I suspect this makes our writing more difficult to enter – because the ground from which the writing is generated hasn't been mapped.

JANICE: You initiated the Women and Words conference in 1983. You've been active over a long time in organizing writers and working with other women collectively. How does this community differ in politics and poetics from other reading communities?

BETSY: I can't speak about this with great authority, because there are communities I have no real understanding of. But I've talked to the various West Word instructors who have taught in other settings, including straight academic workshops. Their experiences of teaching in a feminist environment such as West Word have been amazing. Having taught there myself, I share this feeling. Sometimes I've run into instructors three or four years later who say, 'I've never had a teaching experience like that before or since.' That tells me there is something very specific about the structure in which we are working as teachers and learners, writers and readers, in the feminist com-munity.

JANICE: The year I attended West Word I, there were twenty of us. There was Roberta Buchanan, a poet and professor from St John's, Newfoundland; a woman from Yellowknife who'd just begun writing; a wonderful fisherwoman short-story writer from Cape Breton; Di Brandt, who was completing her first manuscript, which was even-tually nominated for a Governor General's Award; and several ac-complished lesbian writers, Jena Hamilton and Cherie Geauvreau, and others. Within this incredibly diverse group there was a sharing, which recognized women's different experiences in life and in writing. Some of us were beginning, while others had completed novels at that time, but the group didn't appear the least bit judgmental about what each woman had to offer each of us.

BETSY: Yes, there's a recognition that each woman has the permission to name herself, name her wounds. I remember one of the women who was at that first school who had the courage to finally write about being fat for the first time. Someone else wrote about incest. The stories are all different, but what's the same is they've been so seldom told before. There's such an elation about that, because we know the reason these things have been written about so little before isn't artibrary: it has to do with the fact of our gender. Because I left my home country and home territory and extended family, I see writing also as a way of writing ourselves home. Many writers, certainly most feminist writers, have had to leave their homes in some essential way, and that's a lot of what writing is about. It's like writing home, not back to the home you came from, but writing your way towards a home you're making for yourself and for others. For most of the women writers who come to West Word, this is the first time they experience this.

JANICE: It's a terrible irony that we're talking about writing home at the moment Salman Rushdie's life has been threatened.

BETSY: Writing can be dangerous. When you are expected to belong in a home that is acceptable, socially or politically or religiously, but you don't, and you write beyond it – it can be very dangerous.

JANICE: Is writing risk taking, then? If so, what are the risks?

BETSY: Well, in *Serpent (W)rite* the risk was literally feeling I was going to lose myself, my direction, everything, that I'd go off the edge of the page, the world, basically, because I made an intentional decision at the beginning not to monitor where I was going, and to never look back. I wrote it over about three or four years, and never read where I had been. Of course, when I began editing, I had to do some clarifying and tightening, but I was basically wanting to reduplicate that process of being lost. I think we often feel a profound sense of lostness in our society, in 'reality' as we have been told it.

In *Serpent (W)rite* I take that feeling religiously and symbolically back to the garden and Adam and Eve.

JANICE: I want to go into the garden. In *Serpent (W)rite* you take the biblical story and blow language and narrative apart. You make anachronistic, audacious juxtapositions. What provoked this writing?

BETSY: Because I grew up in an orthodox Christian home and community, it was a fairly weighty story in my life, and also it's the gender and ethical frame of reference in North America, whether you grew up in a Christian home or not: Eve, the receiver and bringer of evil and darkness, etc., and Adam, the namer, the one who maintains order and the higher level of being. We keep living it out on a daily basis, that whole scenario. I wanted to go back and look at the implications of that scenario and how inaccurate it was as far as the use of language and translation practices in the first two chapters of the Bible. There is a certain logic that shapes our sense of official reality which is set out in the Bible. I used 'audacious juxtapositions' of disparate texts to dislodge the reader, and myself, out of this grid of perception. I also did it to reveal the sub-texts and collusions of seemingly unrelated phenomenon, because it is these very sub-texts and collusions which quietly maintain the power imbalances in our world.

JANICE: When I was reading *Serpent (W)rite*, I sensed an intimation of change at the end. In the process of writing the long poem, you had worked through a series of textual and feminist problems.

BETSY: Yes, absolutely. One of the main questions in the book was the relation of women and men to language. I do a critique and evaluation of that through the course of the book, from Adam and Eve right up through the contemporary use and deconstruction of language. The word *language* goes back to the word *tongue* and *bilingual*, to the forked tongue of the snake in the garden. But I realized as I was writing that I felt an increasing discomfort with the polarity I was getting into. It was necessary to establish the feminine and how it's been repressed and translated out of existence in terms of the Bible and language, but I didn't want to get into an opposition. What gradually opened up towards the end of the book, via the lesbian body and the two lovers who appear periodically throughout the text, was the presence of four mouths – the two mouths of their faces and the two mouths of their cunts. Consequently in their making love, four mouths were speaking. That opened up the concept of dialects, which has become a central working concept for me since. If you look at the definition of dialects in the dictionary, it's a variety of languages of which no single variety is dominant. To finally move beyond polarity and into dialect was exciting. That's what we're all longing for, a language that has flexible representation and an inherent respect for differences, a language that holds us and respects us in every way, whether we're a Man of Colour or a lesbian working-class woman.

JANICE: Did that movement continue on in *Double Negative*? Does it inform the play you're writing and the new work you're producing?

BETSY: Yes. The concept is something I'll be exploring for a long time. I find it really liberating, and rich.

JANICE: Who is your reading community?

BETSY: Daphne and I interviewed Nicole recently in Vancouver, and we asked her this. She actually responded very similarly to how I would – that there are male experimental, language-centred writers who are interested in her work but who are often threatened or unable to identify with the content. And there are feminists and lesbian feminist readers and writers who identify with the content but often feel threatened by the form and experimentation with language. Yet, there are lots of other people interested as well, often people who are marginalized in other ways and understand the necessity to explore in order to exist. I doubt if it is ever static. In one respect, I have a pretty good sense of who my audience is; in another respect, I haven't a clue.

JANICE: Some lesbian feminist writing is formally banal and non-innovative. How do you see your writing within this context?

BETSY: Writing may not be very innovative or challenging formally, but it can take significant risks in content. Editing *(f.)Lip* helped clarify this for me. Basically, as editors, we've realized that there's important innovation going on in content, form, and language. Sometimes people are working on one or two or all three of these levels. I enjoy all of these ways of resisting and exploring. Some of us love language-centred writing, but it's nice to sit down with a novel that is formally not challenging but in which we find the content a pleasure. In a realist lesbian novel we feel ourselves visible in ways we hardly ever are in other literature. So we need it all. I do have this vision of lesbian feminist writing revolutionizing literature, along with other previously repressed voices, and banal writing runs counter to this vision, but those writers and readers do not likely share my vision. I'm finding that it's Writers of Colour who are taking some of the most significant risks currently.

JANICE: In *Serpent (W)rite* it's not 'in her textuality' but *hors* text – other texts.

BETSY: Yes. In *A Gathering Instinct* the lesbianism was there, but you had to read between the lines and woman's eroticism was still dealt with as mysterious, or in terms of nature. The lovers were of the no-name brand. In *Open Is Broken* the lovers were named. This text was very focused on their intimacy – the passion and experience of two women loving each other. In *Serpent (W)rite* the lesbian lovers' relationship functions as an anchor, and the lesbian writer is actively encountering her outer world with all its overlay of voices.

JANICE: I found it quite disturbing when a nuclear big bang was connected to a heterosexual big bang. This felt like a very reductive, dangerous, and fatalistic parallelism: no matter what we do, we can't change anything because our bodies and behaviours are given.

BETSY: At that point I was full of despair, so it makes sense that you experienced that as a reader. By the time I came to the end of the text, I had arrived at a vision which made me feel much more hopeful. I'm not saying that heterosexual love relationships are doomed, but if they're tied up within that symbology and those dynamics, it's hopeless.

JANICE: Heterosexual women writers are sometimes threatened by lesbian writing. It could be a misreading of lesbian writing as propaganda, or resentful insecurity, or even envy that while lesbianism is no utopia, it does offer and require radically different choices.

BETSY: You can more easily be woman-identified as a lesbian because of the social and intimate context. It is complex because in one regard, I see that as lesbians we are forced to actively confront the raw elements of patriarchal oppression and that these elements are the very substances which are toxic to heterosexual women. Lesbians must deal with them in their concentrated form, 'natural state' shall we say, because we embody the possibility of a woman who belongs to no man. This can be a source of a deep bond between lesbians and heterosexual women if heterosexual women allow themselves to recognize it. Yet, having had the experience of a heterosexual life and a lesbian life, I know that they are remarkably different and that as lesbian writers, we have barely begun to articulate this difference. I find that heterosexual women frequently dismiss or deny this difference and often accuse us of being 'divisive' and 'defensive' when we name ourselves and our other realities.

JANICE: Sometimes lesbian language-centred writing takes on the rhetoric of a vanguard. Is part of the hostility a response to the perceived devaluation of other kinds of writing?

BETSY: As writers we are naturally attracted to certain writing forms and ideas, and we're disinterested, sometimes even turned-off, by others. Experimental writing writes in resistance to the more familiar and valorized forms and ideas. Experimental writers must extricate themselves from the prevailing literary expectations. I'm still puzzled as to why this is so offensive, particularly to the heterosexual feminist writers who have been the most critical of our work. Their most frequent remarks are that our writing is exclusive, difficult to understand, and prescriptive. There's almost this sense of betrayal – that difference is misinterpreted as intentional rejection. Does this spring from a deeply internalized stereotype that we're all alike and consequently that we should have the 'right' to understand each other? There's also a feeling that our work has been privileged, but in fact most of these women writers are in a much more privileged position than any of us who come to experimental work from a slant because we're almost invariably from a different race, a different culture, a different language, or a different sexual orientation.

JANICE: You wrote quite a lengthy response to the 1988 Third International Feminist Book Fair held in Montreal. You recounted how Anne Cameron announced that she was going to give up writing in the voice of Native women because there were now other Native women writers who could explore their own cultural heritage.

BETSY: I had the experience in the sixties of being very active in the Black power and civil rights movements, and I learned a lot in those years, often through pain. I'm going back to some of these lessons now, and I'm relieved that these issues have come to the forefront in Canada within the feminist and literary communities. Even though it's really, really hard, it's absolutely essential. I wrote about my understanding of the practice of appropriation in *Broadside*. This was raised mostly by the Native writers at the International Feminist Book Fair, and it focused particularly on Anne Cameron, because she is so well known for the writing that she's done out of the West Coast tradition. Some of the Native writers, like Lee Maracle and Jeannette Armstrong, have a good rapport with Anne, and they probably realized she could be receptive and understand their concerns. When I was writing the article, I basically came to the point of view that it's a mistake as White feminists to keep our writing totally White. We do have relationships with women, men, and children from different cultures and races. Our world isn't White; it's we who are quickly becoming the minority, and in Canada, particularly in places like Toronto, this is becoming more and more evident. Personally I do not feel comfortable writing from a protagonist point of view as if I were a Person of Colour. I might write about a character or characters who are from different cultures or races, but it is crucial that I cue the reader that I am writing from a White writer's point of view. I know that, say, for me to write as if I were a Native woman would be different from writing as if I were a Chinese woman. At least the ancient Chinese culture is recognized in terms of its validity and contribution to the world. It is a culture and country intact. But I still couldn't do it. Look at how hard it is for us to even understand and articulate ourselves – our own bodies, relationships and culture! As feminists, we know how misrepresented and absent women have been in literature, and we know how urgent it is that we make our voices heard. It is the same for Writers of Colour. When oppressed people say, whether they're Native, Asian, or Black, when they say, 'You are doing great damage to me with your misrepresentations and ignorance, with your greed,' we need to stop, we need to hear that. We have to accept that they know what they're talking about! We have to stop colonizing their culture.

JANICE: How does feminist publishing nurture these differences?

BETSY: To me it makes sense that the debate about racism first took place at a feminist press. Unless the press is devoted to writing by

People of Colour, where else do you have People of Colour working in a small press? Where else could they have questioned our biases, our ignorances, and our White control? The feminist movement is being forced to deal with difference, and we have to find ways to recognize and honour difference if the movement is going to stay together. I think what happened at Women's Press was necessary in terms of the developing consciousness of feminist literature, and ultimately, all literature in Canada and Quebec. But these shifts in consciousness and power never happen without pain and mistakes; it's far too complex for simple resolutions.

JANICE: You originally trained as a visual artist. When did you decide to begin to write, to transfer your interest in creativity from the visual to language?

BETSY: I was painting and writing at the same time for a number of years, and it was sort of like being a non-monogamist. I love them both, but at some point I wanted to go a lot deeper, and I knew I couldn't do both at the same time. I also felt that painting was, particularly at that time, a very elitist art form. How many people see a painting, let alone own one? The attraction was stronger to writing, but painting has informed my writing in form and texture.

JANICE: In *Open Is Broken* you produced sound poems, although your recent work hasn't gone in that direction.

BETSY: I very much enjoy sound poetry. Even in sound, you're dealing with symbol, and therefore with values in language. I love it and would like to do more, but I have been more provoked by my passion for language. Music is a major part of my life – I trained in music, and I'm working on an operatic play. I won't be writing the music, but I'm working with Vivaldi arias and new music will be composed for the play. I guess this is how I'm currently working with sound.

JANICE: Is this a different kind of collaborative work?

BETSY: Yes, in terms of form but not in terms of intent. In collaborative work I believe we undermine – and this is important to me as a feminist – the voice of authority which insists on one way of seeing and saying things and then imposing that perspective on others (which is connected with the concept of universals). To work collab-

oratively is really important to me artistically and politically; instinc-
tually it suits me. Whether I'm doing it with other writers and artists,
or with their texts.

Edmonton, December 1988 – Vancouver, February 1989

Phyllis Webb

Performance

Who is this *I* infesting my poems? Is it I hiding behind the Baskerville type on the page of the book you are reading? Is it a photograph of me on the cover of *Wilson's Bowl*? Is it I? *I* said, *I* say, *I* am saying –

I am the mask, the voice, the one who begins those lyrical poems, *I wandered lonely as a cloud ... I hear the Shadowy Horses, their long manes a-shake ... I am of Ireland / And the Holy Land of Ireland ... I, the poet William Yeats ... I am worn out with dreams ...*

Or am I reading, as they say, 'in person,' in the first person? I step up to the microphone. I wait for you to cough with my damaged lungs. '*I* am with you.' The poem ends. I move into my higher consciousness, my lower voice, my sense of the present, my invocation, my prayer, my tiny faith in the typewritten words before me. The poem begins.

Listen: Do you hear the *I* running away with the man in the green hat? Look again. *I* is off and diving into Fulford Harbour to run with the whales. *I* spout. *I* make whalesong. Passengers on the ferry swarm to starboard to see me disporting myself. *I* / *we* know they are out to get us. Yes, they are mad for education. They'll pen us up at Sealand and we'll die. We don't build big and we can't shoot. *I* commits suicide in the watery commune, the vocal pod. *We* swims on.

I am performing this poem thinking of bill bissett at whose last performance he did not perform. He put on a record and left the room. 'Wow,' as bill would say. But the whales have made it through Active Pass. They pass on the message: *Put on the record.* Sonar pulses ring for miles. Paul Horn is in the Temple of Heaven playing flute ... *Put on the record.*

I devise. You devise. We devise. To be together briefly with the page, the fallen timber. Or with me here standing before you wondering if the mike is on, if my mask is on, *persona*, wondering what to read next, or whether you'll turn the page. Like the state, I do not wither away, though the end is near.

I enter the Edge of Night. I join the cast of General Hospital. *I hear the Shadowy*

Horses, their long manes a-shake ... I am only a partial fiction. *Look.* I hand you a golden jonquil. *Here. Now. Always.* On the outgoing breath of the whales.

From *Hanging Fire* (Toronto: Coach House 1990)

Phyllis Webb

'Read the poems, read the poems. All right?'

JANICE: How has your sense of yourself as a woman writer changed since your early work, which was accomplished within a mainly masculine universe of writers?

PHYLLIS: I suppose one of the marked differences between then and now is that I didn't think of myself as 'a woman writer,' and there weren't many things that reminded me that I was a woman trying to write. I was very young at the time and there were hardly any women writers in this group. Miriam Waddington turned up occasionally, but there wasn't much resonance between the two of us at that time. Aileen Collins was there – she was very quiet – and Betty Layton, and there were a few other women coming and going with the men, usually. Leonard Cohen always brought a new, young, beautiful woman, it seemed to us. But, as I remember it, which may be purely egocentric, I was the only young woman writer in the group, which included people like Irving Layton, Louis Dudek, Frank Scott, and Eli Mandel. Occasionally Al Purdy turned up, and Leonard Cohen, and others, like Robert Currie and Avi Boxer, so it was heavily, heavily male-dominated. But I never isolated that as a problem, and never tangled on the subject of why more women weren't there. They just weren't. But I was learning a lot and was given a whole contemporary poetic culture by these men. The dominant female influence for me at that time was Marianne Moore, but again, Marianne Moore, in a sense, had been handed to me on a plate: Frank Scott gave me her poems; Louis Dudek knew her and sent one of my poems to her for comment. She was approved of because she was a highly intellectual poet, and that happened to appeal to me at the time. Her heavy moral – or light, I guess it is – moral concern interested me, and I was fascinated with the syllabic counting and formal aspects of her work. I was trying to get more control over my material, and so I wrote this long poem called 'Standing'; it was a long-standing poem in which I had a stanzaic pattern and counted the syllables and so on, and that's the one Louis sent her. John Sutherland was another in that Montreal group, of course. My connections were a mixed poetic, sexual, and communal thing; it felt very good as a community of writers, but I am not sure why it didn't bring in more women writers. There may have been a few more that I have forgotten, but when I try to visualize the scene in Layton's living-room, I don't see many women writers, so I was sharing all my problems of writing and excitements and so on with these gentlemen.

JANICE: When did you become more self-conscious of yourself as a woman writer, and when did the issue of gender in writing become more present in your thinking?

PHYLLIS: Not for a long time, really. I suppose not till the early seventies. That's a very long time for me to start thinking about where some of my problems in writing were coming from, like the silences and the difficulty in carrying off a programmed poem or book. Finally I had this overbearing sense that there had been too many fathers, literary and otherwise. I know by 1969 it was conscious, and I wrote a little prose piece in which I dispatched the fathers to the river Lethe, and I saw them sail away. Even when I worked at CBC from 1965 to 1969, we were vaguely conscious that we should be using more women on the program, but it wasn't powerful enough; we didn't go about trying to achieve a balance of male and female in a really direct way. We were conscious of the problem, but now that I look back, we didn't do enough about heavily male-dominated programming there.

JANICE: Your feminist consciousness follows the rise of the second wave of the women's movement.

PHYLLIS: In fact, I was almost too busy working at the CBC at that time to really trouble myself about understanding it at all in my poetry, I was side-skipping and not paying much attention to my poetry.

I had a contretemps with the CBC when I came to the West Coast.

I applied for a job as a CBC summer relief announcer, and was told that they couldn't use women announcers. The man was foolish enough to put it on paper; I went to the Civil Liberties Association, started a case against the CBC, and won. By this time I didn't want the job, the summer was over. But I did have to go and do a bad audition, which was very upsetting of course. After that, I'm glad to say, the CBC started hiring more women announcers, so that now it is pretty well equalized, I think. The Civil Liberties fought a very good case, and I'm rather proud that my consciousness at that point was sufficiently raised to think, 'I have to pave the way for others.' There had always been a problem about hiring women in Vancouver at CBC, and so it started to change things.

JANICE: Your political life began years before this. You were the youngest CCF candidate at twenty-two. How did you come to Left politics?

PHYLLIS: I had a social studies teacher who took us to the legislature, and Harold Winch, the Leader of the Opposition, was presenting his reply to the budget speech. I had grown up in Victoria, but I hadn't been to the legislature before. This had quite a dramatic impact on me because he was a very dramatic speaker and person. The CCF at that time was quite a strong Opposition. I was so impressed with Harold Winch's presentation that I became involved with the CCF at that time. I began to learn about socialism, and, of course, my teachers were not left-wing at all, so I'm sure that they were surprised that this happened. I was very political throughout my four years at UBC. The veterans had returned in 1945 and brought a mature element – political intelligence – to the campus. They started to form political clubs, so I joined the CCF, and the debating club, the Parliamentary Forum, it was called. I did a lot of debating and was very active politically, but not very active in literary things throughout my UBC days. Then I graduated into the election, which was a strange happening. I don't know how I got chosen – I'm not sure it was altogether a democratic process. I graduated, went back to Victoria, and started campaigning.

JANICE: You didn't win, but your presence was an intervention.

PHYLLIS: Oh, no, I didn't expect to win. It was a three-seat constituency, and the CCF put up three women candidates of varying ages, one really quite old, and one for the middle, and one very young. That was quite innovative at the time.

JANICE: While your literary impulses weren't strong at this time, did your politics and writing intersect?

PHYLLIS: They didn't at the time. I did try to write about social subjects, like logging in BC, and those few poems turned out really not to be very good poems. Those that seemed to be slightly poetic were the more lyrical love poems and poems about the sea. But once I got into the area of ideology, the poetry went very bad. I remember this poem about the bare mountains where logging has taken place, and being so appalled and trying to get that onto paper. It's still being written about but is just one of those very difficult subjects. Some people are able to pull it off. I just followed my natural instinct, which was a much more lyrical approach. If there is political content now, it comes in on its own and doesn't *have* to disrupt the poem. But it seemed to me I was going against that impulse and trying to shape the poem to the statement, instead of letting the poem shape the statement in a more integrated approach, which is what I do now. But I was never all that conscious; I just tended to write lyrical poems.

JANICE: Your recent poem 'Pepper Tree' has both political impact, and a strong lyric impulse.

PHYLLIS: Originally it was a prose poem. It began as a lined poem, and then I looked at it and thought perhaps it should be a prose poem. So I tried it as a prose poem, and liked the look and the feel of it. It seemed the right form for that sort of statement, which was political and lyrical and required a surrealist handling as well. So that's how that poem was sent to Nickie Drombolis of Letters Bookstore to be set by Glen Goluska for a broadsheet. Nickie phoned me to say, 'Glen has set it as a tree' – I nearly died – '... a poem as lovely as a tree.' I was rather afraid of seeing it, but Glen is such a marvelous designer typographer, and when I saw what he had done, I was quite pleased with it. Even his line breaks are excellent, and the actual figuration of the tree is not offensive: you don't have to notice it. That was its first publication, and I thought I had to leave it that way when I next published it in the *Malahat Review*. So it is now not a prose poem. I don't know what that says about an editorial intervention as against the fine judgment of the poet herself, because I really did like it as a prose poem and yet I felt it should stay with the first published version.

JANICE: What is your process of writing and revision?

PHYLLIS: I don't always do a lot of revising. There are quite a few unfinished poems. Sometimes it doesn't come off or the original inspiration isn't coming from a deep enough source, and it's more a kind of dissatisfied playing around with something that hasn't been formulated well enough poetically. It's hard to talk about revising in general terms, because each poem is different.

JANICE: Your poems are sometimes translations of your readings of texts, a kind of 'second-hand' writing as you call it. How do your poems circulate in this literary world?

PHYLLIS: It's a kind of self-reflexive world where the assumption is that there is a literate reader somewhere out there who shares some of your imaginative or emotional reactions to a text. What I see in the prose text seems to give me the poetic leaping-off point and a surround of images, or an idea, as with the Loren Eiseley poem, 'The Time of Man,' which came from reading his essay. I not only picked up on the idea of evolution having to progress forward, but also used his images and even quoted sentences. This is what I mean by 'second-hand poetry.' In a sense it is a poetry of theft; I take over the images and use them in a different way or advance the idea along my own course or terrain, like the whooping crane. That was my Canadian-listening to the radio, hearing the annual count of whooping cranes. They were carried by airplane to somewhere else. My awareness was of a vanishing species and this pathetic manoeuvre to stop a natural, or unnatural, process of extinction, a process which all species go through at some point, it seems, in time. 'Marvell's Garden' was very, very much a lifting out of my consciousness, which simply absorbed with great delight all the poetry of Marvell, and then aligned those images according to my poetic impulse at that moment of composition and the exact trajectory of that poem. It is a very personal poem; it alludes to several poems of Marvell, and yet ends up as very much my own poem with my own particular slant on things. To import more objective images from elsewhere, where part of the saying has already been said, may be a way of telling things slant or slanter, rather than writing right out of my own immediate inner space and consciousness. It may be part of the hidden approach to telling the truth, or how not to tell the truth in my poetry. It may be an avoidance technique away from a common language.

JANICE: Can you clarify this 'common language'?

PHYLLIS: I was thinking of Adrienne Rich. Sometimes poetry that is coming out of that search for a common language is not always interesting as poetry and remains stuck in a realist, anti-lyrical narrative tradition. Bronwen Wallace is doing some interesting things and has, for me, captured a common language almost better than anyone else. It has a natural flow, its own music and its own linguistic strength, which is not anti-poetic at all. It's very much in the narrative tradition without losing an imaginative aura. A lot of her poems work very well, whereas others stay on the ground in this search for a common language. Canadian poetry and writing in general has spent enough time in the narrative-realist tradition and needs to leap around a little more crazily. In many ways, it is beginning to give more of that. My essay on 'Unearned Numinosity' [*Grain* 15, no. 4 (1987)] tells a bit more about importing from the outside as an economic strategy in the poem. Name-dropping in poems is obviously an allusive device, but it imports a kind of importance that is not earned. I gain an 'unearned numinosity' by the company I keep in my poetry. Most are writers who are named. I don't always quote from the text; I simply drop names in order to explode a whole literary frame or source or reference of images in history and politics. Even in dedicating a poem to Breyten Breytenbach, you immediately get images of South Africa, of cells, of imprisonment, confinement, political action, courage, and suffering.

JANICE: Your 'unearned numinosity' works paratactically through association. In the poem 'Wilson's Bowl' readers are taken into the universe of Lorca's *duende*. After I read that long poem, I went back to root around in Lorca's essay to find the links between the spirit of death in Lorca's Spanish landscape and your context, Salt Spring Island. Lorca's essay becomes for you a sextant which maps out Salt Spring Island as a space where death becomes natural spectacle, rather than the repressed taboo it is in our culture. How did this transformation of the landscape enable you to talk about death?

PHYLLIS: There was nothing deliberate or conscious about it. It simply came about from the material at hand. Death occurred here on the island, and I was very close up to the event, to the ideas that preoccupied Lilo Berliner, and whose ideas, in fact, influenced me in my changing reactions to the island. At the time I was beginning to get a much more mythical approach to the island, a feeling that there were spirits abroad. This was not my way of dealing or talking about things. I was getting closer to the Indian material and the area of her interest, the petroglyphs. I developed a growing sense that my island experience was beginning to be like a midden. I was shucking off my garbage to make my own midden of meaning. All these images, the caves, the spirit voices, and raven, all became activated for me because Lilo's death made me confront a sense that there was a deadly spirit abroad here. I'd always thought of it as a paradise. Not so! And it was getting worse; there were bad things happening. So my sensitivity to my actual living space became much greater. I became aware of the actual physical direction of where I lived and decided pointing west was not good for me physically. When I moved later to a house with a southern exposure, my spirit was raised and I felt better. So it was like a gradual sensitization to my landscape, and I read a great deal more into it than was probably there. But that served me in dealing with the suicide and the material that it gave me to work with in the poetry, which was so much of that Indian material.

JANICE: I was recently at a talk by Native writer Jeannette Armstrong, who spoke about how Native mythology is invoked by some non-Native writers. Would you respond to this question of the politics of voice, race, and experience in writing?

PHYLLIS: I haven't used the Indian material very much, but in 'Wilson's Bowl' the two people involved were very deep into the study of this material. My own theory about their deaths was that they had gone too far in their White psyches for the psychic and anthropological excavations of meanings without the support of the tribe. They had not been prepared by their backgrounds for this territory that was not theirs. I feel this about a lot of anthropologists. It's very dangerous work. It warned me to stop going any farther into it myself. But over the years I have also said on several occasions that we have taken everything else from the Indians, let us at least leave them their culture, their stories. I don't touch it now, because it does seem to me exploitative. The Indian material has been around me all my life. In fact, my brother picked up on it very early through Emily Carr and related to the Indian culture before I did. I grew up with Indians and totem poles in the immediate environment in the summertime, but never had Indian friends, even though the reservation was next door and the totem poles right there. Indians were paddling out in Brentwood Bay, so my familiarity was there from a very early time. But I only began to feel attuned to mythology when I started working on the petroglyphs. The West Coast stories suddenly felt more real to me than the Greek myths, which felt very distant from me and which I've always had trouble remembering.

JANICE: When I read 'Wilson's Bowl,' I see double. There is a dialogic shifting from incantatory voices in time on the left-hand pages to narrative spatial poems on the facing pages.

PHYLLIS: I didn't write it seeing it on the pages, so that just happened with the layout of the poem.

JANICE: The effect is very powerful because these two interests disrupt each other. Your 'Ghazals' work dialogically also in the associative links and non-links between couplets.

PHYLLIS: I think there is increasingly in my poetry a 'you' who is not necessarily the reader. It's like having a ghost of one's own in the room. I know there's some sort of person-presence I'm addressing the poem to. More and more I want to involve that 'you' in the poem, say, 'You're here. Don't go away,' as I say in 'Leaning,' 'Don't go away.' There is a presence that I feel has to understand the experience of what I'm writing about. So there are increasing *you*s in the poem. It was something that always fascinated me in Atwood's poetry. She had many *you*s, and you never knew if it was the 'you' in the mirror, a 'you' reader, a 'you' alter ego, a shadowy self of some kind, or if it was a strategy of the poem to involve the reader more directly in the experience. I suppose it is simply the reaching out that goes on in the process of writing to create a dialogue. The writer doesn't necessarily want that 'you' to speak. You may not want actual dialogue in the poem or another character coming in, although sometimes there will be another character who will speak and in actual dialogue. But I think in *my* poetry I control the use of this other presence to make a more social environment for the poem, so that it's not just a statement of an isolated person, but assumes an audience, assumes an involved presence whom one desperately hopes is there somewhere when the work is done.

JANICE: Feminist critics have analysed how women writers often find themselves with a schizophrenic split voice or split subject in their writing. There's the one who traditionally has been silenced and there is the one who speaks.

PHYLLIS: It may be, yes. In my *Naked Poems* it definitely happens where there is a kind of persecutory questioning. The interrogator in the last section is definitely an aspect of myself, I think, a kind of superego, making me responsible, in a way, for my statements. Then there is the 'I' strategy of trying to outwit the questioner by ambiguous responses. One of my habitual techniques in life is to remain ambivalent, ambiguous, and mysterious, so that, again, not going around being easily labelled or identified is my refusal to be uncomplex or oversimplified and nailed down or up.

JANICE: Or onto.

PHYLLIS: Yes, and that's actually an insight of the moment. In the *Naked Poems* I do say being 'small like this poem' is less painful. The smaller you get, the fewer areas there are to attack. Is this a paranoid response to the world to avoid the slings and arrows? There's always this attempt to glide away or hide away from a too curious world. This is part of my uneasiness of being questioned in my essay on questioning.

JANICE: But with *Naked Poems* there is a very real social context which provokes dangerous questions. In 1965 there was not a voluminous history of lesbian love poems in Canadian letters.

PHYLLIS: No. And I was very successful in evasive techniques, I gather, because so many people didn't know they were lesbian love poems.

JANICE: The blouse gives it away.

PHYLLIS: Yes, of course, I mean, the clues are there, and the 'she.' Recently at a reading in Toronto I said something about *Naked Poems* as a lesbian love affair, and I could see old friends of mine in the audience being totally startled as if the idea had never crossed their minds. But for anyone who studies them closely, it's perfectly obvious, once you know what's going on. How anyone could read it without knowing, I don't understand, except that so many people just aren't clued in to being prepared to read about that sort of thing. In fact, I had a phone call recently from a student in Ottawa who said in an embarrassed way, 'We're having this problem in class. I'm saying that these poems are about an affair with a woman.' And I said, 'Well, you're right.' And he would go back to his class and say, 'Webb says ...' So they're still puzzled over it. But they are called *Naked Poems*, and it's the naked truth that I am trying to lay out. With my shyness and so on, I suppose I covered my tracks in some way. It's perfectly clear to me what those poems are about. I think a lot of people don't pick up on the lesbian aspect of *Naked Poems* because they speak generally about love. People are moved by the poems and the intensity of the feelings evoked, especially when I read them. So I think they simply say a great deal about love which everybody can relate to, just love, in whatever form.

JANICE: In a homophobic culture don't most people automatically assume that it's a heterosexual love if they're not sure?

PHYLLIS: And find themselves caught up emotionally in the experience of the poems; they're going to identify with their own experience.

JANICE: When you were writing these poems and thinking about what it was to write of a lesbian love affair, did you have literary precedents in mind?

PHYLLIS: Well, no, I just wrote them. Obviously Sappho is echoed in those poems. I'd never really studied Sappho; I just read one or two versions. I guess they stayed with me because I was accused of plagiarism once, and hadn't realized that some poems do echo Sappho's very closely. I just wrote them and then liked what I was doing. The whole book isn't about that relationship at all, since there's the brother-sister thing and the question-answer and the non-linear section. I didn't really think of it as extraordinary because I was just writing out of my experience at the time, and it happened to produce, coincide, or bring on this form of short poems in sequences.

JANICE: There is an erotics of restraint in *Naked Poems* ...

PHYLLIS: The erotics of restraint! Come now! I think that's a misnomer.

JANICE: Why not? There's a restraint to the eroticism in *Naked Poems*.

The restraint fills out the silence around the words, the small, beautiful, fragile poems. That sort of restraint isn't present, for instance, in your ghazals's 'Frivolities,' which are erotic and wildly parodic. The 'frivolous' erotics of 'interstellar' longings are very lush with a different kind of desire.

PHYLLIS: Well, it's totally playful. I don't know where it came from, certainly not out of the experience at that time. But maybe my repressed eroticism is expressed through playfulness. It's really strange, because they didn't come out of anything erotic, but there must have been something going on in my mind at that time if people are picking up on that. It's definitely there, but it's unserious. The poem with the hammock is very sensuous, too. But it was at a stage in my life where memories were returning. Perhaps it's a way of dealing with memories and just feeling that one can play with sexual material with a kind of wickedness. I was having fun writing these things, which is a bit of a change. It was like a holiday, the holidays I never seem to be able to take in real life.

JANICE: And what of your 'interstellar' longings, this desire which moves towards the stars shining?

PHYLLIS: Yes, that's a desire for vast nothingness, really, my nothing desires – a contradiction in terms. That's erotic, I guess, a longing for death as a kind of bliss wherein one imagines it's to be rid of all the rest.

JANICE: But there is a tension between that longing for the bliss of absence and the seductive language, the seductive ...

PHYLLIS: ... silk stockings ...

JANICE: Yes, the seductive language which draws the reader to life and the body. Beverley Dahlen would call this writing out of 'the tradition of marginality' where 'silence arises out of the gulf of oppression and reminds us that language is one of the limits of [the content of life].' The spaces between your lines remind me of these limits and that inarticulate part of what it is to be human.

PHYLLIS: I find all this quite difficult to talk about because if you talk about language and using language, about language and silence in language, it's an impossible task. But I think the idea of oppression and silence is very important, and it's something I'm currently trying to deal with again, because there are those things, and not necessarily oppression, that one does not want to talk about. On the unconscious level the silence is the result of oppression, but also my own experience as a poet. My psyche is taking care of my psyche, and it will not allow disruptive material to erupt until I am ready to handle it at a conscious level. So that I see it very much in psychological terms rather than in political terms. The anxiety that goes into repressing the material creates an enormous amount of discomfort in my life and accounts for the silence, the very uneasy period for me when I'm not writing, which is most of the time. The anxiety gets more intense as the material is approaching revelation, when I'm about to be presented with some poems and my subject. A lot of it has to do with the transformation of form, of that material finding a formal resolution, as well as a manageable psychological resolution. I'm glad that I've become a little more aware of the political aspects of why the material is repressed or is so difficult to deal with. That certainly has to do with society, with my family, my past, and all that shit everybody carries around, and which you don't necessarily resolve throughout the course of your life. Instead of ending up talking about literary ideas, I end up talking about psychology or psychiatry!

JANICE: I don't find this unusual since there is an obvious connection between one's life as a writer and the texts one produces; your writing is brave and you struggle with the sharp edges of life. Ann Mandel calls your writing 'the poetry of last things,' and other critics have noted how you take up difficult material, very painful issues. At their worst, critics have romanticized you into a clichéd suicidal lady poet figure. On the other hand, other critics have talked about the limitations of conflating writing and experience. But as a writer of complex 'last things,' of difficult 'finalities,' the risk of silence must be very acute.

PHYLLIS: You're not on air, you know, just tape.

JANICE: Sorry, Phyllis. It's my thesis speaking! In your early poem 'Lament,' you wrote, 'Knowing that everything is wrong, how can we go on giving birth, / either to poems or the troublesome lie ...?' This critical stance is crucial to your question of silence – 'how can we go on giving birth, / either to poems or the troublesome lie?'

PHYLLIS: Because I'm still in the constant process of, I hope, change. The reply is in the poem, in a sense, and relates to the Buddhist idea of rebirth until perfection is achieved. I'm certainly never going to make perfection this time around, but as a writer, one is always, as far as I'm concerned, seeing the necessity of changing, growing, responding, and processing. If you stop doing those things, you're dead, but if you are perfected in the Buddhist sense, and are not going to go on to a rebirth, then you would stop speaking. There would be no need to go on giving birth to poems or the troublesome lie. But as long as I'm alive, I presume I will have to be doing that. Of course, the other way of not having to do it is simply to give up on the task and just say, 'OK, I've done enough,' which I sometimes do. I think, 'Why do I want to go on with this process?' Or I very frequently get the sense that there is nothing left to write about or write out of, that I'm finished. This is a possibility. Writers dry up. They wear themselves out. They've said everything they have to say – that is a constant fear. But I suppose as long as there is something churning away, there will be the need for the rebirth and the retelling of the lies. I think one would have to be on the way to sainthood to take any other position.

JANICE: Jean Mallinson and Eleanor Wachtel have written about the danger of confusing the author's personal identity with the poetic voice. Mallinson describes a particularly nasty John Bentley Mays article as 'ideologically biased.'

PHYLLIS: To put it mildly!

JANICE: Mallinson then goes on to dismiss Mays's article as an 'extravagant, malevolent, and self-indulgent ... venomous attack ... a maligned combination of rhetorical self-advertisement and desperate, irrational ill will.'

PHYLLIS: Wonderful, wonderful! Isn't that great?

JANICE: How do you respond to criticism of this nature?

PHYLLIS: Again, I'd really need to be specific. I'm not sure I pay a great deal of attention to a lot of criticism unless I feel there is a genuine misreading. Recently, for the first time, I wrote a letter to the editor. From my point of view the published review was simply a very bad misreading, not a close reading of the actual material, the 'Frivolity' section of Water and Light, but reading into it and making a parallel with Naked Poems that, in fact, didn't work. It's similar in its purity to Naked Poems: it's economical and the poems, for the most part, are short, but the subject matter is not repeated. In the review there was definitely a reading into my life, where I had apparently had a love affair that 'went sour.' Well, when I was writing the ghazals, there hadn't been a love affair that had gone sour; that was just not what the poems were about. There was a reading into my life experience which came out of a misreading of the poems. The reviewer brought too much to the poems and then applied it to my life. That made me very angry. I can get extremely upset on occasion, but most often I don't have a very strong response. I did get extremely upset with John Bentley Mays and with Frank Davey. I was genuinely pained and damaged by the Bentley Mays article, but we don't want to go through that again. I became upset over critical responses to my work when there is a misreading of my life obviously coming from a misreading of the poems. There's over-intentionality in their readings. Why they have to relate it to my life, I don't know, but it does seem to lead to critical error, or the other way around.

JANICE: Do you think the critical impulse to collapse the writing into biography is more pronounced in work about women writers? Since patriarchal ideology has associated women with the private experiential world, are women writers perceived as more transparently connected to the 'personal'?

PHYLLIS: Yes, because you know how often I've been called a solipsistic poet. Nowhere has anyone ever called John Newlove a solipsistic poet, and it seems to me he is as much, or more so, than I am. He's a poet I admire very, very greatly, but I have never seen the same kind of attack on his work for his self-absorption and his negativity and his depression and longing for death that is similar to mine in many ways. I have never seen his work critiqued in this way. Nor would I ever learn much about John Newlove's life from criticism. But you might learn a fair bit about mine from criticism or reviews or whatever. But now I am redeemed, it seems. In the latest reviews I am in a state of illumination and grace compared to my old, self-absorbed, solipsistic state. I've been forgiven my sins of the past. I'm amused at someone saying, 'It's all right now. She has matured and gone beyond to a larger universe.' Of course, that is an expectation I have of my own work, that it will mature, and that I will mature, and become wiser and better as I continue to write. God help me if

I didn't get better! But for somebody to say this with surprise, 'You're getting better.' Well, I hope so! Where else can you go except down? I want the poetry to be less self-absorbed, to be bigger and more relevant. I want to be behind the poems paring my fingernails. But I resent it when some smug critic says, 'Now she has reached this higher state.' I don't know why it annoys me so much, except that they repeat all that business about being neurotic and solipsistic. I'm not sure my poetry ever was *all* that self-absorbed, in comparison with, say, John Newlove or Al Purdy or others who write about themselves.

JANICE: Your suicide poems are more ironic than solipsistic. 'To Friends Who Have Also Considered Suicide' is very playful. You've written a number of poems which point specifically to the separation between the author and the poem. I'm thinking about 'Alex,' where the little boy yells, 'Fire, fire!' and then burns up a picture of you. And you quote Roland Barthes in your *Wilson's Bowl* preface: 'I am both too big and too weak for writing. I am alongside it.' Your poem 'Performance' wryly conjugates verbs in order to describe a reader response theory. You write: 'I devise. You devise. We devise. To be together briefly with the page, the fallen timber.' Your writing continually insists on the internal distance between writer and text.

PHYLLIS: Yes, 'Performance' is a theoretical meditation on the lyrical 'I.' Because I have been accused of being self-centred, I've had to examine exactly the uses of the 'I.' This is, again, part of the critical blindness. Once I *write* 'I,' it is not 'me.' Critics don't always go along with a fiction in poetry as they go along with a fiction in fiction. This is part of the power of the lyric, how it has immediacy; it seems to be a straightforward statement coming right on the breath as a first impulse, a direct response to experience. But the 'I' isn't necessarily 'me,' and that is where the critical confusion begins. In 'Performance' I take up the use of the first-person singular and play with it and try to see the variety of ways the 'I' functions in poetry. It's a longish prose poem, but I think I cover a lot of theoretical ground in a short space. I took the opportunity to make a case for myself as having a right to use the first person without having a biographical reading of the poem, so the 'I' can be a trickster figure and remain a shifting 'I.' The 'I' is used strategically in poetry, not always at a conscious level, but in the ultimate product of the poem where one can see or feel a different person who goes along with changes in one's own life over time. But, also, the use of voice and tone, which is part of the strategy of the poem, guides the reader to the appropriate reading. By listening to the voice that's speaking, you find the clues. But not everybody reads with that attuned ear, because they're so focused on the subject matter. I'm never terribly interested in reading about what my poems mean. I am always interested in the technical insight that a critic displays about the work rather than the great thematic stuff. Technique, of course, is the major carrier of the significance of the poem. If you're not writing about important things, then why write? How you convey that interests me. I think that's fairly general among poets.

JANICE: Your own interest in form has led you to break down a number of different poetic forms. Your 'Imperfect Sestina' develops a poetics of failure or transgression, where the poem insists on breaking with convention. Your ghazals and anti-ghazals repeat this process.

PHYLLIS: I'm always rather uneasy working with inherited forms, given forms, closed forms, and yet I seem to be tempted and challenged by them. Once I start on the form, there does seem to be this anarchic part of me that wants to disrupt the form and give it a new life or a new focus or shift it in some way so expectations are disrupted and not satisfied, so it's a challenge to the reader. John Hulcoop has been writing about this disruptive aspect of my personality, that I do not want to conform and am caught between a very conforming personality in some ways and an almost childish need to be a revolutionary of some kind, and to disrupt what is given. It is my way into new territory using the old form, which just happens along; it's handy and I use it. It's too easy to copy and not very hard to write a sestina. The interesting thing is how to write a sestina and *not* write a sestina, how to write a ghazal and *not* write a ghazal. Again, it's elusive and you invoke all kinds of associations from the past about other poems and how that form has been used; you develop a kind of literary historical shorthand. A sestina in our culture is better known than the ghazal, where I import new subject matter just by importing that form. Middle Eastern politics was on my mind at the time, and a whole new series of images was brought in. With the ghazal, there is a convention of using conventional imagery, but it won't have the same meaning for *us* that is has for an Arabic or Urdu writer. It's simply another rich textual source or cultural inheritance that I use while doing something new with it. It's not terribly profound, but it is a way of not repeating exactly but repeating with changes.

JANICE: I want to turn our discussion of breaking conventions back to the issue of women writing. I was listening to Nicole Brossard and Daphne Marlatt identify themselves as writers. Marlatt talks about herself as a feminist writer and defines feminism as not simply a set of ideas or polemic. Nicole Brossard defines herself as 'a woman writer with a feminist consciousness and a lesbian body.' She feels this refusal to name herself as *feminist* writer enables her to speak with the complexity of feminism. How would you define yourself, or would you avoid self-definition?

PHYLLIS: Well, I evade it mainly because I have this horror of being labelled. I have been reassured by various studies that have been done on my work recently that, indeed, I am seen increasingly as a feminist writer. I'm not sure why always or how, or what I've done. It's clearer to me while I'm reading the work. I refuse to identify myself. It makes me uneasy, but again it's a protective measure of what I call my complexity. I don't want to constrict myself with labels, or have others constrict me with labels, but it could be just a coward's way out. In spite of my cowardice or whatever, I'm glad that increasingly feminist critics are seeing my work as progressing through the years towards a feminist stance. It has not been done in a programmatic way in my poetry; it just pops out with an increasing consciousness of what I'm doing. I began thinking of myself as a socialist, a left-wing person, not necessarily a writer, and that was a major identity for me for a long time. And then that shifted to anarchism, and then to feminism. In a sense, I'm still confused about a lot of these issues. I guess I write so little that I am grateful for whatever happens. Though I may say I'm not going to write about these guru figures any more, male figures, I still find myself doing that and cannot bring myself to deny the gifts of the poem in order to conform to my conscious ideologies at the time, which can shift again. Perhaps the unconscious is a truer test of what you really believe and feel and how you experience things. When I wrote my little poem called

'Thinking Cap' as I was about to leave for Detroit, I thought of it as a nationalist poem. Then I saw it also as a feminist poem. I was very pleased with this aggressive invader of Detroit, of going to the U.S. and seeing myself with my red hat arriving as a power, a trickster figure, who was going to steal back. In a sense I had been brought up with William Carlos Williams as the be-all and end-all of poetic correctness. The poem asks, 'Is this my poetic?' It's a poetic I was taught and accepted. It was received wisdom, and now is the time, perhaps, to be questioning the received wisdom of the holiness of the image, of the holiness of the objective poem, and asking, ultimately, is this *really* my way of experiencing and writing poems? So I'm going to snatch the plum – take it back. In a sense I must have felt that part of me had been stolen and not expressed by this received male poetic, the poetic line, the genealogy of our poetic inheritance. It is part of my wonderment about where poetry is going, because I don't see where the next big shift is going to occur. It probably will be in reconstituting a feminist poetic, which is already in process. But I don't think we're anywhere near. It's like starting with the *tabula rasa* and saying, 'All right, now, how do you get back to that?' You don't; we are loaded down with our poetic culture, though it would be interesting to know if some virgin poet could come along with a virgin mind and start writing out of that. Maybe they're doing it? They probably are. I think that I will discover who I am eventually, or what my poetry's about, only as I keep doing it. I can't give you a nice, neat answer about feminism or lesbianism or bisexuality or who I am because I hope I'm still changing –

JANICE: And snatching the plum.

PHYLLIS: Yes – very swift mover, fast-footed Mercury. I tend to the swift dance when I'm confronted with those questions of evasion. But I really see evasion as a psychic strategy, and a rather important one, too, if you're going to be surprised by anything you do, which I like to be.

JANICE: When you talk about your evasiveness and the question of gender and sexuality, your bisexuality is considered as betwixt and between, as quicksilver desire which moves between genders. Bisexuality has been criticized as a sexual practice and its elusiveness is interpreted as an evasion.

PHYLLIS: It's called fence-sitting by those who think it's a choice.

It's transformational. It's being the laurel tree and Diana? Who was it?

JANICE: Daphne.

PHYLLIS: Daphne? Our friend Daphne! We must tell her that. One can attempt to name, I guess, but it seems to me that it is an ability to shift forms or to be transmuted from one state to another. An alchemical image would be another appropriate image for it; and I see it only poetically.

JANICE: In your writing there is much erotic pleasure.

PHYLLIS: It's simply one way of looking at and responding to the world. It is odd that it still has an erotic flavour; I guess it is repression, or sublimation, or memory. As I lose my memory more and more, there are other memories coming along, replacing my practical memory.

JANICE: Earlier we were talking about the revolutionary and conformist tensions in your writing. Isn't this transgressive play concerning the female body a part of women's challenge to the limits of our prescribed symbolic as well as material worlds? Isn't this playfulness important to your poetics too?

PHYLLIS: I just had another thought about playfulness in my poetry; I think I referred to it as an evasive technique, but, of course, women have always been urged to be coy and playful, and they play their little power games. So playfulness could be part of my timorousness about making too disruptive statements that are going to be difficult to deal with. I avoid confrontation. That, of course, is the strategy of women: to manipulate by charm and delight and playfulness. There is a coy kind of thing in the poetry which doesn't come right out and scream and shout and stamp its feet. I hope it doesn't come out as coy, but it is a possible unconscious strategy on my part in order to say unpleasant things ...

JANICE: Seductively?

PHYLLIS: Seductively, yes. True confessions!

JANICE: What kind of unpleasant things do you think you're saying?

PHYLLIS: Let's leave that for the therapist. Read the poems, read the poems. All right?

Saltspring Island, August 1987

Biocritical Essays

JEANNETTE ARMSTRONG, sculptor, artist, writer, teacher, and activist, was born in 1948 on the Penticton Indian Reserve, where she raised her two children. An Okanagan Indian, she received a traditional education through the teachings of Okanagan elders and a BFA at the University of Victoria (1978). During 1979–85 she researched and wrote for the Okanagan Curriculum Writing Project. Her community-based work has extended into work on the Okanagan Community Council (1980–4) and the Tribal Council (1984–8). In 1986 Armstrong became the director of the En'owkin Centre (Okanagan Education Resources) in Penticton. Most recently, she has become the first director of the En'owkin International School of Writing in Penticton, a diploma-granting (through the University of Victoria) creative-writing school organized by and for Native people.

Armstrong continues to write and make visual art while teaching creative writing and performance at En'owkin as well as delivering her powerful oratory performances at gatherings throughout North America. She has written two children's books, *Enwisteetkaw* (Walk in water) (Okanagan Tribal Council 1982) and *Neekna and Chemai* (Theytus 1984). Her noval *Slash* (Theytus 1985) chronicles the Indian movement of the 1960s and 1970s through the eyes of a young male activist. Armstrong's talks on Native and cultural issues are in great demand, and she has published occasional oratory. *Breath Tracks* (Williams-Wallace / Theytus 1991) collects her poems. With architect Douglas Cardinal, Armstrong wrote *The Native Creative Process: A Collaborative Discourse* (Theytus 1991). See Jeannette Armstrong,

'Writing from a Native Woman's Perspective,' in *In the Feminine: Women and Words Conference Proceedings 1983*, ed. Ann Dybikowski et al. (Longspoon 1985), 55–7; 'Discipline and Sharing: Education in the Indian Way,' *Fourth World Journal* 1, no. 2 (Winter 1985–6), 73–88; 'Traditional Indigenous Education: A Natural Process,' in *Tradition Change Survival: The Answers Are within Us* (UBC First Nations House 1988); 'Real Power: Aboriginal Women – Past, Present and Future,' *Status of Women Journal* (1990); 'Bridging Cultures,' *Columbiana: Journal of the Intermountain Northwest* 30 (1989), 28–30; 'Cultural Robbery: Imperialism – Voices of Native Women,' *Trivia* 14 (1989), 21–3; 'The Disempowerment of First North American Native Peoples and Empowerment through Their Writing,' *Gatherings* 1, no. 1 (1990), 141–6; and 'Words,' in *Telling It: Women and Language across Cultures*, ed. Telling It Collective (Press Gang 1990), 23–30. See also Lenore Keeshig-Tobias, 'An Emergent Voice,' rev. of *Slash, Fuse* (March–April 1988), 39–40; Lee Maracle, 'Fork in the Road: A Story for Native Youth,' rev. of *Slash, Fuse* (July 1988), 42; Noel Elizabeth Currie, 'Jeannette Armstrong and the Colonial Legacy,' and Margery Fee, 'Upsetting Fake Ideas: Jeannette Armstrong's *Slash* and Beatrice Culleton's *April Raintree*,' *Canadian Literature* 124–5 (1990), 138–52 and 168–80 respectively; an interview with Hartmut Lutz, in *Contemporary Challenges: Conversations with Canadian Native Authors* (Fifth House 1991), 13–32; and the section on Armstrong in Julia Emberley, *Thresholds of Difference: Feminist Critique, Native Women's Writings, Postcolonial Theory* (Toronto: U of Toronto P 1993).

DI BRANDT was born in 1952 and grew up in Reinland, a Mennonite farming village in southern Manitoba. She earned a BTH (1972) at the Canadian Mennonite Bible College, a BA in Honours English (1975) at the University of Manitoba, and an MA in English (1976) at the University of Toronto. She was married in 1971, and divorced in 1990. With her two daughters Brandt lives in Winnipeg, where in 1993 she completed a PHD dissertation at the University of Manitoba entitled '"Wild Mother Dancing": Maternal Narrative in Contemporary Writing by Women in Canada and Quebec.' She co-edited *Contemporary Verse 2* (1985–8), edited fiction for *Herizons* (1985–6), and since 1989 has been the poetry editor of *Prairie Fire*. Having taught creative-writing workshops across Canada, she teaches English and creative writing at the University of Winnipeg. Her first book, *Questions i asked my mother* (Turnstone 1987) won the Gerald Lampert Award (1987) and was short-listed for both the Governor General's Award and the Commonwealth Poetry Prize. This collection of poetry and prose challenges the authority of the family and a father-centred religion. Her second book of lyric poetry, *Agnes in the Sky* (Turnstone 1990), which won the McNally Robinson Award for the Manitoba Book of the Year, is influenced by the imagism of H.D. and chronicles the experiences of a woman in mid-life who remembers and accepts the loss involved in exploring 'so many different kinds of love.' Brandt is writing her first non-fiction prose book with Patrick Michael Marsh, 'No Tears Allowed: A Prison Biography.' A collection of poems, *mother, not mother* (Mercury P 1992), replies to the poet's query about 'why she can't put down simply, / i am the mother, / & leave it like that.' Short-lined couplets translate 'mother' as child-bearer, lover, friend, daughter, land, nurturer, abuse survivor, and sensual celebrant, 'growing toward beauty / growing old.' See Gary Boire, 'Against Powerful Mal(e)dictions,' *Essays on Canadian Writing* (forthcoming); and Thom Tammaro, 'Di Brandt's *Agnes in the Sky*' *NDQ* 59, no. 3 (Summer 1991), 234–7.

NICOLE BROSSARD was born in Montreal in 1943 and is the prolific author of innovative poetry, novels, essays, and cross-genre texts. In 1971 she received a Baccalauréat at the Université du Québec à Montréal and two years later a Scolarité de maîtrise en letters at the Université de Montréal. She is the mother of a daughter. Brossard contributed a monologue, 'The Writer,' to the 1976 feminist collective theatrical production *La Nef des sorcières* (*A Clash of Symbols*, 1979). In 1976 Brossard also edited a collection of 'new' Quebec writing, *Stratégies du réel / The Story So Far 6* (Coach House 1979). As co-director of a National Film Board documentary, *Some American Feminists* (1976), Brossard encountered Kate Millet, Betty Friedan, Ti-Grace Atkinson, Rita May Brown, and Simone de Beauvoir. She was co-founder and editor of the review *La Barre du jour* (1965–75), re-named *La Nouvelle Barre du jour* (1977–9), and the feminist journal *Les Têtes de pioche* (1976–9), where she editorialized, 'We, as feminists, do not want "power." We want to unmask it in all its forms ... We want space ..., to dance, to discover, to create, to invent a new way of life ... which is no longer conjugated solely in the masculine.' Brossard also founded the feminist press L'Intégrale in 1982 and was president of the Third International Feminist Book Fair in Montreal (1988). With Lisette Girouard she co-edited L'Anthologie de la poésie des femmes au Québec (Montréal: Les Editions du Remue-ménage 1991), and along with Québecoise feminist writers Louky Bersianik and Jovette Marchessault was featured in Dorothy Héneault's creative documentary Firewords (NFB 1986).

Brossard's acute and sensual contributions to lesbian, feminist, and postmodern theory and writing have made her a valued participant and teacher at international feminist and literary events. Her 'fiction-theory' and essays were collected in La Lettre aérienne (1985; The Aerial Letter, trans. Marlene Wildeman, Women's P, 1988). She has twice received the Governor General's Award for poetry: for 'Mécanique jongleuse' suivi de 'Masculin grammaticale' (1974; Daydream Mechanics, trans. Larry Shouldice, Coach House, 1980); and for Double Impression (1984). Other poetry titles include: 'Aube à la saison,' in Trois (1965); Mordre en sa chair (1966); L'Echo bouge beau (1968); Suite logique (1970); Le Centre blanc (1970); La Partie pour le tout (1975); Le Centre blanc (a retrospective collection, 1978); D'Arcs de cycle la dérive (1979); L'Aviva (1985); and Domaine d'écriture (1985). Amantes (1980), translated by Barbara Godard, became Lovhers (Guernica 1986), which writes a delirious space for the 'unprecedented vertigo' of 'my continent woman.' Sous la langue / Under tongue deeply eroticizes language in a translation by Susanne de Lotbinière-Harwood (L'Essentielle éditrice and Gynergy Books 1987). A tout regard and Installations, both published in 1989, won Le Grand Prix de poésie de la Fondation Les Forges. With images by anglo-Canadian artist Christine Davis, Brossard published a deluxe limited edition of ten poems, Thyphon dru (Paris 1990).

A number of Brossard's fictions have been published in translation. The self-reflexive novel Un livre (1970; A Book, trans. Larry Shouldice, Coach House, 1976), invites the reader to play: 'The words are yours.' Sold Out (1973; Turn of a Pang, Coach House, 1976) and French Kiss (1977; French Kiss Or: A Pang's Progress, Coach House, 1986), both translated by Patricia Claxton, invoke the city, a 'muffled world filled with liquid symptoms.' The 'hologram' as a four-dimensional space for the representation of women is introduced in *French Kiss* and extended in *Picture Theory* (1980; *Picture Theory*, trans. Barbara Godard, Guernica / Roof P, 1991). *L'Amèr ou le chapitre effrité* (1977; *These Our Mothers Or: The Disintegrating Chapter*, trans. Barbara Godard, Coach House, 1983) makes way for a non-patriarchal woman to enter the symbolic. *Le Sens apparent* (1980; *Surfaces of Sense*, trans. Fiona Strachan, Coach House, 1989) introduces 'a few characters, all women living in reality, in the middle of a tender and difficult fiction which painfully kept them alive.' *Journal intime* (1984), originally a CBC radio commission, ironically denounces the journal as 'a form of writing which demands too much of me and not enough of who I am.' Divided into four parts (a travel fiction, a critical reading, a translation, and a book), *Le Désert mauve* (1987; *Mauve Desert*, trans. Susanne de Lotbinière-Harwood, 1990) investigates desire and 'reality,' which 'regulate the alternating movement of fiction and truth.' *La Nuit verte du Parc Labyrinthe* (Les Editions Trois 1992), published in French, English (trans. Lou Nelson), and Spanish (trans. Marina Fe), is a series of self-reflexive prose narratives set in Barcelona during the 1990 Fourth International Feminist Book Fair. *A tout regard* (Bibliothèque québécoise 1989) includes 'Mauve' and 'Character / Jeu de lettres,' several 'transformations' or performative creative translations co-authored with Daphne Marlatt as collaborative chapbooks (NBJ, collection Transformance, 1985 and 1986), and 'Polynésie des yeux / Polynesya of the Eyes,' Brossard's only self-translated work.

In 1991 Nicole Brossard was awarded Le Prix Athanase-David, the highest honour the Quebec government can bestow on a writer. See Caroline Bayard, 'Subersions Is the Order of the Day,' *Essays on Canadian Writing* 7–8 (1977), 17–25; Louise Forsyth, 'The Novels of Nicole Brossard: An Active Voice,' *Room of One's Own* 4, nos. 1–2 (1978), 30–8; *Traces, écriture de Nicole Brossard*, special issue of *La Nouvelle Barre du jour* 118–19 (1982); Louise Cotnoir et al., 'Interview with Nicole Brossard on Picture Theory,' *Canadian Fiction Magazine* 47 (1983); Barbara Godard, 'L'Amèr or the Exploding Chapter: Nicole Brossard at the Site of Feminist Deconstruction,' *Atlantis* 9, no. 2 (1984), 23–34; Louise Forsyth, 'Beyond the Myths and Fictions of

Traditionalism and Nationalism: The Political in the Work of Nicole Brossard,' and Martha Rosenfeld, 'The Development of a Lesbian Sensibility in the Work of Jovette Marchessault and Nicole Brossard,' in *Traditionalism, Nationalism and Feminism: Women Writers of Quebec*, ed. Paula Gilbert Lewis (Greenwood 1985), 157–72 and 227–39 respectively; Louise Forsyth, 'Destructing Formal Space / Accelerating Motion in the Work of Nicole Brossard,' in *A Mazing Space*, ed. Shirley Neuman and Smaro Kamboureli (Longspoon/NeWest 1986), 334–44; Lorraine Wier, 'From Picture to Hologram: Nicole Brossard's Grammar of Utopia,' in *A Mazing Space*, 345–52; Clea Notar, 'An Interview with Nicole Brossard,' in *So to Speak* (Véhicule 1988), 123–43; Louise Dupré, 'Nicole Brossard, la quête de l'absolu,' in *Stratégies du vertige* (Les Editions du Remue-ménage 1989), 83–152; Karen Gould, *Writing in the Feminine: Feminism and Experimental Writing in Quebec* (Southern Illinois UP 1990), 52–107; Alice Parker, 'The Mauve Horizon of Nicole Brossard,' *Québec Studies* 10 (1990), 107–119; Alice Parker, 'Nicole Brossard: A Differential Equation of Lesbian Love,' in *Lesbian Texts and Contexts: Radical Revisions* (New York UP 1990), 304–29; Susan Knutson, 'Daphne Marlatt and Nicole Brossard: Writing Metanarrative in the Feminine,' *Signature* 3 (1990), 28–43.

ELLY DANICA, writer, lecturer, and visual artist, was born in Holland in 1947. In 1952 her family moved to Moose Jaw, Saskatchewan. Married at eighteen so that she could escape her father's house, she left husband and young child when she was twenty-five and began an independent life. While recovering from problems with alcohol and prescription drugs, Danica became an accomplished textile artist and read widely while living in seclusion for fifteen years in a rural Saskatchewan church she had converted to a home. At age forty, frustrated by the lack of progress on a novel she was writing, Danica began probing more deeply into her past. The result of this self-analysis is *Don't: A Woman's Word*, an autobiographical narrative which recounts her father's sexual, physical, and psychological brutalization of her from the age of four through childhood.

Danica wrote twenty-two hundred pages of journal notes before she sat down and wrote *Don't* in three weeks. She sent manuscript excerpts to Nicole Brossard, who was teaching at the third summer women's writing workshop, West Word 3, a two-week retreat sponsored by the West Coast Women and Words Society. When Danica was accepted into the workshop, she assumed her writing was simply notes towards a book. Brossard, astonished by the content and writerly innovation, assured Danica her manuscript was not only complete but 'postmodern.' Prince Edward Island publisher and writer Libby Oughton, another student at West Word, published *Don't* through Gynergy Books, a feminist imprint of her Ragweed Press. Danica published the book without prior publicity and called it 'autofiction' in order to minimize attempts by others to dissuade her from publication and to avoid possible lawsuits. Immediately following the publication of *Don't*, Gynergy Press received one hundred unsolicited poetry and prose manuscripts of autobiographical incest narratives. Peter Gzowski interviewed Danica on CBC-Radio, and the response across the country by other survivors of sexual abuse was startling. (Studies vary, but some experts suggest that one in two girl children and one in three boys are sexually abused before the age of eighteen.) The Gynergy edition of *Don't* sold more than ten thousand copies in Canada, and it was translated into German, Dutch, and French, with editions in the United Kingdom, Ireland, and the United States. McClelland and Stewart published a mass-market paperback edition with an introduction by Gzowski.

Through public lectures and workshops Danica has been actively working towards change in the increasingly appalling statistics of child sexual abuse. The book has been widely reviewed for different communities of readers, and even *Alberta Report*, a far-right weekly review, writes that it is more than a 'feminist tract' and quotes Danica's conviction that 'we have to give up this myth of the nurturing nuclear family. It isn't that sweet, charming little environment we see on television.' Danica comments in an afterword to the McClelland and Stewart edition: 'There are now reviews which speak of my courage. I prefer to call it determination. Determination not to let men control or define who I am my whole life' (99). Like other feminists actively engaged in healing the abused and seeking just punishment for the abusers, Danica describes the women wounded by child sexual abuse as 'survivors' not 'victims.' See Peter Gzowski, interview with 'Elly,' *The Latest Morningside Papers* (McClelland and Stewart 1989), 116–30;

Shirley Hartwell, 'Words Speaking Body Memory,' *Trivia* 13 (1989), 48–56; Linda Warley, 'Inhabiting Contradiction: The Female Subject in *Don't: A Woman's Word*,' *Open Letter* 8, no. 2 (1992), 70–80; Janice Williamson, 'I Peel Myself Out of My Skin: Reading *Don't: A Woman's Word*,' in *Essays on Life Writing*, ed. Marlene Kadar (U of Toronto P 1992). For related material see Ellen Bass and Laura Davis, *The Courage to Heal: A Guide for Women Survivors of Child Sexual Abuse* (Harper & Row 1988); Sylvia Fraser, *My Father's House: A Memoir of Incest and of Healing* (Collins 1987); Judith Herman, *Father/Daughter Incest* (Harvard UP 1981); and Liza Potvin, *White Lies (for My Mother)* (NeWest 1992).

KRISTJANA GUNNARS is a poet, and prose writer, translator, and essayist who was born in 1948 as Gunnarsdottir in Reykjavik, Iceland, of a Danish mother and Icelandic father. In 1964 she moved with her family to Oregon, where she learned English and eventually studied English literature at Oregon State University (BA, 1974). She married in 1967 and has one son. In 1969 Gunnars moved to Vancouver, where she became a landed immigrant. She earned an MA in literary studies from the University of Regina (1977) and has studied towards a PHD in English at the University of Manitoba (1981). Having worked as a writer-in-residence and taught at universities across the Canadian West, she currently teaches creative writing and literature at the University of Alberta.

Her book of poetry *One-Eyed Moon Maps* (Press Procépic 1980) was followed by *Settlement Poems 1* and *Settlement Poems 2* (Turnstone 1980), which tracks the written testimonies of Icelandic settlers in Manitoba. *Wake-Pick Poems* (Anansi 1981) is informed by the nighttime mythologies of Iceland's changelings and spinning insomniacs. A collection of short prose, *The Axe's Edge* (Press Porcépic 1983), fictionalizes how Gunnars 'became conscious of a need to listen ... [to] stories that exist prior to being told – the stories told in the private and public writings of Icelandic settlers of the Canadian West. *The Night Workers of Ragnarök* (Press Procépic 1985) collects poems which 'deal in some way with a return to the old country after acculturating in the new' and 'with the inverse situation of a return to the new country after readjusting to the old.' A spare imagistic chapbook, *water, waiting* (Underwhich Editions 1987), invokes 'the movement of the sea' and a 'solemn anxiety / the longing for calm.' *Carnival of Longing* (Turnstone 1989) links poems to an absent lover with prose-poetry queries about the nature of language and writing: 'this is an autumn I cannot contain / in the language on which we are carried.' The fractured numbered 'chapters' of her novel *The Prowler* (Red Deer College P 1989) frame an Icelandic woman's immigrant experience and a self-reflexive fictive meditation on the violence of militarized landscapes and anorexic female bodies. The creative non-fiction *Zero Hour* (Red Deer College P 1991) shifts between a Winnipeg summer and a woman's account of her father's death. In 1992 she published *The Guest House and Other Stories* (Stoddart/Anansi) and a novel, *The Substance of Forgetting* (Red Deer College P), which continues the writing strategies of *The Prowler* and *Zero Hour*. This autofiction explores the nature of desire – 'a perpetual descent into an unknown depth' – in relation to a love affair with a Quebec separatist, friendships with women, and a passion for a new home in the luscious interior of British Columbia, where 'home is where you choose to forget and choose to remember at the same time.'

Gunnar's commitment to 'the translation, the expansion, and the preservation of Icelandic culture, as it exists both in Iceland and in North America,' led her to co-found Gunnars and Campbell, a publishing house for works in translation, and to translate *Stephan G. Stephansson: Selected Prose and Poetry* (Red Deer College P 1988), the work of one of Iceland's greatest poets, who emigrated to Canada at the age of twenty and wrote most of his work on his farm in Markerville, Alberta. Gunnars edited *Unexpected Fictions: New Icelandic Canadian Writing* (Turnstone 1989, where she writes that 'the Icelanders who came to Canada and America were, in fact, *released* from history ... You were able, quite simply, to forget about your past if you wanted ... There is a fresh breeze blowing through the rooms we are looking into.' She has also edited *Crossing the River: Essays in Honour of Margaret Laurence* (Turnstone 1988). See Jane Casey, 'An Interview with Kristjana Gunnars,' *Contemporary Verse* 2 8, no. 3 (1984); M. Travis Lane, 'Troll Turning: Poetic Voice in the Poetry of Kristjana Gunnars,' *Canadian Literature* 105 (1985), 59–68; Pamela Banting et al. 'hiatus Inter Views hiatus,' *Prairie Fire* 7, no. 3 (1986), 110–19;

Paul Hjartarson, 'Transformation of the 'i': Self and Community in the Poetry of Kristjana Gunnars,' in *Canada and Nordic Countries: Proceedings from the Second International Conference of the Nordic Association for Canadian Studies* (Lund, Sweden, 1988), 123–37; Judith Owens, ' "Drawing/in": Wholeness and Dislocation in the Work of Kristjana Gunnars,' in *Contemporary Manitoba Writers: New Critical Studies*, ed. Kenneth James Hughes (Turnstone 1990), 64–78; Diana Brydon, 'The White Inuit Speaks: Contamination as Literary Strategy,' in *Past the Last Post: Theorizing Post-Colonialism and Post-Modernism*, ed. Ian Adam and Helen Tiffin (U of Calgary P 1990), 191–203.

CLAIRE HARRIS, a poet, fiction writer, and editor, was born in Trinidad, where she studied at St Joseph's Convent, Port of Spain. She continued her studies at University College, Dublin (BA Hons., English, 1961); University of the West Indies, Jamaica (Post-graduate Diploma in Education, 1963); and the University of Nigeria, Lagos (Diploma in Mass Media and Communications, 1975). Upon moving to Canada in 1966, Harris began teaching English in separate schools in Calgary. During 1976–9 she edited a set of posters, 'Poetry Goes Public.' Poetry editor of the literary journal *Dandelion* during 1981–9, she was also a founding editor of another Alberta journal, *Blue Buffalo*, of which she was managing editor from 1984 to 1987. Afro-Canadian writers are 'working without a net' in an ethnocentric society, writes Harris, who is 'deeply embedded in the black earth of the West Indies' and influenced by West Indian folk-tales, Spanish surrealists, and Adrienne Rich. Her *Fables from the Women's Quarters* (Williams-Wallace 1984) won the Commonwealth Prize for best first book for the Americas area. These prose and short-lined long poems are often double-voiced. In 'Where the Sky Is a Pitiful Tent' her sensual tropical lyrics are juxtaposed with the brutal oral testimony of Guatemalan revolutionary Rigoberta Menchú. The same year, Harris published her poems *Translation into Fiction* (Goose Lane), which search for a 'new naming' to counteract her representation 'in films and books / [where I] find myself / always here / stripped to skin and sex.' *Travelling to Find a Remedy* (Goose Lane 1986) includes fragmented poems and image patterns to 'test the frail bridge of words / [which] anchors us / islands / in our separateness.' In *The Conception of Winter* (Williams-Wallace 1989) Harris claims that 'this poem will not catch you as you fall / ... it is no use at all   at all / nothing at all / ... it won't beat a drum   it can't dance.' In spite of this, Harris's poems ask difficult questions about how we can engage ourselves in remaking our language and world. *Drawing Down a Daughter* (Goose Lane 1992) is a 'dream collage' of short-lined, concrete, and prose poems interspersed with prose narratives which explore in part immigration and the inheritance of generations: 'Daughter   to live is to dream the self / to make a fiction / this telling i begin / you stranded in landscape of your time / will redefine / shedding my tales / to grow your own.' With Edna Alford, Harris edited *Kitchen Talk: Contemporary Women's Prose and Poetry* (Red Deer College P 1992), a cross-cultural Canadian anthology in which the domestic speaks 'what it means / has meant to be female in the twentieth century.' *Under Black Light* will be published in 1993 by Williams-Wallace. Her work is anthologized in Paula Burnett, ed., *The Penguin Book of Caribbean Verse in English* (1986); Rosemary Sullivan, ed., *Poetry by Canadian Women* (Oxford UP 1989); and George Bowering and Linda Hutcheon, eds., *Likely Stories* (Coach House 1992). See Harris's essay 'Poets in Limbo,' in *A Mazing Space: Writing Canadian Women Writing*, ed. Shirley Neuman and Smaro Kamboureli (Longspoon/NeWest 1986); 'Ole Talk: A Sketch,' in *Language in Her Eye: Writing and Gender*, ed. Libby Scheier et al. (Coach House 1990), 131–41.

SMARO KAMBOURELI was born in 1955 in Thessaloniki, Greece, where she lived until she graduated with a BA in English in 1977. Awarded a Fulbright Scholarship, she travelled to study at State University of New York at Binghamton, New York. In 1978 she moved to Canada to complete her MA on American writer John Hawkes (1981) and her PHD on Canadian poetry (1987) at the University of Manitoba. In 1987 she became a faculty member in the University of Victoria, where she teaches Canadian writing. Her first book, a long prose poem, *in the second person* (Longspoon 1985), begins with a fragmentary commentary about displacement and transformation through immigration; the ongoingness of this process is implied by the title of the preface, 'An Open Parenthesis.' Here 'writing in broken english ... [is] a translation of constrasting systems of perception, a simultaneous rendering of the past and the present.' Journal poems follow two years of inner and actual travels through Canada and Greece documenting the sensual and intellectual life of a woman who encodes loss in new words and diary entries 'as erratic life-liners.' The female writing subject shatters into an eloquent polyphony of 'i. me. you. the other. / one word emotionally multiplied.' Kamboureli is now completing a novel, in part an imaginary life of the Virgin Mary, tentatively titled 'Various Blues.'

Her energetic interest in literary criticism and theory has led to numerous readings, workshops, and lectures in Canada and Europe, and to essays on Canadian writers, including 'Beauty and the Beast: Resistance to Theory in the Feminine,' *Open Letter* 7, no. 8 (1990), 5–27; her co-editing of *A Mazing Space: Writing Canadian Women Writing* with Shirley Neuman; a major contribution to the Canadian women writer entries in *The Feminist Companion to Literature in English* (Yale UP 1991); ongoing editorial work on literary and critical NeWest Press publications; co-editorial work on *Signature*, a journal of Canadian literature and theory; and a critical work, *On the Edge of Genre: The Contemporary Canadian Long Poem* (U of Toronto P 1991). See also her correspondence with Lola Tostevin, 'Women of Letters,' *Tessera* 5 (1988), 13–26. She is currently at work on a book-length study of multiculturalism and ethnic discourse.

JOY KOGAWA, novelist, poet, essayist, and activist was born Joy Nakayama in Vancouver in 1935. She has devoted much of her energy to telling a Japanese-Canadian story and working with others to seek redress from the Canadian government for the internment of twenty thousand Japanese Canadians during the Second World War. 'Some people believe the Japanese community in Canada never recovered. It's not visible now; it's invisible and silent,' writes Kogawa. Her contributions were celebrated when she was made a Member of the Order of Canada. From 1983 to 1985 Kogawa worked actively with the National Association of Japanese Canadians. In 1985 she commented, 'Today, we are still treated as foreigners – by strangers, at parties, in department stores.'

Kogawa is a *nisei*, or second-generation Canadian, who under the War Measures Act in 1942 lost all property and possessions when her family was forcibly moved to a internment camp in Slocan, BC, where Kogawa was educated until the end of the war. In 1945, forbidden to return to the West Coast, her family moved to Coaldale, Alberta. Kogawa studied education at the University of Alberta and taught elementary school in Coaldale for a year before studying music at the University of Toronto, and continuing her studies at the Anglican Women's Training College and the University of Saskatchewan. She married in 1957, had two children, and divorced in 1968.

In the early 1960s Kogawa's first writings were experimental short fictions, but 'because [poetry] was much more accepted then' she changed genres. The first of her poetry was *The Splintered Moon* (U of New Brunswick P 1968). *A Choice of Dreams* (McClelland and Stewart 1974) includes poems which revisit memories of her evacuation during the Second World War, as well as of her visit to Hiroshima, where the poet as tourist encounters 'victims and victimizers in circular flight.' *Jericho Road* (McClelland and Stewart 1977) includes series of lyrics on the pain of a marriage's dissolution. Through detailed images, sometimes mythological, sometimes minimalist, *Woman in the Woods* (Mosiac 1985) considers issues both personal and political.

About her first story, which focused on a white Albertan family, Kogawa comments, 'I had disguised my background to make it acceptable. I denied my identity so thoroughly. Still I don't really think of myself as Japanese.' *Obasan* (Lester and Orpen Dennys 1981; Penguin 1983) won the *Books in Canada* First Novel Award, the Before Columbus Foundation American Book Award, and the Canadian Authors Association Book of the Year Award, and was translated and published in Japan (1983). The novel is narrated by a fictive girl, Naomi, born in 1936 (and therefore one year less wise than Kogawa, according to the author). The narrative includes poetic passages and the silence of a traditional character, Obasan. Kogawa has commented that 'if we never really see Obasan, she will always be oppressed.' The novel's constrasting character, Aunt Emily, is derived from the spirit and archival writings of Second World War, Japanese-Canadian activist Muriel Kitagawa. *Obasan*'s intercultural and intergenerational reach develops a brilliantly effective dramatization of the injustices suffered by the Japanese Canadians during and after the war.

A novel adaptation for children follows *Obasan*'s female protagonist along *Naomi's Road* (Oxford UP 1986). *Itsuka* (Penguin 1992) resumes Naomi's story in a narrative that follows her from her apprenticeship as teacher in a repressive fundamentalist small southern Albertan town to her politicization in the Japanese-Canadian redress movement. The story of Naomi's emotional and libidinal awakening parallels the growing national effectiveness of the dispersed Japanese-Canadian people. While the novel has been criticized as 'too political,' it refuses to simplify the ideological complexities of a long-maligned community and a reluctant, even cynical, federal government.

See Joy Kogawa, 'Is There a Just Cause?' in *Up and Doing: Canadian Women and Peace*, ed. Janice Williamson and Deborah Gorham (Women's P 1989), 157–62; and her 'From the Bottom of the Well, from the Distant Star,' in *Telling It: Women and Language across Cultures*, ed. Telling It Book Collective (Press Gang 1990), 95–7. See also A. Lynne Magnusson, 'Language and Longing in Joy Kogawa's *Obasan*,' *Canadian Literature* 116 (1988), 58–66; Pat Merivale, 'Framed Voices: The Polyphonic Elegies of Hébert and Kogawa,' *Canadian Literature* 116 (1988), 68–82; Marilyn Russel Rose, 'Politics into Art: Kogawa's *Obasan* and the Rhetoric of Fiction,' *Mosiac* 21, nos. 2–3 (1988), 215–26; Robin Potter, 'Moral – in Whose Sense?: Joy Kogawa's *Obasan* and Julia Kristeva's *Powers of Horror*,' *Canadian Literature* 15, no. 1 (1990), 117–39; Magdalene Redekop, 'Interview,' in *Other Solitudes: Canadian Multicultural Fictions*, ed. Linda Hutcheon and Marion Richmond (Oxford UP 1990), 94–101; and the section on *Obasan* in Manina Jones, *'That Art of Difference': 'Documentary-Collage' and English-Candian Writing* (Toronto: U of Toronto P 1993). For a related non-fiction study of the internment of Japanese Canadians, see Ann Gomer Sunahara, *The Politics of Racism: The Uprooting of Japanese Canadians during the Second World War* (James Lorimer 1981), which states that 'forty years after the abuse of Japanese Canadians, there still exists no insurance against it happening again ... The powers of the War Measures Act under which Japanese Canadians were uprooted, detained, dispossessed, dispersed and almost deported remain unaltered' (168).

LEE MARACLE, a Métis writer, was born in North Vancouver in 1950. With her husband, publisher Dennis Maracle, whom she met in 1979, she has raised four children. While her formal institutional education ended in the eleventh grade, she returned to Simon Fraser University in 1987 to study sociology and then creative writing. A life-time West Coast dweller, she has been writer-in-residence at the En'owkin International School of Writing and currently lives in Toronto.

Maracle's work has been published in a number of periodicals, and she has collaborated on several poetry-music tapes with other Native and Black poets in Canada. Her books include *I Am Woman* (North Vancouver: Write-on P 1988), which queries the status of writing: 'The voices of the unheard cannot help but be of value. But how can one squeeze one's loved ones small, onto the pages of a three dimensional rectangle, empty of their form, minus their favorite colors and absent of the rhythm of the music that moves them?' In a series of illustrated first-person testimonials, her subjects range widely: 'Women's Movement,' 'Isn't Love a Given?' 'Education,' 'Law, Politics & Tradition.' Her voice 'does not intend to write for ... the European in the land.' Maracle interpellates and calls to these potential readers, turning the tables of White privilege: 'It is inevitable, European, that you should find yourself reading my work. If you do not find yourself spoken to, it is not because I intend rudeness – you just don't concern me now.' *Bobbi Lee: Indian Rebel* (Women's P 1990), an expanded first-person narrative about a young Métis girl, was written in the 1970s and presented orally before its first publication. In the 'Prologue' to its second edition Maracle describes the book's history as 'a reduction of some two hundred pages of manuscript to a little book. What began as a class to learn how to do other people's life history, turned into a project to do my own ... In the end, the voice that reached the paper was Don's [a White editor], the information alone was mine.' The narrative tells the autobiographical story of Bobbi through childhood and adolescence, her childbearing, and her participation in Native politics. Interwoven is a plea for Native justice and self-determination which includes a first-person commentary on the events at Oka. *Sojourner's Truth and Other Stories* (Press Gang 1990) maintains the voice of the storyteller in short fictions which combine character portraits, journal entries, and short-line poetry; several are direct narrations with 'the poetic terseness of the dilemma.' 'Worm' is a teaching story for her children. 'Who's Political Here?' revisits the 1970s to review some of the characters in *Bobbi Lee*. Another returns to 'World War I' and cautions the reader not to fix Maracle's story but to 're-imagine' it. In 'Eunice' the narrator examines current feminist cultural politics while portraying her response to a White woman whose 'life was shaped by her desire for feminism outside the isolation of agoraphobia.' In *Oratory: Coming to Theory* (North Vancouver: Women Artists' Monographs 1990), an essay with photographs, Maracle challenges the European scholar's 'alienated notion which maintains that theory is separate from story,' and asks, 'What is the point of presenting the human condition in a language separate from human experience: passion, emotion, and character?' The female protagonist in the novel *Sundogs* (Theytus P 1992) is a university student who is inspired by Elijah Harper's stand against the Meech Lake Accord and joins a First Nations group in solidarity with Oka Native activists.

Maracle participated in and co-edited *Telling It: Women and Language across Cultures* (Press Gang 1990). She contributed to the Renga poetry of *Linked Lives* (Editions Trois 1991). Her forthcoming work includes another novel, 'Raven's Song,' forthcoming from Press Gang. See Lee Maracle, 'Moving Over,' *Trivia* 14 (1989), 9–12; 'Just Get in Front of a Typewriter and Bleed,' 'Ramparts Hanging in the Air,' and 'Afterword,' in *Telling It*, 37–41, 161–72, and 173–5 respectively; and an interview with Hartmut Lutz, in *Contemporary Challenges: Conversations with Canadian Native Authors* (Fifth House 1991), 160–79.

DAPHNE MARLATT, a poet, novelist, essayist, editor, and teacher, was born in Australia in 1942 and spent her childhood in Malaysia until 1951, when her family immigrated to Vancouver. She studied English at the University of British Columbia (BA, 1964) and translated some of Francis Ponge's early poems for an MA in comparative literature at the University of Indiana (1968). Her novella 'Sea Haven' was published in *Modern Canadian Stories* (Ryerson 1966). *Frames of a Story* (Ryerson 1968), a poetic revision of 'The Snow Queen,' and the spare-languaged *Leaf/leafs* (Black Sparrow 1969) were followed by *Rings* (Georgia Straight Writing Supplement 1971), the inside-out story of the birth of her child and dissolution of her marriage. This text is reprinted with other journal entries and poems in *What Matters: Writing 1968–1970* (Coach House 1980). *Vancouver Poems* (Coach

House 1972) and *Our Lives* (Truck 1975; Oolichan 1980) write a verbal economy of Vancouver life from public streets to private collective living. Marlatt's attachments to the landscape and mythologies of British Columbia, as well as its writing community, are evident in *The Story, She Said* (BC Monthly 1977), a collaborative retelling of a trip to Prince George, and in *here & there* (Island Writing Series 1981), a poetic travelogue through the Kootenays.

A number of Marlatt's books on travel and immigration focus on what it means to be 'other.' Her own immigrant experience created 'a perfect seedbed for the writing sensibility.' The long-lined poetry of *Steveston* (Talonbooks 1974; Longspoon 1984) is a 'documentary' of the everyday lives of Steveston's Japanese-Canadian fishing community 'that undercuts its own status as documentary.' The prose of *Zócalo* (Coach House 1977) narrates a trip to Mexico with a lover. 'In the Month of Hungry Ghosts' is a series of letters and poems written from Penang and published in the *Capilano Review* 16–17 (1979), 45–95. And *How Hug a Stone* (Turnstone 1983) maps out the contradictions Marlatt and her son discover on a visit to extended family and England.

Touch to My Tongue (Longspoon 1984) is Marlatt's first collection of lesbian love poems, dedicated to Betsy Warland, with whom she has lived since 1983. Her formally innovative novel *Ana Historic* (Coach House 1988) invents the history of a forgotten BC woman settler through the evolving consciousness of a female narrator, who writes herself 'Not a Bad Ending.' *Double Negative*, with Betsy Warland (Gynergy Books 1988), is a collaborative series of love poems and prose which rhythmically document a train ride through Australia. *Salvage* (Red Deer College P 1991) in part revises some of her earlier texts to recuperate feminist concerns which 'had lain buried' as an unrecognized sub-text. Travel narratives, *Zócalo*, 'In the Month of Hungry Ghosts,' and *How Hug a Stone* are republished in *Ghost Works* (NeWest 1993).

A woman of letters, Marlatt has been active as an editor of *Tish* (1963–5), the *Capilano Review* (1973–6), and *Island* (1981–4), and she co-founded and co-edited *Periodics* (1977–81) and *Tessera* (1984–). In 1988, as Ruth Wynn Woodward Chair of Women's Studies at Simon Fraser University, Marlatt organized a conference and then co-edited a 'transformation,' rather than a proceedings, with Sky Lee, Lee Maracle, and Betsy Warland: *Telling It: Women and Language across Cultures* (Press Gang 1990). Her interest in translation has evolved in creative collaborative French and English 'transformations' with Nicole Brossard, including *Mauve* (NBJ/Writing 1985) and *Character/ Jeu de lettres* (NBJ/Writing 1986). A number of her poetics essays are published in *Tessera* (nos. 1–3, 5–6, 8–9; 1984–90). Marlatt comments on the politics of lesbian unity in her imaginary interview 'Changing the Focus,' in *Inversions: Writings by Dykes, Queers and Lesbians*, ed. Betsy Warland (Press Gang 1991), 127–34. *Words with You* (Guernica 1993) collects collaborative works with Betsy Warland.

See Barbara Godard, 'Body I: Daphne Marlatt's Feminist Poetics,' *Canadian Review of American Studies* 15, no. 4 (1985), 481–96; Christina Cole, 'Daphne Marlatt as Penelope, Weaver of Words: A Feminist Reading of *Steveston*,' *Open Letter* 6, no. 1 (1985), 5–19; Janice Williamson, 'Speaking in and of Each Other: An Interview with Daphne Marlatt and Betsy Warland,' *Fuse* 8, no. 5 (1985), 24–9; the special issue of *Line* (13[1989]) on Marlatt; Brenda Carr, 'Collaboration in the Feminine: Daphne Marlatt/Betsy Warland's "Reversed Writing" in *Double Negative*,' *Tessera* 9 (1990), 111–22; Susan Knutson, 'Daphne Marlatt and Nicole Brossard: Writing Metanarrative in the Feminine,' *Signature* 3 (1990), 28–43; Brenda Carr, 'Between Continuity and Difference: An Interview with Daphne Marlatt,' and Janice Williamson, ' "It gives me a great deal of pleasure to say yes": Daphne Marlatt's Lesbian Love Poems *Touch to My Tongue*,' in *Beyond Tish*, ed. Douglas Barbour (NeWest/Line 1991), 99–107 and 171–93 respectively; Stan Dragland, 'Out of the Blank: Daphne Marlatt's *Ana Historic*,' and 'Creatures of Ecstasy: *Touch to My Tongue*,' in *Bees of the Invisible* (Coach House 1991), 152–71 and 172–90 respectively; and the section on Marlatt in Manina Jones, *'That Art of Difference': 'Documentary- Collage' and English-Canadian Writing* (Toronto: U of Toronto P 1993).

ERIN MOURÉ, poet and essayist, was born in Calgary in 1955. She studied for two years at the Universities of Calgary and British Columbia. Since 1976 she has worked for CN and then VIA Rail, crisscrossing Canada on the passenger trains in various capacities until 1984, when she moved to VIA's Montreal headquarters, where she works as senior officer, Customer Relations and Employee Communication. Her first poetry book, *Empire, York Street* (Anansi 1979), was nominated for the Governor General's Award. *The Whisky Vigil* (Harbour Publishing 1981) chronicles the 'Mrs. Jekyll & Mr. Hyde' symbiotic despair of alcoholism and ends with 'Divorce from You: 'my heart is a huge room where / the furniture is dusted.' The poems in *Wanted Alive* (Anansi 1983) invoke diverse stories of loss, from those 'shot in Zimbabwe with the shout of joy caught / in their mouth' to 'the woman hurt all her life / by money, walking away / from it.' This collection includes a series of 'Seven Rail Poems' and also features a poetic utopia – 'In the Brief Intervals between Their Stuggles Our People Dream' – where workers dream 'of taking over, the day after cutback; / ... crossing the country in 4 days on schedule, / manned by rail workers / deaf to government intervention.'

Mouré's writing will continually focus on the dailiness of living and work, which she eventually calls 'wurq,' in order to refuse the domestic/public distinction encouraged by a genre of male 'work' poetry. The political urgency of the everyday in Mouré's poems is underscored by the epigraph from César Vallejo in *Domestic Fuel* (Anansi 1985) – 'Someone cleans a rifle in his kitchen. / How dare one speak about the beyond' – and a number of poems challenging militarism and nuclear armaments. Biting satire and a rhetoric of philosophical argument inform a number of these poems, including 'Poem Rejected by the Globe & Mail,' where 'The Revolution is over! There is no more sense in teaching your children to earn money / ... Teach them to live on little, to take apart Chryslers / & boil them ... Sleep, Ontario.' Lesbian love poems record the awkwardness of public censorship: 'I want my lips to feel kissed by you, / to feel natural / & not   so crooked or so rare.' These poems mark an intensified concern that 'the language [confront] itself & its assumptions in the poem.'

Fuelled by the stimulating intellectual companionship of Montreal writer Gail Scott, concerns about language become increasingly central in *Furious* (Anansi 1988), which won the Governor General's Award. A sometimes outlandishly quirky humour and an incisive critical wit sharpen poems like 'Goodbye to Beef.' A series of prose pieces, critical companions to the *Furious* poems, include this revisionary look at the vernacular, often characteristic of Mouré's poetic language: 'It's the way people use language makes me furious. The ones who reject the colloquial & common culture. The ones who laud on the other hand the common & denigrate the intellect, as if we are not thinking.' She has defended herself from charges of elitism: 'Literal meanings of the "accessible" just place women, and working-class people, as the lowest common denominator in the reproduction of the social order. It's the cannon-fodder mentality.' Her writing challenges fixed versions, playing with the prepositional logic of a non-objectified lesbian eros in 'Rolling Motion': 'lifted upward airborne soft face into under into rolling over every upward motion.' *WSW (West South West)* (Véhicule 1989) includes linked poems of melancholia and desire, a haunted writing which spatializes the interior of 'our imperfect, fleeing minds.' Six cycles of poems in *Sheepish Beauty, Civilian Love* (Véhicule 1992) mark out a social and personal ground where language is both material and play. From the cellular to the macro-political Mouré confronts the junctures of civic and personal space we inhabit, the pain of cultural violence embedded there, the absurdity of a 'poem in which a chicken constantly interrupts,' and despite all of this, the reach of one woman towards another, the 'leg kiss,' the 'will to tenderness, even in the face of its absence.'

See Erin Mouré, 'To Speak of These Things: A Letter,' *Canadian Fiction Magazine* [*Tessera* issue] 57 (1986), 132–5; 'Poetry, Memory and the Polis,' *Trivia* 13 (1988), 66–73, reprinted in *Language in Her Eye: Writing and Gender*, ed. Libby Scheier et al. (Coach House 1990), 201–8; 'It Remained Unheard,' *Dandelion* 15, no. 2 (1988), 79–85; 'Watching the Watchwords,' *Books in Canada* 18 no. 8 (1989), 3–4. See also Peter O'Brien, 'An Interview with Erin Mouré,' *Rubicon* 3 (1984), 25–44, reprinted in *So to Speak: Interviews with Canadian Writers*, ed. Peter O'Brien (Véhicule 1986), 230–49; Robert Billings, 'Changes the Surface: A Conversation with Erin Mouré, *Waves* 14, no. 4 (1986); Stephen Scobie, 'The Footnoted Text,' in Signature, Event, Cantext (NeWest 1989), 71–81; Sonja A. Skarstedt, 'Poetry and Feminism: The Requisite Duo,' *Poetry Canada* 10, no. 4 (Winter 1989–90), 10–11; Susan Glickman, 'Speaking in Tongues: The Poetry of Erin Mouré,' *Essays on Canadian Writing* 43 (Spring 1991), 133–43; and an interview with Janice Williamson, 'Can't We Talk about the Alberta Flag?' *Prairie Fire* 13, no. 4 (1992–3), 74–82.

M. NOURBESE PHILIP, a poet, novelist, essayist, lecturer, and lawyer, was born in Moriah, Tobago. At age eight she moved with her family to Trinidad. In 1968 she received a BSC (Econ.) from the University of the West Indies and moved to Canada. At the University of Western Ontario she completed an MA in political science (1970) and an LLB (1973). After practising law from 1975 to 1982, she devoted herself to writing and raising three children with her husband. Her first book of poetry was *Thorns* (Williams-Wallace 1980). *Salmon Courage* (Williams-Wallace 1983) explores questions of gender and race in various forms from lyric to parodic. The title poem celebrates 'swimming against the tide' ... / in time to the spawning / grounds of knotted dreams.' A novel for young people, *Harriet's Daughter* (London: Heinemann 1988; Toronto: Women's P 1988), was first published in England, having been rejected by a number of Canadian publishers because 'Black protagonists don't sell books.' The novel opens in the midst of the 'Underground Railway Game' and follows the fantasies and everyday life of fourteen-year-old Margaret (who has renamed herself 'Harriet' after Harriet Tubman) and Tobagonian friend Zulma. In 1988 Philip won the Casa de las Americas Prize for the manuscript version of *She Tries Her Tongue; Her Silence Softly Breaks* (Ragweed 1989). This collection of serial poems includes an essay on her poetics, where she states her conviction that 'the challenge ... facing the African Caribbean writer ... is to use the language in such a way that the historical realities are not erased or obliterated, so that English is revealed as the tainted tongue it truly is [having been] used to brutalize and diminish Africans.' The poems revise the myth of Proserpine and ask, 'Might I ... like Philomela ... sing' in a language which is not a 'foreign l/anguish'? *Looking for Livingstone: An Odyssey of Silence* (Mercury P 1991) is a novel of the fantastic based on the imaginary prose and poetry records of The Traveller's anthropological inner and outer journeys in search of her silence and the explorer 'Livingstone-I-presume.'

Philip was awarded a Guggenheim Fellowship for Poetry in 1990. A founding member of Vision 21, a multi-disciplinary, multi-racial collective formed around issues of racism in the arts, she has taught creative writing at York University and currently teaches part-time at the University of Toronto. Her work has been anthologized in Paula

Burnett, ed., *The Penguin Book of Caribbean Verse in English* (1986) and Rosemary Sullivan, ed., *Poetry by Canadian Women* (Oxford UP 1989). Philip's influential essays, including 'The Disappearing Debate or How the Discussion of Racism Has Been Taken Over by the Censorship Issue' and 'Gut Issues in Babylon: Racism and Anti-Racism in the Arts,' are collected in her *Frontiers: Essays and Writings on Racism and Culture* (Mercury P 1992). See also her 'The Absence of Writing or How I Almost Became a Spy,' *Brick* 39 (1990), 26–34; and Leslie Saunders, 'Marlene Nourbese Philip's "Bad Words,"' *Tessera* 12 (1992), 81–9.

GAIL SCOTT, novelist, short story writer, essayist, and journalist was born in Ottawa and grew up in a bilingual community in eastern Ontario. She studied at Queen's University (BA, 1966) and at the Université de Grenoble (1967). In 1971 she gave birth to her daughter, Anna. During the 1970s she worked as a journalist in Montreal and was one of the first anglophone writers to report on and interpret Quebec's national struggle, particularly through her writing about Quebec's cultural politics for major English-Canadian news agencies, magazines, and newspapers. One of the founding editors of *Spirale* (1979–82), a Quebec cultural review, she also co-founded and co-edited the feminist critical and creative-writing journal *Tessera* (1984–9). A contemporary of such Quebec feminist writers as Louky Bersianik, Nicole Brossard, and France Théoret, her thinking and writing developed in part through active participation in the Québécois postmodern writing scene. Influences range 'from Walter Benjamin to the surrealists to Jane Bowles.' *Spare Parts* (Coach House 1982), five surreal picaresque short stories, revealed her interest in narrative innovation. Daring sentences, often short and sharp-edged, make cinematic quick-cut synaesthetic effects, as in: 'After the hot came the cold. The fog fell. The Peace Tower stuck up like a Sherlock Holmes mystery. Trying to see was like trying to draw tiny drops back from across your eyes. Veils of tears.' A novel, *Heroine* (Coach House 1987), translated into French in 1988 and German in 1990, records the narrator's fractured bisexual recollections in her bath about how an 'English heroine (of a novel) might look against the background of contemporary Quebec.' From this vantage point she constructs her history, rooting through Quebec feminist politics and poetics (influenced by French post-structuralist and feminist theory) and the sexual politics of the Left. A playful ambivalence leaves unresolved the narrator's dilemma: 'The question is, is it possible to create Paradise in this Strangeness?' Her critically and formally innovative essays, *Spaces Like Stairs* (Women's P 1989), several of which were first published in French, include 'Paragraphs Blowing on a Line,' which queries the poetic quality of her prose language work: 'Why must I get involved with this forward movement of time the novel seems to require, when the voice of the notes, the woman's voice beckons me towards poetry?' *Main Brides, against Ochre Pediment and Aztec Sky* (Coach House 1993), a novel, refines her narrative method. Scott suggests 'the old forms essay novel have moved forward maybe two post-moderns one for women one for men ours circular ...' See Barbara Godard, review of *Heroine, Border/Lines* 11 (1988), 50–1; Lou Robinson, 'Our Litanies, Our Transfusions: After Reading *Heroine* by Gail Scott,' *Trivia* 13 (1988), 31–41; Mary Meigs, 'Surreal Senses,' review of *Heroine, Canadian Literature* 122–3 (1989), 222–3; Barbara Carey, 'On the Edge of Change: An Interview with Gail Scott,' *Books in Canada* 18, no. 6 (1989); Lorna Irving, 'Words on the Prowl: Québec Literature and Gail Scott's *Heroine*,' *Québec Studies* 9 (1989–90), 111–20; Camille Norton, 'The Music of Wolves: After Reading *Spaces Like Stairs*, by Gail Scott,' *Trivia* 15 (1989), 31–41; Sherry Simon, 'En Manque,' *Spirale* 74 (1987); George Bowering, 'Paragraphs Blowing on a Line,' review of *Spaces Like Stairs, Hungry Mind Review* 13 (1990), 16; Gerald Hill, 'Across Reference: A *Heroine* Dictionary,' *West Coast Line* 5 (1991), 45–56.

LOLA LEMIRE TOSTEVIN, poet, essayist, novelist, and translator was born in the francophone community of Timmins, Ontario. As a child, she studied as a convent boarder, an experience which provided the setting for part of her first novel. She also studied at the Collège St Thomas d'Aquin in Ottawa, the Université de Paris, the University of Toronto, and the University of Alberta. She married in 1962 and raised two children before publishing her writing. She teaches creative writing at York University, and her work is informed by her readings in French feminist theory. *Color of Her Speech* (Coach House 1982) centres on the way difference is ordered hierarchically when power privileges particular discourses and speaking positions. Thus her poetry insists on the relation between women and language and linguistic minorities like the franco-Ontarians. (See, for instance, her poem 'femspeak: jargon / gutteral voiceless / sound ... in Quebec we say / argot/ argoter to cut / ... the semantic cut / cunt / woman's cant / rant / rent.') In *Gyno-Text* (Underwhich Editions 1983) the embodied language of a maternal subject is made strange and inventive through a minimalist graphemic and aural form. *Double Standards* (Longspoon 1985) searches for a writing adequate to a woman's narrative when women's 'stories' provide insufficient 'vehicles for her use.' The poetics of negation in 'do not be deceived by appearances / I am not a woman' is also evident in the painful revelation of 'This Is Not a Poem.' *sophie* (Coach House 1988) plays on the absence of women in philosophy and includes a series of erotic heterosexual love poems, 'Song of Songs'; a series of French poems, 'Espaces vers'; along with wickedly ironic poetic and prose critiques of the Western male intellectual tradition, including a prose narrative lampooning a semiotics colloquium with a vibrator's electric muscle. Her first novel, *Frog Moon*, is forthcoming, as are *Cartouches* (Coach House), a new collection of poems, and her collected essays, which include among others: 'Breaking the Hold on the Story: The Feminine Economy of Language,' in *A Mazing Space*, ed. Shirley Neuman and Smaro Kamboureli (Longspoon/NeWest 1986), 385–91; 'Diana Hartog: Poetry beyond Revision,' *Brick* 29 (1987), 9–13; 'Women of Letters' [a correspondence with Smaro Kamboureli], *Tessera* 5 (1988); 13–26; 'Daphne Marlatt: Writing in the Space That Is Her Mother's Face,' *Line* 13 (1989), 32–9; and 'Contamination: A Relation of Differences,' *Tessera* 6 (1989), 13–14; See Shirley Neuman, 'Importing Difference,' in *A Mazing Space*, 391–405; Janice Williamson, 'To pen a trait: The Feminist Reader and the Poetry of Lola Lemire Tostevin,' *Line* 9 (1987), 95–108; Danny O'Quinn, Restore Me with Apples,' *Open Letter* 7, no. 5 (1989), 37–51; Charlene Diehl-Jones, 'Body/ Language,' *In/Versions* 1, no. 1 (1990), 8–13, and 1, no. 2 (1990), 7–10; Smaro Kamboureli, 'Theory: Beauty or Beast,' *Open Letter* 7, no. 8 (1990), 5–27.

BRONWEN WALLACE, poet, short-story writer, feminist columnist, and film-maker, was born in Kingston, Ontario, in 1945, where she died of cancer in 1989. She studied English and taught creative writing at Queen's University (BA, 1967; MA, 1969). Writer of the Kingston *Whig-Standard* feminist column and a long-time feminist activist in the women's community, she collaborated on films with film-maker and social worker Chris Whynot, with whom she raised her son. Her first book of poems, *Marrying into the Family*, was published with *Bread and Chocolate* by Mary di Michele (Oberon 1980) and establishes her focus on women's lives. *Signs of the Former Tenant* (Oberon 1983) and her next collection extend the *Common Magic* (Oberon 1985) of poetic language. Concentrating on women's experience, she formulates a body consciousness where 'thought is no different from flesh.' Poems in *The Stubborn Particulars of Grace* (McClelland and Stewart 1987) shift between sexual politics and the dailiness of coming to wisdom. She won a number of poetry awards, including the regional award for the Commonwealth Poetry Prize (1989). Storytelling which 'tries to explain the fit of things' fascinates the plain speech of the brave gritty figures in *People You'd Trust Your Life To* (McClelland and Stewart 1980), a collection of short fiction. *Keep That Candle Burning Bright and Other Poems* (Coach House 1991) collects her last prose poems, a section of which are dedicated to country singer Emmylou Harris. *Arguments with the World* (Quarry 1992), a selection of Wallace's journalism and essays, was edited by Joanne Page. See Bronwen Wallace, 'Why I Don't (Always) Write Short Stories,' *Quarry* 37 (1988), 69–77; Margaret Atwood, review of *Common Magic, Journal of Canadian Poetry*, 2 (1987), 120–3; an interview with Brenda Cantar in *Arc* 20, (Spring 1988); and 'Bronwen Wallace: Particular Articles,' a special issue of *Open Letter* (7, no. 9 [1991]).

BETSY WARLAND, poet, essayist, cultural activist, and editor has Norwegian roots and was born in 1946 in Fort Dodge, Iowa, where she married (1969) and studied painting at Luther College (BA, visual arts, 1970). Soon after moving to Canada, where she became a citizen in 1981, she worked with other feminists to establish the Toronto

Women's Writing Collective (1975–81), which co-sponsored Land-scape, a poetry festival for Toronto women writers, and a women's reading series, Writers-in-Dialogue. Her first collection of poetry, *A Gathering Instinct* (Williams-Wallace 1981), gives language a visual 'interior design.' Warland's organizational energy was central to the success of the 1983 Canada/Quebec gathering in Vancouver of over eight hundred women for workshops and readings. In addition to initiating and coordinating the conference, she co-edited with others *In the Feminine: Women and Words / Les Femmes et les mots Conference Proceedings 1983* (Longspoon 1985). She was active in developing collaboratively the West Word Women's Writing Retreats and co-founded *(f.)Lip: A Newsletter of Feminist Innovative Writing*, which she co-edited (1986–9). She also co-edited *Telling It: Women and Language across Cultures* (Press Gang 1990), the 'transformation' of a conference on women writers marginalized by racism and/or homophobia.

A Gathering Instinct was followed by *Open Is Broken* (Longspoon 1984), which reveals a more openly lesbian eroticism of pleasure, strength, and vulnerability. Her fascination with 'in her textuality,' the connections between women writers, is marked within her collage texts as well as in this book's address 'for Daphne [Marlatt],' whose erotic poems, *Touch to My Tongue*, are reciprocally dedicated. This dialogue continues in collaborations with Marlatt, which include 'Reading and Writing between the Lines,' *Tessera* 5 (1988), and *Double Negative* (Gynergy Books 1988). The main body of her long poem *Serpent (W)rite (a reader's gloss)* (Coach House 1987) is dispersed as marginalia – notes upon notes cut across a generous library of texts from post-structuralist to radical feminist theory, anthropology, Eastern philosophy, children's rhymes, theology, and linguistics. Echoing pre-Christian matriarchal mythology, gnostic texts, and patriarchal elements in the Bible, Warland confronts her own Christian fundamentalist childhood and listens for the voice of a 'suscipe cyprine' Eve. An essay collection *Proper Deafinitions: Collected Theorograms* (Press Gang 1990), includes formally innovative explorations of lesbian eroticism, feminist consciousness, mother-daughter relations, racism, the medicalization of the female body, and child sexual abuse. Warland edited *Inversions: Writing by Dykes, Queers and Lesbians* (Press Gang 1991), an anthology of essays by Canadian, Quebec, and U.S.

women. Collaborative works with Daphne Marlatt are collected in *Words with You* (Guernica 1993). *The Bat Had Blue Eyes* (Women's P 1993) was transformed into a performance script for the 1993 Vancouver Women in View Festival. She is currently working on an operatic play. See Janice Williamson, 'Speaking in and of Each Other: An Interview with Daphne Marlatt and Betsy Warland,' *Fuse* 8, no. 5 (1985), 24–9; Di Brandt, 'Interview with Betsy Warland,' *Contemporary Verse* 2 11, no. 4 (1988), 42–7; Susan Standford Friedman, 'When a "Long" Poem Is a "Big" Poem: Self-Authorizing Strategies in Women's Twentieth-Century "Long Poems,"' *LIT* 2 (1990), 9–25; Brenda Carr, 'Collaboration in the Feminine: Daphne Marlatt / Betsy Warland's "Reversed Writing" in *Double Negative*,' *Tessera* 9 (1990), 111–22.

PHYLLIS WEBB, a poet, essayist, teacher, and former broadcaster, was born in Victoria, BC, in 1927. Twenty-two years later she graduated with a BA in English and philosophy from the University of British Columbia and ran unsuccessfully for the CCF in a provincial election, the youngest candidate ever. During the fifties she did graduate work at McGill University, worked as a secretary, began her radio broadcasting career on a freelance basis, and was associated with writers like F.R. Scott, Louis Dudek, Eli Mandel, Miriam Waddington, and Leonard Cohen. Along with Eli Mandel and Gael Turnbull, Webb was featured in *Trio* (Contact 1954). *Even Your Right Eye* (McClelland and Stewart 1956) was written while Webb travelled through England and Ireland. After a year in Paris, Webb taught at the University of British Columbia (1960–3) but returned to Toronto, where she worked for CBC Public Affairs and later became executive producer of the radio series *Ideas* (1967–9). *The Sea Is Also a Garden* (Ryerson 1962), dedicated to Webb's 'mothers,' includes several insightful parodic poems about death and suicide, which for some unselfconscious critics became the basis for a reductive mythology of Webb as merely melancholic. She has taught creative writing at the University of British Columbia and the University of Victoria, and was writer-in-residence at the University of Alberta (1980–1). Since 1969 she has lived on Salt Spring Island, where she established a local chapter of Amnesty International.

Naked Poems (Vancouver: Periwinkle 1965), through a minimalist series of 'non-linear' images and questions, effectively translate an absent lesbian lover through the language traces of her body in a room. The poems are reprinted in *Selected Poems 1954–1965* (Talonbooks 1971) with an extended introduction by editor John Hulcoop and in *Selected Poems: The Vision Tree* (Talonbooks 1982), a fine gathering of poems which features a perceptive introduction by West Coast poet and editor Sharon Thesen. In *Wilson's Bowl* (Coach House 1980) her youthful political interests and an earlier trip to Russia inform the 'Poems of Failure,' inspired by the anarchist 'sweet old Prince / Kropotkin.' These poems, 'born out of great struggles of silence ... wayward, natural and unnatural silences, my desire for privacy, my critical hesitations, my critical wounds ... a strange gestation,' consider 'Crimes,' including anti-war and anti-fascist poems, and a poem on the 'the question as an instrument of torture,' which is also the subject of an essay. The long poem 'Wilson's Bowl' traces the sorrows and songs of a double suicide. The essays and adapted radio scripts collected in *Talking* (Montreal: Quadrant 1982) include 'On the Line,' an essay which traces her influences through Adrienne Rich among others. *Water and Light: Ghazals and Anti Ghazals* (Coach House 1984) presents Webb's beautiful and anarchic revisionary couplets of the Persian ghazal poetic form: 'A lozenge of dream / sticks on my tongue / Soulange, Stonehenge / sugar-mite, maple – / a candy poem.' 'Leaning' addresses the reader: 'And you, are you still here / tilting in this stranded ark / blind and seeing in the dark.' The titles in *Hanging Fire* (Coach House 1990) 'are "given" words, phrases, or sentences that arrive unbidden ... tracking ... hidden themes, connections, a sub-rational.' Webb's ironic and articulate fury is evidenced in works like 'There *Are* the Poems,' where poets 'burrow into the paper to court in secret the life of plants, the shifty moon's space-walks, the bliss, the roses, the glamorous national debt. Someone to talk to, for God's sake, something to love that will never hit back.'

Webb has also published the afterword to the New Canadian Library edition of Gabrielle Roy's *Windflower* (McClelland and Stewart 1991), and the following essays: 'The Muse Figure,' in *In the Feminine*, ed. Ann Dybikowski et al. (Longspoon 1985), 114–16; 'Unearned

Numinosity,' *Grain* 15, no. 4 (1987), 9–11; and, 'Message Machine,' in *Language in Her Eye*, ed. Libby Scheier et al. (Coach House 1990), 293–6. For essays on Webb's work see Jean Mallinson, 'Ideology and Poetry: An Examination of Some Recent Trends in Canadian Criticism,' *Studies in Canadian Literature* 3 (1978), 93–7; Stephen Scobie, 'I and I: Phyllis Webb's "I Daniel,"' *Open Letter* 6, nos. 2–3 (1985), 61–8; Cecelia Frey, 'The Left Hand of Phyllis Webb,' *Prairie Fire* 3, no. 3 (1986), 37–49; Pauline Butling, 'Paradox and Play in the Poetry of Phyllis Webb,' *A Mazing Space*, ed. Shirley Neuman and Smaro Kamboureli (Longspoon/NeWest 1986), 191–204; Susan Glickman, '"Proceeding before the Amorous Invisible": Phyllis Webb and the Ghazal,' *Canadian Literature* 115 (1987), 48–65; John Hulcoop, *Phyllis Webb and Her Works* (ECW P 1991). Pauline Butling edited a special issue of *West Coast Line* (5 [1991]) on Webb's writing.

JANICE WILLIAMSON, writer, critic, teacher, and sometime activist, was born in 1951 in Brandon, Manitoba. In 1952 her family moved to Ontario, where she grew up in Pickering. After travelling through Europe and West Africa, she received her BA from Carleton University in 1975 and her MA from York University in 1981. She completed her PHD at York University in 1987 with a dissertation titled 'Citing Resistance: Vision, Space, Authority and Transgression in Canadian Women's Poetry.'

In the early 1980s Williamson was a volunteer in the Women's Press 'social issues' manuscript group and a collective member of *Border/Lines: Cultures, Contexts, Canadas*. She participated in a socialist-feminist action group, and in 1983 she was arrested for non-violent civil disobedience in protest against the production of the guidance system for the cruise missile at Litton Industries. This experience led to her editing with Deborah Gorham *Up and Doing: Canadian Women and Peace* (Women's P 1989), a collection of social history, feminist theory, autobiographical narratives, interviews, and creative work. In 1991 she co-founded Women's Action for Peace in the Gulf.

Her creative work was sparked by West Word I, a 1985 women's writing retreat led by Daphne Marlatt and Gail Scott and co-organized by Betsy Warland and Gloria Greenfield, among others. This initiated work on *Tell Tale Signs: Fictions* (Turnstone 1991), an illustrated collection of prose fictions, creative documentary, and prose poems, which includes the chapbook *The Journals of Alberta Borges* (Greensleaves 1991).

In 1987 Williamson moved to Edmonton, where she is associate professor of English at the University of Alberta. She has published essays on Canadian women writers, feminist cultural studies, and the West Edmonton Mall. She co-curated and wrote with Bridget Elliott *Dangerous Goods: Feminist Visual Art Practices* (Edmonton Art Gallery 1991). With Claudine Potvin she edited *Women's Writing and the Literary Institution* (University of Alberta 1992). A poetry chapbook, *Altitude* x 2 (disOrientation P 1992), is part of a work in progress.

Picture Credits

JEANNETTE ARMSTRONG courtesy of Greg Young-Ing

DI BRANDT courtesy of Jack Simpson

NICOLE BROSSARD courtesy of Germaine Beaulieu

ELLY DANICA courtesy of John Sylvester

KRISTJANA GUNNARS courtesy of W.C. Christie

CLAIRE HARRIS courtesy of Lennox K. Harris

SMARO KAMBOURELI courtesy of Maria Gilli

JOY KOGAWA courtesy of John Flanders

LEE MARACLE courtesy of B. Hemsing

DAPHNE MARLATT courtesy of LaVerne Harrell Clark

ERIN MOURÉ courtesy of Erin Mouré (self-portrait)

M. NOURBESE PHILIP courtesy of M. Nourbese Philip

GAIL SCOTT courtesy of Josee Lambert

LOLA LEMIRE TOSTEVIN courtesy of Jerry Tostevin

BRONWEN WALLACE courtesy of Chris Whynot

BETSY WARLAND courtesy of Daphne Marlatt

PHYLLIS WEBB courtesy of Déstrubé Photography